Daniel Farson has relished life on various levels. As the son of the American foreign correspondent, Negley Farson, he travelled through Europe as a child and was evacuated to America and Canada in the War. Having pursued a journalistic career for a period after Cambridge, he joined the Merchant Navy and sailed round the world washing dishes. This was followed by a startling burst of 'spurious fame' when he became one of the first celebrities of ITV with such series of his own as *Farson's Guide to the British*; *Farson in Australia*; and the entertainment programme, *Time Gentlemen Please!* The latter was filmed while he was living in Limehouse – before it became fashionable – and prompted him to take over a pub of his own on the Isle of Dogs, The Waterman's Arms, which revived Music Hall and became a famous tourist attraction.

In 1964 he turned his back on television and his role as 'personality' in order to write. Since then, 22 of his books have been published including his best-seller on *Jack the Ripper*; his biography of his great-uncle, Bram Stoker, *The Man Who Wrote Dracula*; his autobiography *Out of Step*; a memoir of Henry Williamson (author of *Tarka the Otter*), *Henry*; and the historical novel, *Swansdowne*, on convicts sent to Van Diemen's Land in the last century. In 1986 he returned to Tasmania to research the sequel. *Wanderlust*, an anthology of his father's travels, gave particular satisfaction, and he contributed the introduction to the Penguin republication of *Caucasian Journey* (1988).

A prolific travel writer, largely for the *Daily Telegraph*, Daniel Farson was one of the first writers to forecast the popularity of Turkey as a new centre for holiday-makers; his *Traveller in Turkey* (Routledge, 1985) expressed his love for the country and the people. Farson also wrote the introduction to the Thames & Hudson photographic book *Turkey* and regards Turkey as his second home – 'not just for the beauty of the country, which is infinite, but the friendliness of the Turks and the rewarding bonus of their humour.'

COLLINS INDEPENDENT TRAVELLERS GUIDE

TURKEY

DANIEL FARSON

Series Editor Robin Dewhurst

Collins
8 Grafton Street, London
1988

William Collins Sons & Co Ltd
London · Glasgow · Sydney
Auckland · Toronto · Johannesburg

First published in 1988
© Daniel Farson 1988

Maps by Kevin Jones Associates

BRITISH LIBRARY CATALOGUING IN PUBLICATION DATA
Collins Independent Travellers Guide to Turkey.
1. Turkey—Description and travel—1960
—Guide-books
915.61'0483   DR 416

ISBN 0 00 410971 6

Typeset by Ace Filmsetting Ltd, Frome, Somerset.
Printed and bound in Great Britain by Mackays of Chatham.

Dedication

With gratitude to Mrs Gülsen Kahraman, whose advice was invaluable, as always.

With admiration for Mr Çelik Gülersoy, for restoring the former glories of Istanbul.

With friendship for Liam Carson and Gabrielle, fellow travellers in Turkey.

Note

While every effort has been made to ensure that prices, hotel and restaurant recommendations, opening hours and similar factual information in this book are accurate at the time of going to press, the Publishers cannot be held responsible for any changes found by readers using this guide.

Prices in Turkey can be a very confusing subject. The country suffers from a chronically high rate of inflation (between 30 and 40 per cent) but, on the other hand, the Turkish lira is frequently devalued against Western currencies. This means that the actual costs of your trip remain about the same – though the numbers constantly change. In this guide, prices are based on the rate current at time of writing, about L 1,475 to the pound (or about L 900 to the US dollar). Remember that, as Turkey becomes more popular, prices are subject to larger increases.

This book will prove useful when comparing costs between one hotel and another, for the price differential is likely to remain reasonably consistent, although it must be stressed that the actual prices quoted will always be subject to revision.

Contents

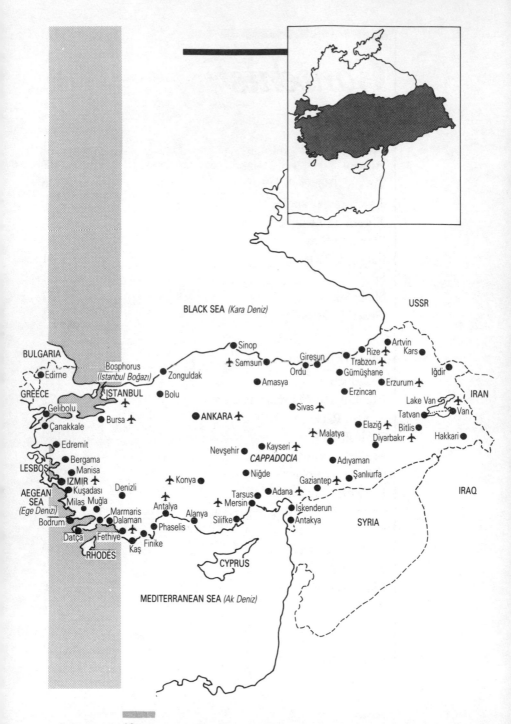

BLACK SEA *(Kara Deniz)*

USSR

BULGARIA

GREECE

Edirne

Bosphorus
(Istanbul Boğazı)

Zonguldak

ISTANBUL

Gelibolu

Bolu

Çanakkale

Bursa

ANKARA

Sinop

Samsun

Amasya

Giresun

Ordu

Rize

Trabzon

Gümüşhane

Erzincan

Sivas

Artvin

Kars

Erzurum

Iğdir

Lake Van

Tatvan

Van

IRAN

Edremit

Nevşehir

Kayseri

Malatya

Elazığ

Bitlis

Diyarbakır

Hakkari

Bergama

Manisa

CAPPADOCIA

Adıyaman

LESBOS

IZMIR

Kuşadası

Denizli

Konya

Niğde

Gaziantep

Şanlıurfa

IRAQ

AEGEAN
SEA
(Ege Denizi)

Milas

Muğla

Antalya

Tarsus

Adana

Mersin

Bodrum

Marmaris

Dalaman

Alanya

Silifke

İskenderun

Datça

Fethiye

Phaselis

Antakya

SYRIA

Kaş

Finike

RHODES

CYPRUS

MEDITERRANEAN SEA *(Ak Deniz)*

Introduction

'Arid, harsh, backward, unfriendly' – all these are misconceptions, the opposite of the truth. Those who have never been to Turkey believe that the land is barren, yet if you travel south from Trebizond (Trabzon) you go through an alpine landscape famous for its thirty-six shades of green, and when you sail into Marmaris on the Mediterranean coast you could be entering a pine-clad fjord in Norway. Apart from Central Anatolia, the soil is so fertile that Turkey provides the larder for the Middle East, with the promise of even greater supplies when the south-eastern plains are irrigated by the reservoir project planned for a new Mesopotamia by damming the Tigris and Euphrates.

Many people think that Turkey is unsophisticated, yet a vein of civilised appreciation is reflected throughout the country with the Turkish passion for flowers and trees, and their zest for good food and drink to be savoured in the open air under a trellis of vine leaves.

Another common idea is that the Turks look tough, and there is an element of truth in this. Fortunately, Turkey is a strong country with an army of nearly 650,000 men; the West is inclined to take this strength for granted, and visitors are sometimes disconcerted by the sight of soldiers patrolling with guns at airports, though of course this is done for *their* protection. At Heathrow, pistols in pockets may be more discreet but are just as plentiful. A quick look at the map and Turkey's neighbours – the Soviet Union to the north; Iran and Iraq at war; and Syria to the south – should make us thankful for Turkey's strength.

Even so, on first impression Turkish people often look severe, with little time for effusiveness or the histrionics of the Greeks – that is, until they smile. This is one of the revelations as you grow to understand Turkey: the realisation of a sharp sense of the ridiculous, which is similar to British Edwardian humour at its best. Eccentricity is welcomed in Turkey for, unlike the English today, the Turks like to see their visitors having a good time. Remarkably tolerant, they warm to people who like Turkey: their pride in their country is open and should be respected.

As for honesty and friendship, I can think of no people so trustworthy. Distances may prove longer than expected and journeys can be tiring in the heat of midsummer, but the Turkish countryside is so varied and exhilarating that only a boring person could be bored. The

Turks themselves are the constant reward. Never underrate them. They are the least devious of people themselves but they can spot falseness instantly. Their hospitality is so gracious that it would be a crime to abuse it. Instead, try to reciprocate in the most thoughtful way you can, which does not mean offering money.

Above all, try to explore Turkey for yourself: there is more fun in making your own discoveries by chance than being led by any guidebook. This guide is intended for the independent traveller who wants to see the main attractions and then go round the corner. Though I hope my recommendations may prove helpful, I do not pretend that this guide is comprehensive. And rates of exchange vary, favourite restaurants change hands, timetables are altered – so it is vital to check for yourselves. If things should go a bit wrong, that is a vital part of travel, and the sun will surely shine tomorrow (though I have to admit that I struck a freak spell of rain when I visited southern Turkey early in May 1987). Nowadays the weather seems erratic everywhere, but usually less so in Turkey. May can be a perfect time of year, and if you are able to choose I urge you to visit Turkey in the off-season months of May, June, September and October when the weather should be idyllic and it is cheaper and less crowded too (see p. 30).

Turkey is vast: it is more of a continent than a country. Races meet but do not mix, and different regions embrace yet remain separate. The very names convey the romance of the east: Iskenderun near Antioch; Tarsus to Antalya; Troy (Truva); Urfa; and Istanbul, where Europe faces Asia across the Bosphorus.

There is surprise to titillate every adventurous taste. Turkey is not just a place to visit, but the rare experience of a lifetime. As a Turk once told me proudly, 'East is east and west is west, but Turkey is something else.' It may sound glib but you will find that it is true.

History

Those who think of the Turks as 'barbarians' are probably unaware that Turkey was one of the earliest centres of civilisation, and that the Ottoman Empire at its peak rivalled those of Rome and of Britain and was just as feared, just as respected, and just as powerful. The Ottoman Empire covered an equally large area of the civilized world, stretching to Persia and the Caucasus in the east, to Hungary in the north, and the coast of Africa, Egypt and Morocco in the west. This background accounts for Turkey's sophistication today.

To travel through Turkey without an interest in the past would be the waste of a rare opportunity. Ancient sites, such as Aphrodisias, are now being excavated, which promise to equal Ephesus (Efes), once one of the Seven Wonders of the World, and those in Greece today. If you travel down the Aegean and Mediterranean coastline, you can literally stumble on ancient ruins in places like Patara and Phaselis without another person in sight. The more you can learn, the richer your experience will be. Meanwhile, this is a brief guide to the various influences which have shaped Turkey into the country you see today.

BC	
6000	Anatolia was the centre of an agricultural society, succeeded 1,000 years later by the Hatti and then by the Hittites.
2000	**The Hittites** were concerned in controlling the diverse nomadic tribes of Asia Minor.
1680–50	Labarnas I, the real founder of the Hittite Empire, was a unifying force who marched towards Aleppo. His successor, Mursilis I, conquered Babylon, establishing the Hittites as the dominant power in the Near East.
1590	Mursilis I was assassinated, and a dispute followed until a new, humane code of law was drawn up. The Hittites had the wisdom to establish an *entente cordiale* with their defeated enemies such as the Hurrians in the east of Turkey, near Lake Van, who were made feudal vassals rather than slaves.
1375–35	Pressing further south, Suppiluliumas I, the first great Hittite leader, reached the Lebanon and embraced Egypt too, where the widow of the boy-king Tutankhamen asked for one of his sons to marry and reign as one of the Pharaohs. This state of truce did not last, and was

13

followed by war against Ramses II (1292–25) who stretched the Egyptian Empire to include Syria.

1296 | Ramses was defeated decisively, though not killed, by the Hittite king Muwatallis in the Orontes valley (near today's Syrian border). Hattisilius III, brother of Muwatallis, signed a peace treaty with Egypt, consolidated by the marriage of one of his daughters to Ramses, which led to a long period of peace.

The Hittites, however, remained an enigma. They vanished off the face of the earth so completely in a national migration around 1200 BC (probably due to the influx of hordes from Asia) that their empire was unknown to the Greeks and Romans, and the reference to it in the Bible was considered legendary. Only in the last 150 years have its traces been unearthed, after a French explorer came across the ruins of a city in Central Anatolia in 1834, and rock carvings were found on the west coast unlike anything known before. A British archaeologist in the 1870s claimed that the indecipherable inscriptions found in Syria were those of the Hittites; in 1906 a German discovered a store of inscribed clay tablets on the site of Boğazköy; and ten years later a Czech deciphered them with the tremendous realisation that the Hittites once controlled much of Asia Minor, under the rule of an early constitutional monarchy, with no single common language. Eight languages have been found in Boğazköy alone. Their origins are still a mystery: they are partly Indian, the Indians having come across the Caucasus from Asia.

1250 | The barbarians from the north superseded the Hittites; Hattusa, the capital, was burned in 1200. (Remains found at Karatepe are neo-Hittite, dating from 700 BC; they are not typical of Hittite culture). Anatolia reverted to tribal domination while the coastline was occupied by the Greeks, their first influence. In eastern Turkey, the Urartian civilisation flourished in the area around Lake Van.

1100 | The Greek coastal settlements developed into independent states loosely joined together. The Ionian Greeks held Smyrna to Miletus; the Dorian and Lycian Greeks were south of ancient Halicarnassus (today's Bodrum).

540 | The Persians moved into Anatolia but proved a benevolent occupying force, although the coastal areas were forced to pay tributes. Otherwise, the Greek and Persian cultures progressed together.

356 | **Alexander the Great** born, the son of Philip II of Macedonia who was dedicated to the overthrow of the Persians and the liberation of the Greek coastal colonies.

336 | Philip II was assassinated when he was ruler of Greece, planning his great expedition which was taken over by his son. Alexander started his extraordinary conquest of Asia Minor, transporting his

Macedonian troops across the Hellespont (better known to us as the Dardanelles) two years later. They took the same route as Xerxes I, the son of Darius I of Persia, who dared to build a bridge of boats across the Hellespont 130 years earlier, triumphed at Thermopylae and looted Athens before he withdrew. When Alexander was half-way across, it is alleged that he sacrificed a bull to Poseidon, the Greek sea-god, and poured a golden cupful of wine into the swirling water as a further appeasement to the gods. Landing on the other side, he hurled his spear into Persian soil as a symbol of his attack, and led his men ashore.

333   By this time Alexander had conquered most of Asia Minor, with many cities wise enough to welcome him without a show of resistance, awed by his advancing reputation. Only one place opposed him, and he regarded that as irrelevant: the mountain city of Termessos above Antalya, which released an avalanche of boulders when he rode into the valley below on his way north, probably misled by the citizens of Phaselis where he had established his winter headquarters on the coast. Several of his soldiers were killed and his own horse injured, but this time Alexander turned away, claiming he could not be bothered with such an insignificant eagle's nest, but he set fire to the Termessian olive trees as he went.

Alexander's greatest victory came with the defeat of the superior force of the Persian Empire led by Darius III, followed by his peaceful occupation of Egypt where he founded the city which he named after himself – Alexandria. Darius reassembled his troops only to be defeated for the second time. Seeking new worlds to conquer, Alexander stretched his men to the utmost as he forged his way towards India, advancing as far as the Ganges where he was forced to turn back due to the discontent of his homesick and nearly mutinous army. His death was an anti-climax, caused by fever in Babylon in 323.

323   With no heir apparent (apart from an unborn son), Alexander's empire was fought over by his three leading generals, including
280   Seleucus. A Hellenistic period began, bringing a Greek influence to art, architecture and literature.

190   The Seleucids (named after the general) were defeated after Antiochus III (son of Seleucus II) tried to free Greece from the Romans but was routed by the Roman army at the Battle of Magnesia in 190 BC in the province of Lydia. This was the beginning of **Pax Romana**. To begin with, Anatolia benefited from two hundred years of peace and prosperity. Cities moved from the safety of the high acropolis to the flatter land below, and trade moved freely without obstacle. Then the tranquillity was ruffled by a series of foreign invasions, including that of the Goths, who ransacked what they could before they were repulsed.

15

AD

288 | Constantine the Great (288–337) chose the Greek town of Byzantium to be the new capital of the Roman Empire, rededicating it as New Rome in 330, which was soon after renamed Constantinople (the city of Constantine).

Allegedly seeing a flaming cross above him before his crucial victory over his rivals in 312, Constantine embraced the Christian faith, though he was not baptised until his deathbed. Before he moved to Constantinople, he convened the historic Council of Nicaea (Iznik today) in 325. On his death, he divided his empire among his sons.

330 | **Byzantium:** the Byzantine Empire, now established in Asia Minor, was to last with various upsets, for 1,100 years.

527 | Emperor **Justinian** (ruled 527–65) brought the Empire to a new peak, embracing the Balkans, Italy and North Africa. Known as 'the Just', he codified Roman law, encouraged Hellenistic culture and built the new St Sophia in Constantinople.

1071 | **The arrival of the Turks:** Asian nomads, known to the Chinese as *Tu.küe*, were threatened by the Mongols and migrated to the east, bringing their newly acquired Islamic faith after forming the Seljuk/ Turkish dynasty in Persia. Capturing most of Anatolia from the declining Byzantine Empire at the end of the eleventh century, the Seljuk Turks settled in Konya and ruled from the Hellespont to Arabia and India until the arrival of Genghiz Khan.

1204 | Led by the Venetians, the Crusaders looted Constantinople and the Emperor retreated to Nicaea.

1241 | The Mongols swept across the eastern borders and seized Erzurum. Two years later, the Seljuk and Byzantine armies were routed by the Mongols.

1261 | Byzantine rule was restored in Constantinople by the Emperor of Nicaea, Michael VIII, after he formed an alliance with his Genoese rivals.

1281 | **The Ottoman Empire:** the Ottoman or Osmanlı Turks emerged under Osman I, the founder of the dynasty. For 640 years they ruled from the three successive capitals in the north, Bursa, Edirne and Istanbul, removing control from Anatolia.

1449–53 | Constantine XI called in vain on the Western Church for military support. Mehmet II was able to take the supposedly impregnable city of Constantinople by blockading the Bosphorus after he had dragged his ships overland to the Golden Horn. Emperor Constantine was killed in battle when the Janissaries stormed the city; Mehmet rode to St Sophia calling for the *müezzin* to restore Islamic prayer. Constantinople became Istanbul and the Byzantine Empire was over.

1495 | The birth of **Süleyman the Magnificent** who reigned from 1520 to 1566. He lived up to his name, establishing Istanbul as one of the greatest centres of civilisation in the world. He conquered Belgrade in 1521 and stormed the Crusader castle in Rhodes after a long and devastating siege the following year. He occupied Hungary in 1526 where the appalling weather turned the roads into quagmires and offered as much resistance as the enemy. His empire stretched to North Africa where Charles V, the Hapsburg Emperor, sent sixty-five galleys and four hundred troop ships, carrying 12,000 sailors and 24,000 soldiers, to seize Algiers, under the leadership of Cortez. It was the Turks, however, who seized advantage of torrential rain and Charles lost 12,000 men. But the Turks lost Tunis to Charles in 1535 and, though Süleyman posed a real threat to Venice and Spain, his naval warfare was ultimately unsuccessful. So was his siege of Vienna (1529), largely due to more freak weather which delayed his armies.

1565 | His worst defeat came in 1565 with the siege of Malta which the Crusader Knights defended with exemplary courage, inspired by their belief in eternal salvation should they die fighting Islam. Altogether, 20,000 Turkish soldiers were killed in battle, an astonishing number considering their distance from the Turkish mainland, and proof of the ease with which massive armies could be transported across the Mediterranean. The Turkish navy was finally repulsed but, in the middle of the century (largely due to the audacity of the pirate Barbarossa from Lesbos) Süleyman had controlled the Mediterranean with constant raids on the Italian mainland. Probably he stretched himself too far.

Apart from his martial skill, Süleyman was a benevolent ruler, according to the standards of his time, and was known to the Turks as 'the lawgiver'. As he grew older, he became more lax, moving his harem and eunuchs to the Topkapı Palace which already housed the government, so that the two became fatally entwined. His grand vizier Rüstem Pasha, an intimate confidant responsible for much of the Sultan's triumph, was strangled on his orders in 1536, possibly due to the machinations of Süleyman's ambitious wife Roxelana, who was more concerned with the acquisition of her own power than of his. She also brought about the shocking murder of Süleyman's eldest son Mustafa, in order to gain the succession for her own son Selim II, 'the Sot'.

1571 | Under Selim, the slow decline of the Sultanate began. The Christian fleet under Don Juan of Austria decisively defeated the Turks at the naval Battle of Lepanto. The real power shifted to the Janissaries (an élite army corps recruited from Christian conscripts and famous for its discipline) who rebelled, but were finally abolished by Mahmut II in 1826.

1862 | Turkey had now become known as 'the sick man of Europe', constantly threatened by Russia who looked longingly at the Bosphorus and the access to the Mediterranean. The threat had brought the Allies hurrying to Turkey's defence to avoid such a seizure in the Crimean War (1853–56).

1876   With the Ottoman Empire gradually crumbling, resistance was embodied in a group who formed the Committee for Union and Progress, known in the West as 'the Young Turks'. They rebelled against Abdül Hamit, forcing him to declare a new constitution which he then revoked, killing their leader in the process.

1908   The Young Turks deposed Abdül Hamit and took charge of the government led by Enver Pasha, a revolutionary finally defeated by his own vaulting ambition.

1914–18   Turkey entered the First World War on Germany's side, largely due to British incompetence in failing to respond to a situation that was originally in their favour. The ultimate tactlessness came when the British impounded a Turkish battleship which was being built by Armstrong's on the Tyne and had been paid for by public subscription with collection boxes on the bridges of the Golden Horn and in every Turkish village. The Germans, advised by Liman von Sanders, the astute head of the German mission, moved in smartly and restored Turkish national pride with the presentation of two German warships instead, despatched at once to Constantinople though this was technically an act of war. The *Goeben* and the *Breslau* sailed through the Dardanelles on the orders of Enver Pasha, a possible alliance with Russia was abandoned and, though Turkey was still officially neutral, the warships, classified as part of the Turkish navy, retained their German crews.

1915   Istanbul was in a state of turmoil, torn apart by rival factions. A bold concept by Winston Churchill, then First Lord of the Admiralty, could have resulted in the seizure of the city if the British fleet had sailed through the Dardanelles on the first attempt and not turned back due to lack of nerve after ships were sunk, almost accidentally, by Turkish floating mines.

Another crucial factor worked against the British: by the time their forces rallied it was too late. With German supervision, the Turks recovered confidence and a young officer called **Mustafa Kemal** (1881–1938) happened to be the right man in the right place at the right moment. The British forces were close to victory – at times only a matter of yards and minutes away – but due to Kemal's extraordinary resistance at Cape Helles ('I don't order you to attack,' he told his men, 'I order you to die. In the time which passes until we die other troops and commanders can take our places') he held the ridges which dominated the narrows below. Taking advantage of British inertia after the landing at Suvla Bay, Kemal held his ground again. Finally the Allies had to evacuate ignominiously though, ironically, this withdrawal was the one triumph of their whole campaign. Kemal emerged as the 'saviour of Gallipoli' and the new leader to be reckoned with. Kemal Atatürk (the 'father of the Turks', as he became known) is in many ways the most remarkable political figure of the twentieth century, who transformed his country with skill and courage, and sometimes a necessary ruthlessness – an achievement which is still undervalued in the West today. In his own country, his memory is revered with portraits and statues in his honour in the smallest village in every corner of Turkey. In most towns, the statue or statues of Atatürk are the dominant feature, and all are different. In spite of the recent encroachment by Islam, Atatürk's reputation remains sacred and woe betide any visitor foolish enough to doubt it.

1920   After the First World War, the Allies took their revenge and threatened to carve Turkey up leaving little but skin and bones, but two developments saved the Turks. In the normal course of events, Tsarist Russia would have clasped the longed-for channel of the Bosphorus with open arms, but the leaders of the Revolution were preoccupied with their own problems and regarded the 'revolutionary' movement in Turkey with fraternal sympathy. Conversely, the Greeks, who had been bribed with the promise of Turkish territory, now demanded their reward in full and more, claiming most of Turkey's Aegean coast. Supported by the Allies in theory if not in practice, the Greeks occupied Smyrna (Izmir today) with a force of 20,000 men. This humiliation provided Atatürk with the necessary incentive: thousands of his countrymen joined his National Movement in Ankara, which was the new Turkish headquarters.

1922   The Turkish War of Independence ended with the Greeks being driven out of Smyrna with loss of life and the destruction of much of the old city by fire. It was a cruel victory but it was a battle won. Kemal Atatürk became the first President of the Turkish Republic (proclaimed in 1923) and an astonishing period followed with his Westernisation of Turkey – virtually the inspiration and fulfilment of one man. Religious courts were replaced by the Swiss Legal Code, a new alphabet was introduced, the Koran was banned in schools, the fez and yashmak were banned as well, and Sunday was declared a day of rest.

Atatürk's determination to pull Turkey into the twentieth century could be described as fanatical but, unlike most fanatics, he was a man who enjoyed the human pleasures of life to the full, and even had his share of so-called 'weakness of the flesh' which helps to explain his identification with the people and their reciprocal devotion. And, unlike most fanatics, he was successful. He died at the Dolmabahçe Palace on 10 November 1938; as the tugs pass by on the anniversary of his death today, they still sound their sirens in respect for this extraordinary man.

1939–44	Turkey adopted a sensible, if precarious, neutrality in the Second World War.
1950	The Democratic Party, rival to Atatürk's People's Party, won the election; Adnan Menderes held office for ten unsatisfactory years.
1960	The army took over and Menderes was executed.
1965	The Justice Party was returned in the General Election but Turkey rapidly approached civil war.
1971	The army intervened, but the country was close to anarchy, with shooting in the streets.
1980	General Evren, the head of the Turkish army, took over as President and restored order with Turgut Özal as the Prime Minister, responsible for the security which distinguishes Turkey today.
1987	At the end of November, further proof of Turkey's democratic process was confirmed in the first free elections since the military coup of 1980, with 93 per cent of the electorate going to the polls, returning Prime Minister Turgut Özal with an overwhelming majority. Mr Özal declared: 'Turkey will become economically more liberal than most Western European countries.'

Architectural style

Hittite, Greek and Roman, Byzantine, Seljuk and Ottoman are the main influences in Turkey. For the layman like myself there is the immediate need to comprehend the distinctions between the early civilisations which dominated the ancient world.

This was not a case of standing stones, primitive implements, scratched murals or mystifying, lumpish erections like Stonehenge. For anything comparable you have to look south to the Pharaohs of Egypt with their sumptuous design, or to China for the ultimate refinement. The temple to Artemis at Ephesus, and the mausoleum at Halicarnassus were included in the Seven Wonders of the Ancient World, and the statues on the top of Mount Nemrut (first century AD) deserved to be another.

A recent exhibition in Istanbul was symbolised by the trellised sun-disc of the Hittites – a splendid design which, incidentally, is more reminiscent of the Aztecs than of European culture which was backward by comparison. The Greek and Roman styles, eventually inter-mingling, reached a peak of perfection in cities like Ephesus and Aphrodisias, and the ports of Priene, Cnidus and Side were superior to the Roman colonisation of Western Europe where the climate was less conducive.

For the traveller, there is the danger of a surfeit of places to see. A Seljuk doorway anywhere else would bring the tourists flocking, not just for the understandable surprise, but also for the astonishing beauty which one should never take for granted in Turkey. There is the additional excitement that many of the ancient sites are still being excavated. In Patara, Olympos, the marshes below Caunus and the island of Gemile there is just a hint of the full marvel to be unearthed.

To travel through Turkey is enjoyable even if you haven't the faintest interest in the past, but if you have such curiosity and wish to learn the rudiments of the different architectural styles, then you will travel with a sense of history and your stay will be infinitely more rewarding.

The Hittites

Architecturally, the Hittites were noted for the contrast of the thickness and heaviness of their walls and the delicacy of their gold and silver ornaments, used 4,000 years ago in religious ceremonies. These can be seen in the Hittite Museum in Ankara. The Yazılıkaya sculptures near Boğazköy are tremendous: reliefs of figures 2.5 m tall apparently in procession, marching along the walls of two galleries, the men in short tunics and pointed hats, the women (or goddesses) in long skirts, wearing jewellery. The Hittite lions, their mouths open in a roar intended to frighten off intruders, still guard the citadel of Boğazköy.

The Greeks

Settling along the coast of the Aegean around 1100 BC in large numbers, the Greeks established a confederation of cities. The Dorians followed, settling further south around the Datça Peninsula with Cnidus as the great port at the end, where the Aegean meets the Mediterranean. It is necessary to realise that these seas were as busy as any of the great waterways today.

Inevitably the Greeks moved inland, into Anatolia, replacing the Hittites. Further south, from Dalyan to Kaş, the Lycians left their distinctive mark with humped sarcophagi (you can see one in a back street of Kaş today) or those standing petrified in the waters of Kekova. Even more remarkable are the columned tombs in the shape of a portal carved into the cliffs at Dalyan, one of the loveliest sights in Turkey with the river flowing underneath; they are less accessible, and consequently more mysterious, than those at Fethiye.

The Greeks built their amphitheatres, recognisable because they moulded them out of the terrain whereas the Romans erected a structure behind. These theatres are a yardstick, not only of the civilisation (there are few signs of barracks or prisons), but to gauge the size of the population which was roughly ten times that of the audience. This is frequently exaggerated: a television presenter who claimed blithely that one of the smaller theatres seated 250,000 people was thinking in grandiose terms which would have daunted even Cecil B. de Mille. In fact, the theatres vary enormously in size: that at Miletus held 20–25,000 spectators, a figure scarcely conceivable today. The smaller

Lycian sarcophagus

Columns (l-r) Doric, Ionic, Corinthian

Hittite lion at Boğazköy

Greek amphitheatre

Medusa head

Lycian cliff tombs at Demre

Mosque at Edirne by Sinan

Seljuk doorway

Roman amphitheatre

theatre of Termessos is just as remarkable due to its precarious position in the mountains; it held a more manageable 4,000 people who watched the plays by the light of oil-lamps.

Another point of recognition are the columns which supported the roofs of the temples, since destroyed by the elements or the calculated act of later dynasties – the Byzantines who pulled down the Temple of Athena at Assos, and the Christians who were guilty of similar destruction at Aphrodisias. Enough remains to astound one: in Uzuncaburç, in the hills behind Silifke, roofless columns surround the former temple of Zeus; at Priene five lonely columns achieve a remarkable effect of serenity, overlooking the plain where the great river once meandered and met the sea.

In the most basic, layman's way, here are some means of identifying them:

Doric: severe, slightly tapered towards the top which is stark and undecorated; used to support wooden buildings, with twenty fluted indentations around the heavy column. Few examples survive: one is the Acropolis above Edremit.

Ionic: far more elegant, untapered and thinner with twenty-four flutes. The base is moulded (unlike the Doric style) and the top of the capital is decorated with a twirl on either side like a ram's horns.

Corinthian: this is the most elaborate, a work of art with a capital of cascading leaves. It is richly impressive, though the Ionic style is simpler and sublime. The Romans also used acanthus leaves to ornament their triumphal arches (a new innovation) – at Hadrian's Archway in Antalya, with lions' heads above.

The later Romans deserve the credit for continuing the best of the Greek tradition, developing a Hellenistic style (Pergamon and Aphrodisias are examples); they even completed the Temple of Apollo in Didyma as the Greeks intended.

Byzantine: new and larger churches replaced the early temples and the Byzantine influence progressed in two easily identifiable stages. The basilica, more secular, followed a rectangular design with two rows of columns dividing the area lengthwise, and a low, timber roof. The dome was added in the sixth century AD, using arches to support the concave circle, and buttresses outside to enhance the space. The greatest example can be seen in Ayasofia in Istanbul. The churches in Cappadocia, below the ground as well as above, with their early frescoes of Christ, were designed in a unique troglodyte style and are striking proof of Christian perseverance.

Seljuk: an instantly recognisable style used in the intricately carved stonework of the doorways of caravanserais and theological schools, rising to a steep, triangular point. One look convinces us that this influence came from Persia in the East. The importance of the entrance was due to its use as a public audience with those in authority.

The Ottoman or Osmanlı influence: this achieved the full splendour of the mosque with ornately tiled minarets and patterned walls (as in Erzurum) reaching perfection in the age of Süleyman the Magnificent and his architect Sinan in the sixteenth century. A truly Turkish style was established for the first time – the harmony of the great dome flanked by minarets, already referred to, with a blaze inside of Iznik tiles in their unique blue.

The Ottoman style continued until the nineteenth century when it was replaced by a sort of Turkish baroque exemplified by the palaces of Dolmabahçe and Beylerbeyi on the Bosphorus, yet even these are startling feats of architecture whose appeal increases with time, while the smaller Pavilions so lovingly restored, such as the Malta Pavilion in Yıldız Park, are simpler works of art whose beauty you can appreciate with the advantage of a drink or cup of *çay* or *kahve* instead of the stuffiness of museums.

Turkey Today

Area: 780,576 sq km
Population: 53 million
Tourists: 2½ million a year, and rising

Turkey is changing fast. A backward nation of 12 million when Kemal Atatürk declared the Republic in 1923, the population will be close to 70 million at the end of the century and that of Istanbul alone might equal the whole of Greece. Inevitably, such speed is accompanied by the usual spread of building and industrialisation which does not improve the countryside, however desirable it is in itself. Fortunately, Turkey is vast – more of a continent than a country – and able to absorb such development and more to come, for it is vital to the economy that the scope of agriculture be expanded too, with such immense projects as the Atatürk Dam embracing the basin of the Tigris and Euphrates, irrigating an area twice the size of the Netherlands. The landscape will be changed and villages submerged, but far greater fertility will follow. Conservationists are worried, but it can be argued that even the need for a power station on the Gulf of Gökova is a necessary, if deplorable, part of the new Turkey.

Admittedly, there is anxiety over the rise in inflation, estimated at 30 per cent (the highest in the OECD), with interest and repayments on substantial debts of $30 billion. On the credit side, Turkey is enjoying the benefits of an open economy, with a better standard of living for those in the shanty towns of Ankara and Istanbul, the injection of foreign currency due to tourism, a realistic exchange rate which has boosted exports, a lack of strikes, and a greater security than the country has enjoyed for years. If all continues well, the outlook for the 1990s is highly favourable, with Turkey as a possible flourishing member of the EEC.

Membership of the EEC

As far back as 1963, the President of the European Community stated that 'Turkey is part of Europe', yet her application is still being considered, much to the mortification of the Turks themselves. Apart from implacable opposition from Greece, there are several debatable reasons for the delay. These are partly the result of ignorance, a vague suspicion that Turkey, with her rapidly increasing population, is an uncomfortable and uncertain proposition. Then there is the vexed question of human rights, though Turkish prisoners now have the right of appeal to the European Human Rights Commission. In 1987 less than 0.2 per cent in a referendum opposed the motion to allow former political leaders like Süleyman Demirel and Bülent Ecevit (both former Prime Ministers) to campaign for political office in subsequent elections. Those who accuse Turkey sometimes forget, however, that political dissidents are also known in other countries, such as Northern Ireland, which is part of the United Kingdom. If you want to familiarise yourself with the Turkish political situation, the *Daily News*, written in English, is extraordinarily frank by any standards, not hesitating to criticise the government or to support the former Prime Minister Süleyman Demirel in his bid for a return to power. Any doubts you may have about censorship are likely to be confounded. It is well edited and useful for the latest news on what is happening inside Turkey.

From sheer expediency, Turkey's role as a member of NATO is crucial to Western Europe and America, placed as it is between the USSR and the Middle East, with the recent threat of Islamic fanaticism spreading from Iran. Does the West really wish to embrace Turkey's friendship or risk her possible shift towards the East? No wonder that the Turks are bewildered by Europe's continuing hesitation and apparent indifference.

Religion

Turkey is part of Islam and an estimated 99 per cent of the population is Muslim. You will hardly be aware of this, especially in the cities where people drink even during the fast of Ramadan (*Ramazan* in Turkish), though this is against their religion. It is only in Eastern Turkey, or similar remoter regions, that you come face to face with such rules yourself and are expected to observe them.

Any confusion is due to the drastic reforms of Kemal Atatürk which were deliberately secular, aimed at breaking the established traditions of centuries. The fez was banned, and women were encouraged to abandon their veils, a fashion which caught on quickly when it was decreed that prostitutes should keep on wearing them. Atatürk was determined to bring Turkey into the twentieth century and become part of Western Europe, and he realised that Islamic laws were an obstacle. But these Islamic roots lie deep, and today there are signs that they may be growing back. In Eastern Turkey, the abstinence of Ramazan has always been observed scrupulously, but it comes as a shock to be woken in the Pera Palas Hotel in Istanbul by the drums and flutes outside which signal the last opportunity to eat, around 3.30 a.m. A few years ago, people might have opened their windows and yelled 'Shut up!' This is no longer the case. But perhaps the threat should not be exaggerated. A poll in the newspaper *Milliyett* in 1987 showed only 7 per cent wanting the strict Sharia law insisted upon by Islam fundamentalists, forbidden under Turkish law. Only 18 per cent worship the requisite five times a day, though 54 per cent observe Ramazan. The future could well show a shift in favour of Islam fostered by the active training in religious schools, but it is right to emphasise that the more moderate Muslim traditions can be a controlling influence.

Apart from the drumbeat of Ramazan, the sound which makes you aware that you are in Islam is the chant of the *müezzin* – usually relayed from the top of the minaret by loudspeaker, nowadays – proclaiming that 'There is no God but Allah and Mohammed is his Prophet.' The prayers are spoken five times a day, preceded by meticulous washing which explains the wash-basins and taps encircling the mosques. These ablutions – of face, hands, forearms and feet – are obligatory: for moral as well as physical cleaniness.

More recent than Christianity, the Muslim religion was started in Mecca in the sixth century when the Prophet Mohammed received instructions from God which formed the basis of the Koran. Islam acknowledges Jesus and the Bible. There are five precepts: the adherence to faith; prayer; almsgiving; the fast of Ramazan, and the pilgrimage to Mecca, which remains the ultimate affirmation (anyone who goes there is known as a *hacı*, such as the present Prime Minister). Mosques include niches which face in the direction of Mecca (*kıble*); and all prayers (*mihrab*) are also said facing Mecca.

Advice

Though visitors are welcome, it is courteous to observe the formalities if you enter a Turkish mosque: leave your shoes outside, do not wear shorts or short skirts (which are inadvisable anyway), and cover your head and shoulders if you are a woman (a shawl is often provided at the entrance). If you have slip-on shoes, wear them to save you trouble if you know you will be visiting several mosques. Keep reasonably quiet: chattering can be a nuisance even if you are not a Muslim, for mosques are havens of serenity and quiet in contrast to the surrounding bustle.

Ramazan

The most important religious fast in the year, Ramazan lasts for thirty days; the date is slightly different each year due to the Muslim calendar. Neither food nor drink must pass the lips of the true Muslim from sunrise to sunset. Then a cannon booms out the signal that it is time to eat again, and people hurry to the bakers for fresh bread and go home for a massive meal, terminated by the drums at half past three or four o'clock in the morning. It is just as well to find out the exact dates of Ramazan before your visit. After climbing to the stone figures on

Mount Nemrut at dawn, I was eager for a cup of tea or some refreshment when we descended and could not understand it when we were greeted with shrugs and the unconvincing explanation that the 'tea' had not yet arrived. As this was a place plainly intended for travellers like myself, it seemed curious indeed, until I was refused even a glass of water at our next stop and the obvious truth dawned at last – this was the first day of Ramazan. I mention it to show how strictly the rules are observed in remoter Central and Eastern regions where it is unwise to be seen eating fruit in public, smoking, or even taking a drink from a public fountain. Reserve these excesses for your hotel where such behaviour is tolerated.

Şeker Bayramı 'Sugar Festival' lasts for three days – a cheerful celebration of the end of fasting, when gifts are brought to family and friends, and sweets given to children. This is a universal practice: the officers on board ship still present their men with cakes or biscuits, as they have done for centuries. Banks are closed and resorts like Bodrum are crowded with visitors. This is a time for music, dancing, food and drink, not to mention smoking and sex, which are also frowned on during Ramazan.

Kurban Bayramı This is a longer version of Şeker Bayramı, lasting for four days, which falls two months and ten days later. It starts with a Festival of Sacrifices, notably the ritual slaughter of a sheep. Usually this is performed discreetly in someone's back garden; occasionally in an open street, the blood flowing down the gutter to the understandable dismay of unsuspecting tourists. In fact, the ritual is less gruesome than it sounds: I have been deeply impressed by the solemnity, the way that the sheep is caressed beforehand, and despatched with a razor-sharp knife which is more merciful than an abattoir where the noise and smell of blood can terrify the waiting animals. The sacrifice is not a mere gesture but has the practical purpose of feeding the poor, as the meat is cut up and distributed by the rich to their less fortunate neighbours to whom such a meal is a rare treat. Even the sheepskin is not wasted, but given away.

The Weather and When to Go

Freak weather (which seems to strike all parts of the world nowadays) caused an exceptionally heavy snowfall in the winter of 1986–87 and heavy rainfall along the coast in the following spring. Eastern Turkey in any case usually has heavy snow and intense cold from October to April, so it is best to travel there in early June, which avoids the religious taboos of Ramazan, which usually falls in May.

Summers are hot, often unpleasantly so for tourists who have to take their holidays in July and August when the temperature at Marmaris can reach 92°F/33°C with thirteen hours of sunshine and uncomfortable humidity. Even at sea, such heat can be stifling if you do not worship the sun.

The Black Sea is variable, with rain even in summer, and heavy snow in winter. Central Anatolia endures hot summers and intense cold in winter. The Mediterranean enjoys a mild winter, with sudden bursts of rain which pass quickly. The Aegean has the most moderate climate of all: hot summers, but not as fierce as those further south, and mild winters. The best months for travel along the coast are May and June, and September and October. These are the best months for Istanbul too, which can be quite cool and wet, but April and early November can be good, too.

Travelling Around

By air

To Turkey Regular flights go from many major international airports direct to Istanbul – also to Izmir and Antalya, though these are less frequent in winter. However, flights on national airlines are usually expensive, and by far the best are the many tour operators active in the air charter business which now offer seats (when they are available) for less than half the national airlines' prices. A list of these is available from the Turkish Tourist Office, or you can telephone direct to the agencies concerned (see pp. 68–9) or check in your local travel agency.

Dalaman Airport opened for charter flights in 1982, transforming arrivals and departures for holiday-makers who are heading straight for the coast. Strategically placed inland, Dalaman is little more than an hour's drive from Marmaris in the west and Fethiye in the south, and is used by the Yacht Cruising Association and Island Sailing who frequently have spare seats for sale on their private charter flights. A new local airport, promised near Bodrum, for smaller aircraft will cut hours off travel time.

Students should remember that they are likely to be eligible for discounts – within Turkey, too – so take your proof with you.

Inside Turkey There are internal flights to Samsun, Trabzon, Izmir, Dalaman, Ankara, Sivas, Erzurum, Kayseri, Elazığ, Antalya, Adana, Malatya, Diyarbakır, Van, and Gaziantep. Istanbul has two airports, internal and international; the service is efficient and cheap – for example, around L 62,000 single to Antalya and L 75,225 single to Van.

By train

To Turkey The train journey to Turkey from Britain is a marathon. The best is the overnight Tauern Express from Ostende, with sleeping cars, which arrives in Munich the next morning to catch the Istanbul Express in the evening, going through Yugoslavia and Bulgaria with sleepers as far as Belgrade. Visas are needed and you would be wise to bring your own refreshments. The second-class single fare is approximately £135.

Distance Chart

Adapazarı see Sakarya
Antalya see Hatay
İzmit see Kocaeli
Mersin see İçel
Şanlıurfa see Urfa

An altogether more elaborate alternative would be to consider travelling on the Orient Express. If you wish to indulge yourself by taking one of those proverbial journeys of a lifetime, full details are available from Venice Simplon-Orient-Express, Sea Containers House, 20 Upper Ground, London SE1 9PF, tel.: 01-928 6000. This comes close to emulating the original glamour of the old Orient Express, by taking you across Europe from London to Paris, Zürich, St Anton, Innsbruck, Verona and Venice, where you transfer to a ferry for Istanbul. This luxury tour departs from London on Thursdays and you leave Venice on Friday for Istanbul. It is, as you might expect, expensive (£1,625); but it would certainly be a memorable way to travel to Istanbul.

Inside Turkey
The train service is often and inexplicably overlooked, partly because those Turks who can afford to do so, prefer to fly. Yet a long train journey to a place like Van in the east gives a unique insight into the country and is wholly enjoyable if you have stocked up with favourite food and drink. The cabins are comfortable and astonishingly inexpensive. There are express services between Istanbul, Ankara and Izmir; otherwise Turkish trains are not for the impatient but for those who wish to relax with no regard for time. When Turkish trains are good they are excellent, though admittedly this is usually for long distances such as Istanbul to Ankara, Erzurum and the east.

I was personally delighted with my journey from Istanbul where I left the Golden Horn by ferry and crossed the Bosphorus to the station at Üsküdar, Haydarpaşa Garı, climbing up the steps through the domed entrances of decorated glass, to find the train impatient to start its journey. This ended at Tatvan three days later on the edge of Lake Van, and we continued by boat for a further five hours to Van on the other side. My train compartment was clean and comfortable and, though the 'restaurant' consisted of a couple of tables occupied usually by the buffet staff, they were friendly and many of their own meals to which I pointed proved surprisingly good. Do not expect a wide choice, and bring your own treats if you are greedy or obsessional. The charming gesture of the young waiters who picked wild flowers from the field during a long delay, producing a posy on the dinner-table later, was more than compensation for the lack of brusque efficiency. Better the Turkish rough-and-tumble any day.

The cost of crossing Turkey from one end to the other is almost nominal, not much more than L 29,300.

By bus

To Turkey
You can ask about and take the cheapest bus available direct to Ath-

ens. Then continue by local buses to Salonika, Kavala and Xanthi to Istanbul. This may introduce you to new depths of discomfort but in retrospect it could be just as much fun as the lush Orient Express – more so if you are young. At least you are spared the neutered hell of airports.

Inside Turkey This service is magnificent: comfortable and extraordinarily cheap – around L 7,000 for an overnight journey from Ankara to the coast, or from Bodrum to Izmir. The network reaches every corner, and is one of the most reliable and extensive means of travelling in Turkey.

Try to travel early in the morning or overnight, to avoid the heat of the day and the waste of valuable time. Journeys of several hours are broken by stops which provide relief and the chance for a cup of tea or something to eat at one of the excellent roadside *lokantas*, but they also prolong the time involved. There is no point in growing impatient, but arm yourself with fruit and a good book. Travelling from Bodrum to Izmir in the afternoon would have seemed interminable except that I read the whole of Conrad's *Heart of Darkness*.

Two points to remember: the depot or *otogar* is usually on the outskirts of the city, or outside it altogether – as in Erzurum. Also, there are several bus companies to choose from, so if you do not find a service which suits your timetable, try another company nearby.

Once on board, everyone is friendly, from the boy who provides free bottles of water and pours freshening cologne into your palms, to the driver who may pay you the compliment of allowing you to sit in front. This has the best view, with the possible penalty of a radio-fanatic as the driver switches incessantly from one station to another (especially when he hits on pleasing music) with an alarming lack of concentration on the road ahead. The sign above him is discouraging: 'Trust in Allah'. If you are making a long journey in the summer, it is better to sit behind one of the roof skylights unless the bus is air-conditioned, and ask the boy to have it opened if necessary. A 200 km journey takes approximately four hours and costs about L 3,000 – marvellous value.

By car

To Turkey Driving can only be recommended if you have time to waste or have sadistic feelings towards your car, for it involves going along vile roads in Yugoslavia and you have to obtain a transit visa beforehand which is valid for only 48 hours if you continue through Bulgaria. The journey is close on 3,000 km and takes four to five days. Obviously, you are advised to seek the assistance of the AA or RAC who will supply detailed information.

Turkish Maritime Lines operate a car-ferry service from Venice to

Izmir, which continues to Istanbul. This departs every Saturday at 9 p.m. in high season (mid-June to end of September) and every fifteen days in April, May and the first half of June. It arrives in Izmir on Tuesdays at 1 p.m. and departs at 4 p.m. on the same day, arriving in Istanbul on Wednesday at 10 a.m. Details are available from Sunquest Holidays (see p. 69) or: Turkish Maritime Lines (Türkiye Denizcilik İşletmeleri), Denizyolları Ac., Rıhtım Caddesi, Karaköy, Istanbul. Tel.: 1440207/1455366. Telex: 24810 DZYLTR. There are also offices in Ankara, Izmir and Mersin.

Inside Turkey

Most of the main roads are good, though there can be sudden stretches where the road is about to be resurfaced or reconstructed and you have to proceed at a dusty crawl. The outskirts of Marmaris resemble an area recently blitzed. Heavy, long-distance lorries can slow you down but are less overpowering than they are in most countries, and the roads can be refreshingly empty in eastern regions like Lake Van, where driving is a pleasure.

Car hire gives you freedom at a cost. It is not cheap at around L 290,000 a week, plus petrol, which varies in price from city to city. A Turkish hire firm might be slightly cheaper; otherwise the names will be familiar – Avis, Budget, National Europcar and Hertz, with offices in the main centres like Kusadası and Antalya, in addition to Istanbul and Izmir. Remember, too, that charges are invariably higher than estimated, with a 10 per cent tax in addition to the cost of petrol.

In some parts of Turkey, driving can be exceptionally hazardous: you may be startled to find yourself being overtaken on bends, cut up, or subjected to a prolonged blare on the horn. Be prepared to pull in if you suddenly find that you're driving towards a large vehicle which is overtaking slowly on your side of the road: lorries are the worst offenders. Obviously the best advice is to ensure you do not allow yourself to retaliate in similar fashion, and to avoid night driving if at all possible.

If the worst should happen, however, and you find yourself involved in an accident, you must inform the police – whether or not anyone has been injured – as an official report of the incident is essential. Repairs can be carried out in towns (garages can be found on principal highways and grouped in special streets), and there are official agents in Istanbul, Ankara and Izmir dealing in spare parts for foreign cars.

If it is necessary to leave a vehicle in Turkey, either for repair or because it is a write-off, it must be delivered to a customs office in order that the vehicle's endorsement on your passport can be cancelled. Without this cancellation you will not be allowed to leave the country. If you are leaving the vehicle for repair only, make it clear to the customs office that this is the case, because any vehicle which is not reclaimed within three months is considered to be abandoned and steps are taken to dispose of it.

By taxi and dolmuş

**Inside
Turkey**

Taxis are reasonable – less than half of what they cost in Britain, for example – but always agree on a price beforehand if you are outside Istanbul, if you are going some distance, or if you notice that the meter is mysteriously 'out of order'. Otherwise, they are good value.

You can share a taxi within towns or for shorter distances. Also there is a form of mini-bus (slightly more expensive) which is fine for connections in remoter areas (such as Ortaca to Dalyan) but less so for longer journeys when you should aim for the quickest service possible. The *dolmuş* is an entertaining, shared experience though it can be irksome if you have to be somewhere on time, for it stops constantly as more and more people and their animals are squeezed inside until the vehicle resembles the Marx Brothers' cabin in *A Night at the Opera*. *Dolmuş* means 'stuffed' and the name could hardly be more accurate. It does not depart until it is so full that it can hardly move, but there is the considerable advantage that it will stop to pick you up, or drop you off, *anywhere*. As you wait for a passenger to deliver a bale of cotton or fetch a favourite goat, this is a good way of absorbing the countryside. The destination is confirmed from the sign on the front window and cries from the driver and his friends. Fares are taken on board, another person squeezes in breathlessly, and you trundle off at last – a jolly, carefree jaunt.

Where to Stay

A century ago there was scarcely a hotel in Turkey. The concept was something new – a Western invention. Until then, the place for the traveller to stop at was the Seljuk *hans* or caravanserai, dating back to the thirteenth century, usually placed one day's journey apart on the caravan trail. Protected by strong walls, they resemble fortresses with a courtyard inside, a mosque, bedrooms, kitchens and even baths. They were self-contained and welcomed travellers and their animals free of charge. This was due to the generosity of the rich who lent the land as a charity but also as a shrewd form of safekeeping, for the caravanserais were regarded as a necessity and were safe from the hands of any acquisitive sultan. Many examples can be seen today, in Edirne and Kusadası (now a splendid hotel), with three others near Kayseri.

If you were not on the caravan route, or found that the caravanserai was too far, there was no problem – you simply knocked on the nearest door and you were admitted as 'a visitor from God', a courtesy still practised today. If you misbehaved yourself you might be killed once you continued on your journey, but while you were a guest your presence was sacrosanct.

Until 1839, when the sultan gave rights to minorities and foreigners, there were few independent travellers from abroad apart from those on diplomatic business, but after the reforms they poured in for reasons of trade and needed somewhere to stay. Finally, the British embassy grew tired of housing unwelcome guests and encouraged a hotel opposite to look after their surplus visitors. It was known, predictably, as the Hotel Angleterre and was claimed to be the first hotel in Turkey, if not in all the Orient. As it opened in 1841, only two years after the sultan's reforms, the English acted with haste, probably thankful to be rid of the businessmen who were demanding accommodation.

One of the owners was Egyptian, a small man with a moustache, with a photograph of Queen Victoria on one wall and one of himself on the other. He was dictatorial, insisting on a long dining-table, rather like a ship's, with himself as the captain, and he told his customers what newspaper to read – even the novelist Pierre Loti, who did not return but built his own house above the other side of the Golden Horn. However, the sunsets and the views were known to be magnificent. More recently, the Angleterre has been renamed the Alp.

In 1892, the Pera Palas opened for the first passengers off the Orient

Express, carried from the station by sedan chair; the original china can be seen in the hotel today, in a glass case, with the intials W.L. denoting *wagons lits*. Of all the hotels in Istanbul, the Pera Palas conveys the splendour and romance of old Turkey.

The original owner was Jewish-Lebanese and on his death the property was divided among four charities (which must be unique). The profits are administered today by the management headed by Mr Hasan Süzer, one of the great hoteliers in the world.

The first truly Turkish hotel was not opened in Istanbul until after the First World War. Today there is a profusion, but it is wise to book in advance for they are often full in the tourist season. Outside Istanbul and the main cities such as Izmir and Ankara, hotels are less prevalent (though there is usually a good one in every town). This presents a problem in view of the sudden tourist explosion; one solution, drastic yet doubtful, is the construction of holiday villages or complexes on a massive scale. At their best, these are excellent, designed with care and imagination among existing trees and shrubs and laid out with colourful flower beds. Two that spring to mind are the Akçay Turban Holiday Village (Turban is a reliable name to look out for), with buildings kept deliberately low, flanked by palm, mulberry and magnolia, with borders of luxuriant lilies, geraniums and roses: there was even honeysuckle around the door of my chalet. The food and service are first-rate and there is the obligatory spacious swimming-pool beside the sea. Another is the Holiday Village at Marmaris with plenty of facilities for the family; individual chalets are set so skilfully among pine trees that the place is invisible as you sail into the bay.

At their worst, the complexes are impersonal, concrete stalags with the evident influence of their Germanic investors – you could be anywhere in the world, especially as the Germans seem to expect the Turks to adapt to their (topless) way of life, instead of adapting to the country they are in. If you make the effort of travelling to Turkey, it is Turkey you ought to see. You may ask why, if people are happy lolling on the beach all day, paying 'pearls' or beads at the bar, and eating international food, it should be begrudged. The answer is simple: Turkey offers so much more. On the credit side, such 'villages' serve as useful bases to explore and they provide invaluable shock-absorbers for the legions of tourists now pouring in from all over Europe.

Pansiyons

For me, the most agreeable accommodation of all is the small, private hotel or *pansiyon*. This is hard to find anywhere in the world nowadays, when modesty is almost a filthy word, yet rewarding when you do with none of the hassle of reception desks, piped muzak in the dining saloon, sanitised loos, or a disenchanted staff who take no personal interest because they know they are unlikely to see you again. *Pansiyons* are the perfect compromise and should be nurtured and cultivated for the future. They prove so successful that I hope they have signposted the way in places like Kas, Bodrum and the village of Dalyan, where you can stay for under L 9,000 a night and eat your breakfast by the side of the river with the Lycian tombs carved in the cliffs opposite, an orange tree in the foreground, and the caiques chugging gently out to sea laden with bales of cotton. The bed might be slightly hard and the room extremely simple, but for me this is the height of luxury.

Checking your room

Even if it goes against your sense of reticence, you have nothing to lose in asking to see your room beforehand and much to gain – even a grudging respect. Arriving at Bodrum to find it full up as usual, my helpful taxi-driver stopped at a *pansiyon* next to the sea indicating that it was as good inside as it appeared. Fortunately, I kept him waiting, for the room I was shown proved to be a small, airless cell without windows. It is easier to make your stand at the outset and find what you want, rather than move in meekly and complain afterwards.

Tourism

The Turkish tourist industry is at a crucial point. The temptation to cash in on Turkey's belated popularity must be irresistible; also there is the *need* to cash in by providing as many facilities and beds as possible. At the same time, Turkey is one of the few parts of the Mediterranean which remains comparatively unspoilt and this is the reason why people want to go there. It's the old story of killing the goose that lays the golden eggs.

Fortunately, the Turkish authorities are aware of the danger and restrict the growth and height of new buildings within a certain distance from the sea. Consequently, the coastline is spared the towers which scar the Spanish Costa Brava, casting shadows on the sand. Also, to be fair, most of the new concrete complexes (around Kemer, for example) are hidden out of sight so they are hardly offensive visually unless you are staying there. Best of all, places like the miles of beach at Patara, with the ancient city behind, have been declared protected areas and this is taking effect. The first pension at Patara, which opened this year, is set inland with admirable discretion, considering that residents will have to be driven two kilometres before they see the sea. Unfortunately, such foresight is rare. The same conservation should apply immediately to Dalyan where the delta itself is threatened by the construction of a large hotel at the end of that magical sandbar where the loggerhead turtles used to nest. Tarnish such places with pollution and you tarnish them for ever.

In the spring of 1987 I was asked to address some students at the Boğaziçi University who were studying the effects of tourism, and these are some of my notes: 'Tourism will happen; for the economy it *must* happen, it is both desirable and inevitable. But it can be controlled. There is a real risk that in encouraging mass tourism too quickly – in doing too much, too soon – you will destroy the unique qualities of Turkey, the beauty and the friendliness, which are why the more discerning traveller wants to come here today. Money is the excuse, but I believe that more money will be earned in the future if you conserve today. If only for reasons of greed, it is madness to act with haste. Time is on Turkey's side. Do not think of five years ahead but fifty or a hundred. Not your children but your grandchildren.'

Fine phrases, but the students were unimpressed: they knew all this already. And it was encouraging to learn that if it's a choice of turtles or tourists, they are on the side of the turtles. After all, there will always be tourists – a threatening rather than a threatened species. Fortunately, the Turkish coastline is so crenellated with inlets and bays that there is room to accommodate both. Meanwhile, the peace of Dalyan is unique and should not be jeopardised.

Eating and Drinking

Turkish food reminds one of the range of the Ottoman Empire, which brought paprika to Hungary and coffee to the gates of Vienna, while importing the national dishes of the conquered lands and adapting them accordingly. Turkish food is both basic, reflecting the charcoal grills of the nomads, and elegant, deriving from the succulent morsels fed to the sultans.

I say food, rather than cuisine, for it is the freshness of the produce rather than the conversion it undergoes which makes it exceptional. Many would disagree with me here: the *maître d'hotel* at the Divan in Istanbul, famous for its first-class restaurant, told me that there are three great cuisines in the world: French (which no one would disagree with), Russian and Turkish. This is a curious claim, ignoring Chinese cooking which must be more imaginative than Russian. Also, if I am to be scrupulously honest, I must admit that Turkish meals can become monotonous. It helps to recognise this so that you can make your choice carefully and seize on new dishes as well as the old dependables.

Circassian chicken

For example, there is one outstanding national dish to look out for which is seldom on the menu because it is troublesome to prepare. This is Circassian Chicken, *Çerkez Tavuğu*, brought to Istanbul by the slave girls from the Caucasus, allegedly the most beautiful in the harem and possibly beloved because they were able to whet the appetites of the sultans with this incomparable taste, a blend of chicken and pounded walnuts.

In former days, with ample time to spare, the women of the household pounded the walnuts interminably in a pestle and mortar, releasing the walnut oil which formed a paste. This was spread over cold boiled chicken which was also pounded, though I prefer the small pieces which are often used instead. The other ingredients are garlic, paprika and chicken stock, and a couple of spoonfuls of vegetable or olive oil, or French walnut oil if it is available. Today, with the genius of the blender and the addition of a slice of white, crustless bread (soaked in cold water and squeezed dry), the thick sauce can be made in seconds, mixed with the chicken pieces and spread smoothly over the top, garnished with walnut halves. It may not be traditional but it works beautifully.

41

Mezes

Circassian chicken illustrates the Russian influence; the concept of numerous side dishes, as the basis for the meal, reflects the Chinese. There is one recommendation I should pass on immediately. The *mezes* epitomise all that is best in Turkish food, especially if you have a taste for garlic, yoghurt, aubergine and olive oil. These appetisers can range from a simple salad of tomato, cucumber and green pepper, or slices of melon with white cheese, to a lavish array of glorious *hors d'œuvres* which revive past memories as well as appetites. Everything is freshly prepared, without the deception of yesterday's dishes revamped to resemble today's. To resort to that sort of culinary subterfuge is alien to Turkish taste.

In fact, the *mezes* are so tempting that one procedure is vital in order to save you frustration and disappointment. *Never* order your entire meal in advance. If you do, all the dishes, hot and cold – *mezes*, fish, meat and dessert – will arrive simultaneously, and your expectation of a gradual meal to be relished at leisure is dashed. If several of you are eating, you will be wise to order a number of separate *mezes* to start with and re-order if one proves especially popular, but you will be hardly able to do so if the rest of the meal appears to be waiting impatiently.

If you are in a rush, ignore this advice completely. But if you are in such a rush, it is hardly worth sitting down to a decent meal to begin with!

As the range of *mezes* tends to be overwhelming (though sometimes predictable), it helps to know what dishes to look for, lined up behind the glass cabinet as if on parade, waiting to be identified. Obviously it is a matter of taste, but I find the simpler the dish is, the better – a purée of aubergine (we would call it a 'dip'), rather than the famous *İmam Bayıldı* (aubergine stuffed with tomatoes and onion, liberally covered with oil) which gained its name when an İmam, a Muslim holy man, fainted with delight because of its fragrance. Dishes of beans and vine leaves or green peppers stuffed with rice, small currants and pine nuts, spiced with olive oil and lemon juice, are unfailing too. Some more favourites are:

Liver and red peppers (*Arnavut Ciğeri*): this is a sharp-tasting Albanian dish with small pieces of liver stirred in *rakı* then drained and fried in hot oil in a heavy pan for just two minutes, served on onion rings and strips of red pepper.

Stuffed mussels (*Midye Dolması*): mussels stuffed with rice, pine nuts and the tiny currants or black grapes which enhance any rice dish, and various spices.

Russian salad (*Rus Salatası*): this *hors d'œuvre* was once popular in Britain, and one can understand why: a pleasing combination of diced vegetables and mayonnaise. There are also less exotic versions of plain potato salad, though 'plain' is a libellous description for something so appetising.

Tarator sauce: made from nuts and garlic, excellent over boiled vegetables.

Stuffed vine leaves (*Dolma* or *Yaprak Dolması*): cool, stuffed vine leaves are probably best without meat – simply fresh young leaves, folded round a stuffing of the excellent Turkish rice, those superb black currants (the size of peppercorns) and pine nuts, with herbs and spices.

Yoghurt and cucumber (*Cacık*): another incomparable national dish – yoghurt, chopped cucumber and garlic with olive oil poured on top unless you specify *yağsiz*.

Haydari: this is a version of the above with a taste which is even sharper and cleaner – simply yoghurt, garlic and parsley – good with *rakı*.

Aubergine (*Patlıcan*): comes in many forms – cold, fried slivers with yoghurt, and puréed. All the purées are recommended.

Fish-roe purée (*Tarama*): this looks like the Greek *taramasalata* and even resembles the taste, but for some sad reason it lacks the infinite delight of that incomparable Greek starter – even though that came, perversely, from Turkey in the first place.

Soups   As most Turkish dishes are served lukewarm rather than piping hot, you may wish to start with soup in the winter.

Red lentil soup (*Kırmızı Mercimek Çorbası*): the orange-red lentils turn yellow in the cooking. Prepared with stock, onions and egg yolks, this is a satisfying, nourishing soup, especially welcome if you are hungry.

Chicken soup (*Tavuk Çorbası*): with pieces of chicken, egg yolks and cream.

Carrot soup (*Havuç Çorbası*): with carrots, beef stock, egg yolks and milk.

'Wedding soup' (*Düğün Çorbası*): this famous soup includes two pounds of lamb, vegetables, egg yolks and lemon. It should be cooked for several hours, but there is a simpler version.

Börek   Though these can be eaten with the *mezes*, I prefer them on their own, for they are served hot and should be devoured at once. The name is probably derived from the prefix *bur* meaning to wrap or twist, for these are rolls of pastry filled with cheese or, better still, cheese and spinach, or meat, and deep-fried until crisp.

They can be served like slices of cake, but the most popular method is to keep them to the size of small cigars – hence *sigara börek* (or *böreği*). The cheese is Turkish *feta*, the herb is finely chopped flat-leaf parsley, and the pastry paper-thin sheets of filo.

This is one of the few dishes which arrive hot and make a marvellous complement to glasses of cool white Turkish wine, which is probably bad for your digestion unless you have the willpower to cry 'enough' and move on to the next course – if you still have room.

Fish   The range of fish is astonishing, the price depends on where you go: fashionable Pandeli's above the entrance to the Spice Bazaar in Istanbul is especially popular with American tourists, or the pontoon restaurant tied to Galata Bridge where fishermen fry their catch in hot oil and press it between fresh bread, offering the simplest and possibly the cheapest fish dinner to be found in the great city. At first I was discouraged by the thought of any fish plucked from the murky water of the Golden Horn, even though the amateur fishermen who line the bridge seem to have surprising success, but the fish served in the pontoon restaurants are taken from the cleaner Bosphorus.

This waterway, leading to the Black Sea, is dotted with villages famous for their fish restaurants. Tarabya is the most popular, with an impressive view of vast Russian tankers looming in the distance and jaunty tugs battling through the choppy water in the foreground revealing the strength of the currents.

On my first visit I was taken to a banquet at the Facyo which made me aware that Turkey is surrounded by coastline apart from her eastern borders. It is claimed that the Bosphorus alone has sixty varieties of fish, and I was served on this occasion with red mullet caught outside; *kalkan*, resembling turbot, from the Black Sea; bass from Marmara; and giant prawns from Iskenderun in the south of the Mediterranean.

Seafood and fish can be expensive, even exorbitant when no price is marked on the menu. Lobster is hardly worth the extravagance, and crab is usually disappointing. Conversely, sauté of octopus (hot or cold) is delicious and cheap, and so are the fried rings of squid (*kalamar*) and shrimps (*karides*), when these are in season and plentiful.

A really large fish is a wise choice if there are several of you to share it; small fish tend to be dry and bony though much loved by holiday-makers. Of course it's a matter of personal taste.

Salt-cured tuna (*Lakerda*) and smoked sturgeon: rival our own Scotch smoked salmon.

Swordfish (*Kılıç*): may be startling but this is one of the best items to order if you see it on the menu, especially in flat steaks gently simmered in oil, butter and lemon juice.

Marinated swordfish (*Kılıç Şiş*): using oil and lemon juice and grilled in cubes on skewers with bay leaves in between. The taste of swordfish is subtle and should not be disguised by too strong a sauce or accompaniment.

Sea bass (*Levrek*): particularly good if charcoal-grilled over dry fennel.

Uskumru Dolması: cold mackerel, baked and stuffed with pine nuts and herbs.

Anchovies (*Hamsi*): best when really fresh, caught in the Black Sea.

Meat   It is vital to realise from the outset that there are numerous versions of this important Turkish food. To ask merely for *kebab* is similar to asking for 'beef' in Britain. Because it sounds tempting and familiar, many people ask for *Şiş* (*Shish*) *Kebap* and leave it at that, with little idea of what they might be missing.

Şiş Kebap: *large* portions of lamb, often interspersed with small onions, squares of green pepper, and tiny tomatoes, none of which cook at the same pace. The idea is frequently better than the reality, though it is saved by the addition of rice.

Çöp Kebabı (pronounced 'chop' kebab): I find these *small* pieces of lamb strung together on wooden skewers preferable to the grander version above. The lamb has nothing else in between and you are given several of the skewers. It is cheaper, too.

On my first night in Istanbul, I smelt my way to a modest, bustling kebab saloon downstairs, just off Taksim Square (52 Sıraselviler Caddesi), and ordered *Çöp Kebabı* which was served with a marvellous paste of tomato, herbs and spices. Washed down with a bottle of beer, the meal cost less than L 3,000 and is one of the most enjoyable I can remember. In Turkey, more money does not necessarily mean better food.

Köfte Kebap: small meatballs of minced lamb. This dish can vary but is usually first-rate.

Adana Kebabı: a tastier version of the above which comes from Eastern Turkey and is highly spiced. Instead of being round, these balls are flatter and served on flat skewers accordingly.

Döner Kebap: slices of lamb which are stacked, compressed and impaled on a revolving spit (originally a sword), and sliced off as they cook; served with the flat bread known as pitta (*pide*). *Döner* is commonplace and reliable, particularly tasty if the slices are slightly crisp. It is a far and better cry from the British version which lingers day after day and includes pork, a shocking idea to the Turks. *Döner* is excellent for filling up a hungry family.

Sauté: if you are travelling and stop at a place where they need to prepare the meal especially, you could break the monotony by asking for

45

a *Sauté* of lamb (*kuzu*) or mutton (also veal), which is prepared quickly in a heavy black pan called a *saç*, a Turkish version of a wok. Small pieces of meat are simmered in oil with onion, garlic, red pepper, tomato purée and a profusion of such herbs as flat parsley and dill, with probably a spoonful of yoghurt, too. The result is marvellous.

Güveç: similar to the above, though closer to a stew than a goulash, baked in round, individual earthenware casseroles which achieve something miraculous in the cooking. I brought some of these dishes back to England and they do seem to contain the taste in a most remarkable way.

Bonfile: an all-purpose word to describe various cuts of steak: can be a treat.

Accompaniments With all the above dishes rice is the perfect accompaniment, better than chips, though these are readily available too.

Turkish rice tastes – well, that is the point, it actually has *taste*. And as it is a vital part of most meals, enormous care is taken in the preparation. In the old days, young girls had to prove their skill in making *pilav* before their prospective mothers-in-law would give their consent. There were other tests, too, such as making the unfortunate girls wear high wooden sandals in the *hamam* as proof of their deportment, but the *pilav* initiation sounds more sensible. The constant addition of butter and seasoning results in a dish good enough to eat on its own. The art is in recognising the right amount of liquid to be absorbed by the particular type of rice, for this varies considerably.

İç Pilav: one of the most delicious versions – at its simplest, with currants (small raisins the size of peppercorns known as 'black grapes') and pine nuts. This probably has the addition of a considerable amount of butter after the rice has absorbed the meat or chicken stock, spices and herbs. There can be small pieces of lamb's kidneys or chicken livers too but, as so often, the simpler can be the better.

Stuffed cabbage (*Etli Lahana Dolması*), with minced lamb, is recommended. So is *Mantı*, a form of Turkish ravioli, and *Pide*, Turkish pitta, served in special Pide Saloons, a flat, doughy bread with various ingredients on top, good for hungry families. Turkish bread is excellent and is a crucial part of every meal.

Desserts Turkey has a hot climate so puddings are out in summer and fruit and ice creams are in. Ices are made with a resinous substance which is purer than the additives we resort to, though slightly tacky. Children will love them. The fruit is incomparable – a simple slice of melon (*kavun*) to start with, or a fresh fruit salad with nuts and honey and a separate bowl of yoghurt to finish.

Depending on your taste, you may like the custards such as *Keşkül* – an almond custard made with cream, milk and rice flour, decorated with chopped almonds and pistachios and fresh pomegranate seeds. There are numerous cakes and pastries, the most famous being *Baklava*, the origin of *milles feuilles*: layers of thin filo pastry with a base of crushed nuts. It is delicious with a cup of Turkish coffee. Almond creams, cold saffron rice dishes and *Kadın Göbeği* (Lady's Navel Fritters), small golden rounds with a hole in the middle topped with whipped cream, are other delicacies. There are also versions of *crème caramel.* If you find such dishes tempting, experiment as you go along and you may find treats in store.

Breakfast The perfect start to any day is the clean, fresh taste of home-made yoghurt and honey, with the possible addition of fresh fruit. Insist on this wherever you are, unless you prefer the usual Turkish breakfast of white cheese and black olives. Yoghurt is as commonplace as toast in Britain, so if there is any excuse ignore it and keep on insisting. Eggs are usually available too, if not on any menu. Boiled eggs vary in the timing and tend to be served on plates with teaspoons so tiny they hardly bring a morsel to your lips. This is odd, since shops abound with highly decorative egg-cups. You could buy one of these and supply your own spoon, if you can be bothered. *Omlet* is an invaluable standby. Even if cooked in oil and served flat and open the taste is excellent, probably due to the quality of the free-range eggs.

Taking your time Throughout any meal there is no sense of impending curfew or a hovering staff anxious to see you leave, as there often are in other countries. So long as you are eating and enjoying your meal, the restaurateur is content. Consequently, eating out is one of the rewards of travelling in Turkey, especially if this is, literally, out of doors – under the protection of a trellis of vine leaves, with the chance of a swim beforehand and a contented doze afterwards.

However simple the food and drink, this is the height of luxury, a form of good living which the Turks understand instinctively because they appreciate it as well. No 'last orders' or 'time gentlemen please'. If customers are still talking and eating, lunch only finishes when dinner begins.

Tipping This is not obligatory, for there is usually a service charge included in the bill. However, the cost is so much less than it is at home, and the service more attentive, that it seems churlish not to leave an approximate 10 per cent if you have enjoyed your meal. Then everyone is happy.

Drink

One of the pleasant surprises in Istanbul, and they are legion, are the open-fronted corner kiosks which sell freshly squeezed fruit juices, ranging from orange to strawberry. Also there is *Ayran*: a popular national drink of yoghurt and milk whipped together that can be refreshing if really cold, unless there is too generous an addition of salt. I am sure it is delicious when you get it right – possibly with the sharpness of goat's yoghurt and no salt whatsoever – but the taste varies surprisingly and I am usually disappointed, though it is worth persevering.

Tea (*çay*), is the universal drink, brought at the drop of a carpet. I have seen an elderly irate Englishwoman demanding milk with her tea at breakfast, and finally obtaining it. But she was fierce indeed and it is hardly worth such trouble. It is easier to ask for a slice of *limon* and even some *bal* (honey), if you prefer that to sugar. There are various kinds of herbal teas which are excellent as well as health-giving.

Coffee (*kahve*) is sublime if you like the sooty taste as I do. This is not something to be drunk with milk or cream (the idea is odious) but a glass of cool water (*su*) helps, and be careful not to drink the sediment at the bottom of the cup. Indeed, if you want more than a taste, ask for a large cup. If you want it heavily sugared ask for *şekerli*; without sugar, *sade*; but best is medium – *orta*.

Many people believe they cannot live without Nescafé (as mistaken as thinking that you cannot survive without television), and most places will supply it. Personally I find it offensive when visitors arrive with their own small tin and demand cups and boiling water in order to make their own coffee – and it doesn't go down too well with the Turks either, if you are strangers. Turkish coffee is one of the great tastes of the world, so at least give it a chance.

Beer and spirits

Efes beer is better than Tuborg; Tekel is also recommended. I have no experience of Turkish whisky, though it is allegedly terrible, and Turkish gin is vile. Brandy is tough and pleasing, but choose the most expensive brand. Conversely, Turkish vodka is excellent and good value. If you bring a bottle home, insert the peel of a lemon and keep in the fridge for five hours, and you will have gained a marvellous vodka martini. While in Turkey, a first-rate drink I recommend is vodka with a bottle of pure fruit juice, such as cherry – *vodka ve vişne*. These juices are also welcome on their own, especially in hot weather.

Wine

Surprisingly, Turkey is one of the largest producers of wine in the world. If you are a wine drinker, you will be satisfied, if not exactly ecstatic. You can experiment with local wines, some of which are highly presumptuous, but several names are wholly reliable: Doluca is recommended (it is also called Villa Doluca) and is probably the best dry white, though Kavak (Kavaklıdere) runs it close and is usually cheaper.

Rakı

I have left *rakı* to the last, for this is a law (or law breaker) unto itself. A national spirit, it has been described as 'liquid dynamite' and even that is an understatement for the effect can last longer than any explosion. Though *rakı* has such distant relatives as anisette and, even closer, the Greek *ouzo*, there is nothing quite like it. *Rakı* is a drink for the mood of the moment and takes possession with alarming speed: if you are happy it makes you ecstatic, if you are depressed it creates misery, and if there is something seriously wrong it can drive you mad. Yet, when all is well, it produces a rare sense of well-being and can prove the friendliest spirit when approached sensibly as the Turks do from experience – as an accompaniment to food, or *mezes* at the very least: yoghurt is the perfect antidote.

Whatever you do, drink *rakı* at leisure and not with delirious speed.

The drink is remarkable also for seldom giving you a hangover – a traditional hangover, that is, with throbbing head and shaking hand. Instead it simply leaves you disembodied. Then the only cure is to have another *rakı* and you're on top of the world again. A few days on this fatal treadmill and you are such a zombie that your entire holiday is in danger of surrender.

I cannot resist the lethal stuff myself but a wiser, inner me (quickly suppressed) warns me that it is folly to start on the *rakı* before six in the evening. I pass on this advice with the benefit of personal experience. Benefit! That is hardly the word.

Some basic words

Some names to assist you (with some examples of phonetic pronunciation) are:

Apple	*Elma*	
Apricot	*Kayısı*	Ky-easy
Banana	*Muz*	
Cheese	*Beyaz Peynir* (this is white cheese)	
Cherries	*Kiraz*	
Chicken	*Piliç*	peel-ich
Coffee	*Kahve*	car-vay
Cold	*Soğuk*	
Eggs	*Yumurta*	you-merta
Grapes	*Üzüm*	
Honey	*Bal*	barl
Hot, warm	*Sıcak*	
Lemon	*Limon*	
Lemonade	*Limonata*	
Orange	*Portakal*	
Pepper, black	*Kara biber*	
Red mullet	*Barbunya*	
Red sea bream	*Mercan*	
Salt	*Tuz*	

Sardines	*Sardalya*	
Spinach	*Ispanak*	
Strawberries	*Çilek*	chill-ek
Sugar	*Seker*	
Water	*Su*	soo
Water, still mineral	*Maden Suyu*	mah-den soo-yoo
fizzy mineral	*Maden Sodası*	
Cheers!	*Şerefinize!*	sherry-fay

Sport

With the Aegean and Mediterranean regions of Turkey increasing in popularity as holiday destinations, it is likely that any sport in which you participate – if such is your interest – will be connected with the sea. For more detailed information on any of the activities listed below, contact the Turkish Information Office in your own country.

Sailing
There are marinas at Kuşadası, Bodrum, Kemer and Antalya, and in the holiday village of Altın Yunus at Çeşme, and the multitude of coves and bays around the Turkish coastline are ideal for mooring sailing boats. You should note, however, that there are various areas along the coastline where you are forbidden to moor your boat, and it is also advisable to avoid sailing back and forth across Turkish and Greek waters if you do not wish to encounter difficulties when entering either country.

Underwater diving
This is permitted in certain areas under the guidance of local authorities, but it must be stressed that on no account should you attempt to leave the country with any historical souvenirs you may have found in Turkish coastal waters.

Fishing
No licence is necessary if you wish to fish in non-prohibited areas, but there are a few restrictions to observe regarding the minimum sizes of fish that can be landed and the maximum number that any one person is allowed to catch. Full details, including information about fishing zones, can be obtained from the Department of Fisheries in Turkey by writing to Tarım, Orman ve Köyişleri Bakanlığı, Su Ürünleri Daire Başkanlığı, Ankara.

There are, of course, a number of land-based activities on offer in Turkey, if such a consideration plays a part in your holiday plans.

Football
This is almost a national obsession, and every large city has a stadium, should you wish to attend a match. Ask at your hotel for details of forthcoming games.

Skiing
There are a number of centres and resorts offering skiing facilities, particularly from January to April. Among these are Uludağ, Saklıkent, Köroğlu, Palandöken, Sarıkamış, Erciyes and Elmadağ.

Other sports
In addition to its more esoteric sports such as camel-wrestling (see p. 57), Turkey has good amenities for those interested in mountaineering and hunting, as well as a number of camping and spa centres.

Shopping

Bargaining

Bargaining is a serious game, to be played politely. The shop-owner will entice you inside like a fisherman playing a trout, and once you rise to the bait he will keep you there with further glasses of tea which do not arrive for several minutes, giving him time to impress his customers with his wares. Tea, coffee, even *rakı* involve no obligation on either side, though the unrolling of dozens of carpets thrown on the floor in front of you makes me increasingly uneasy if I do not intend to buy. But do not worry: this is part of the ritual, too, and though such attention may seem excessive, remember that the seller does well enough if he lands a single purchaser each day.

You are not expected to bargain in ordinary shops, of course, but when purchasing carpets and *kilims*, copperware and normal tourist souvenirs. In such cases, bargaining is expected, but there comes a point when it can turn sour if your offer is so absurdly low that it becomes insulting. If you are asked for L 10,000, try offering L 6,000 and work from there. Do not look as if you care desperately, or rubbish the goods unless they are really indifferent. A better ploy is to say what fine workmanship it is, but you simply cannot afford such a price. Sense the moves of the game and everyone should end up smiling.

Advice

If you see something you really like, buy it on the spot instead of waiting for the end of your visit or your return to Istanbul, in the hope of finding something better. I remember a plate outside the mosque at Iznik which I still regret. On one of my first visits to Turkey, I admired a *kilim* in Marmaris but assumed that the Covered Bazaar in Istanbul would offer a wider range. It did not. After interminable displays, I had to admit defeat. On my next visit, though I was travelling alone, I bought a splendid *kilim* in Diyarbakır, lost it, found it again, and bought another at a hotel in Adıyaman which was literally carpeted with *kilims*, of faded pinks and mustards. Though it was a chore to carry these everywhere, I bought a sack which made transport easier. Today they are two of my favourite possessions and I am thankful that I acted impulsively. When you have no doubt, buy rather than delay.

Carpets and *kilims*

A Turkish carpet needs no recommendation: it involves a considerable sum of money, but a good-quality carpet made from pure wool and using no artificial dyes is an investment. You can test the genuine article by looking at the back, which should be uneven if hand-made. If you pull at a knot and it comes out, it's factory made, and if the colour comes off when wiped with a wet handkerchief, then it's an artificial dye. But your *eye* should be able to guide you best of all.

Silk carpets made near Istanbul are especially fine, while those of wool often come from the busy market town of Kayseri. Personally, I prefer *kilims* – tougher, simpler, jollier and cheaper. Apart from the possibility of buying a first-rate *kilim* for under L 147,500 (though prices are increasing all the time), I find the colours subtler and the patterns more imaginative than those of carpets which are slightly cloying in contrast. Of course this is a matter of taste as well as cost, and such a viewpoint would seem heretical to those who know more about carpets than I do. Also, I admit that I should be delighted to own a traditional carpet as well as my *kilims*, if I could afford to do so.

You may find the best carpet and *kilim* shops outside Istanbul, in remoter towns like Datça. Personally, I shun the smart carpet shops aimed specifically at the tourist trade, by arrangement with tour operators who wheel their coachloads inside. For one thing, you pay more for the little lectures and salesmanship; for another, it is more fun to bargain on your own over the traditional glass of tea.

Though many shops are open most of the time, they are usually closed on Sunday, especially the bazaars in the big cities – including Istanbul. Otherwise, hours are both earlier and later than you would expect.

Other best buys

Leather This is outstanding, but resist flattery unless you are satisfied yourself rather than convinced by others. Leather jackets are particularly good in Marmaris, though most of these in fact come from Istanbul. Belts for men and women are exceptional, too.

Jewellery Gold and silver can be a particular bargain, for though they are sold by weight, they vary in price and you may well be fortunate. Semiprecious jewellery is attractive and plentiful. Necklaces, bracelets and earrings make generous presents and do not take up too much space.

Onyx Onyx should be bought in the Cappadocia region where there are local onyx factories and displays of ashtrays, jars, egg-cups and so on for you to choose from. Personally, I am never 100 per cent sure about onyx, but it certainly *looks* expensive, yet proves surprisingly cheap.

China Turkish plates are a must, wonderfully decorative with imaginative patterns or calligraphy. Again, these vary in price and are not necessarily dearer at tourist stalls outside popular mosques.

Copperware Abundant in the Covered Bazaar in Istanbul, round copper trays are both attractive and useful.

Scarves Again, seize the opportunity. The ladies who sell silk scarves outside the fortress above Alanya may seem rapacious but their goods are genuinely good value.

Turkish delight   *Lokum* is an obligatory gift to take back with you. It varies greatly, from loose bits in grocers' shops – which at least you can see – to the small, succulent squares tasting of mint, pistachio, lemon or rose-water, sold in boxes at the tea-shop in Istanbul's Divan hotel. Another *lokum* specialist is Hacı Bekir in the smart shopping street of Istiklal on the way to Taksim Square.

Honey   Buy honey to take back especially if you like a particular flavour, such as the dark pine honey available in Marmaris. It is sealed in flat metal containers to make it easier to pack, and you can also buy honey-combs.

Spices   Another must, spices are easily available, fresher and cheaper than at home. A visit to the Spice Market (Mısır Çarşısı) next to the New Mosque, near Galata Bridge in Istanbul, is an interesting experience and highly recommended. Take your time and seek the advice of the shop-owners and their assistants who will be anxious to help. Paprika, cinnamon and, above all, saffron are good value.

Herbs   You may have a personal favourite; remember, too, that the various herbal teas are delicious, apart from curing every malady known under the sun.

Nuts and fruits   Whole kiosks are devoted to nuts – try to choose one where the turnover is high. I have an aversion to chickpeas, but recommend pistachios and especially the pine kernels which are used in savoury rice; also the small raisins known as *kuş üzümü*, the size of peppercorns.

Clothing   Cotton shirts and blouses and wool shirts are also good buys, as are cotton towels.

General points   Remember that you can buy most things in Turkey, so do not feel you need to pack *everything* in order to cover every eventuality. Items such as serrated knives for fruit and taking on picnics, for example, you can buy on arrival.

Equally, however, certain items should be taken with you. You are advised to stock up with camera film before you go. Other items which can prove useful include a plug for the washbasin, and a mosquito machine to plug in at night to kill the beasts.

General Basics

Banking and shopping hours

Most shops close on Sundays – even the Covered Bazaar. Government offices close at weekends, and so do banks. Otherwise banks are open from 8.30 a.m. to 12 noon and from 1.30 to 5 p.m. Post offices provide an exceptional service: they are open from 8 a.m. to midnight, Monday to Saturday, though there can be occasional and regional variations. Giro's Postcheque service enables you to cash cheques up to a limited amount *anywhere* in Turkey at a post office.

Shops are generally open from 8.30 a.m. to 1 p.m., and from 2 to 7 p.m. The Covered Bazaar in Istanbul is open from 8.30 a.m. to 7 p.m.

In the Aegean and Mediterranean regions, government offices and other establishments close during the afternoon in the summer.

Currency and currency regulations

Turkish currency The monetary system is the Turkish lira (L). Coins in circulation are of 5, 10, 25, 50 and 100 lira, and banknotes are in denominations of L 10, 20, 50, 100, 500, 1,000, 5,000 and 10,000.

Currency regulations No limit is imposed on the amount of foreign currency which can be taken into Turkey, but not more than the equivalent of US$1,000 in Turkish currency can be taken in or brought out of the country. For this reason, you should not neglect to make a currency declaration if you calculate that you may still be carrying more than $1,000 worth of Turkish currency at the end of your trip.

Exchange slips You should keep the exchange slips provided when converting your currency into Turkish lira, since you may be required to produce these when converting your Turkish lira back into your own currency or when taking souvenirs out of Turkey. This precaution is simply to prove to the authorities that such transactions have been made in legally exchanged foreign currency.

Plastic money In the main tourist areas, major credit cards are accepted in hotels, restaurants and many shops, and money can be drawn against them through cooperating banks. As yet, however, they are not extensively recognised in the more remote areas of Turkey. Travellers' cheques

55

Exchange rates

and Eurocheques can be cashed in any bank upon production of appropriate identification.

For currency exchange, banks normally offer a marginally better rate than hotels.

Documents needed to enter Turkey

Nationals of EEC countries, the United States, Australia, Canada and New Zealand require only a valid passport for a visit to Turkey lasting up to three months. If you wish to extend your visit by a further three months, contact the nearest Turkish embassy or consulate.

Electrical current

Turkish current is usually standard 220 volts AC, so transformers are not required for European appliances, though there is a small area in Istanbul still using 110 volts. However, you will need a plug adaptor if your appliance has square, not round, pins.

Embassies and consulates

● **Britain:** Embassy – Sehit Ersan Caddesi 46/A, Çankaya, Ankara; tel. 127.43.10.
Consulate – Meşrutiyet Caddesi 34, Tepebaşı, Istanbul; tel. 144.75.40.
● **United States:** Embassy – Atatürk Bulvarı 110, Çankaya, Ankara; tel. 126.54.70.
Consulate – Meşrutiyet Caddesi 104, Tepebaşı, Istanbul; tel. 151.36.02.
● **Canada:** Embassy – Nenehatun Caddesi 75, Gaziosmanpaşa, Ankara; tel. 127.58.03.
● **Australia:** Embassy – Nenehatun Caddesi 83, Gaziosmanpaşa, Ankara; tel. 128.67.15.

Festivals and entertainment

Apart from the major fast of Ramazan and the two main celebratory festivals of Şeker Bayramı and Kurban Bayramı (see p. 29), the other public holidays and feasts – when banks and post offices close – are 1 January, 23 April, 19 May, 30 August and 29 October.

Festivals

15–16 January:	**Selçuk**, Camel Wrestling
March:	**Erzurum**, Troubadour and Ski Festival
23 April:	National Sovereignty holiday and Children's Day
20–30 April:	**Manisa**, Mesir ('power-gum') Festival
April–May:	**Emirgan**, Tulip Festival
5–12 May:	**Ephesus**, Arts Festival
May:	**Marmaris**, Yacht Festival
19 May:	Atatürk Commemoration, Youth and Sports day
May–June:	**Antalya**, Film Festival with plays staged at Aspendos
25–27 May:	**Denizli**, Pamukkale Fete
Mid-June:	**Edirne**, Wrestling Festival
June, 3rd week:	**Rize**, Tea Festival
20 June–15 July:	**Istanbul**, International Arts Festival; sound-and-light at the Blue Mosque
1 July:	**Samsun**, Fair
7–31 July:	**Bursa**, Folk Festival
7–10 August:	**Troy**, Drama Festival
20 August:	**Izmir**, International Festival
30 August:	Victory Day, with military parades
15 September–5 October:	**Mersin**, Fashion Fair
17–22 September:	**Çorum**, Hittite Festival
Mid-September:	**Ürgüp**, Cappadocian Wine Festival
28–29 October:	Republic Day
10 November:	Anniversary of Kemal Atatürk's death in 1938: at 9.05 a.m., the entire country observes a minute's silence, while cars blow their horns and ships sound their sirens in respect.
6–8 December:	**Demre**, Festival of St Nicholas
14–17 December:	**Konya**, The Whirling Dervishes

Television

Television is still a novelty in Turkey and visitors may be surprised by the television-gardens where rows of young men sit in rapt attention watching a flickering epic or, better still, a game of football since the game is a national obsession. It would clearly be absurd to go to Turkey to watch television when there is so much else to see, though the two channels can provide distraction.

Entertainment

For information on visiting entertainers, check with the English language *Daily News*.

Cinema

At the cinema, films are usually dubbed in Turkish.

Forms

One of the exasperating penalties of travel is the constant announce-ments in airports, which you cannot hear, and from your pilot on the plane, which you do not wish to hear – 'We are flying at 33,000 feet' is the sort of news which could only be of interest if it happened to be 33 feet. Arriving at your hotel, exhausted and short-tempered, you face the ritual of the questionnaire, either verbal ('Are you two people?' 'No, I just look like that') or written, as a form is thrust before you like an exam paper, demanding such useless information as the place where your passport was issued, and when. Whereas the criminal would have such nonsense at his fingertips, the honest man rarely has the remotest idea of such details as his passport number.

This antiquated procedure has enraged people for years, especially if they check into a different hotel every night and wish to change and wash without delay. Before the war, my mother could bear it no longer when she saw a sign in a Munich hotel – 'Dogs not admitted, Jews not wanted' – and signed in as Dr and Mrs Rosenbaum of Jericho with myself as Master Reuben Rosenbaum. My father was unamused but by this time she had a taste for such permutations and the next night we blossomed as Featherstone Haugh Haugh Featherstone from Cranleigh, while in Sweden we were transformed as Fernando Alvarez of Chihuahua from Mexico, and I was Master Ramon Alvarez. Finally, she went over the top with Mr and Mrs Hirahito Tagashi of Tokyo. Realising that no concierge ever paid the slightest attention to what she wrote, she gave up the contest.

It remains problematical if any of these forms are examined, and if so what good is achieved unless you *are* a master-criminal travelling under your own name? But it could save time to photocopy the basic facts, such as the origin of your passport, and give this with a bright smile to the receptionist asking him or her to fill in the form for you while you sign your name with a flourish and hurry to the lift. It might just work. Even if it doesn't, you will always have the facts to hand.

Health

No inoculation is needed for Turkey, although some doctors do recommend vaccination against diseases such as cholera and hepa-titis. Insurance is advisable on any long adventurous journey, but there should not be any need to take special precautions other than to ensure, if you intend to visit both the European and Asian sections of Turkey, that your policy covers both areas. Even the risk of drinking the local water must be exaggerated, but it is best to be on the safe side and ask for bottles of water (*su*) in your hotel bedroom (or mineral water, the excellent *maden suyu*), if only to refresh yourself. The Turkish chemist, *eczane*, has an excellent range to cure most ailments, and most local doctors speak English. Check the newspapers for duty chemists open to provide a twenty-four-hour service or dial 011 for information. British prescriptions are valid in Turkey, though you should of course ensure you take a good supply with you if you use a particular drug or medication regularly.

The nationals of those countries with whom Turkey has such bilateral agreements (e.g. Malta) are treated free. Otherwise, clinic fees for state hospitals are L 500 during business hours, and L 700 for an emergency. At university hospitals, fees vary from L 1,000 to 2,000. Treatment fees vary according to the type of medical attention necessary: whether a blood transfusion is required, medicine is prescribed, the type of room occupied, and so on.

In emergencies you could contact the American hospital in Istanbul, Güzelbahçe Sokaği 20, Nişantaşi (tel.: 031 40 50), or the Hacettepe medical centre attached to the university in Ankara (324 22 40).

Homosexuality

Be discreet. Surprisingly, there do not seem to be fixed laws for the age of consent or homosexuality in general, but it would be unwise to trespass on Turkish tolerance for your behaviour could be observed. The Turks are remarkably uncritical, but they do not like homosexuality paraded in front of them.

Unlike Western Europe or America it is hardly a problem and certainly not an issue in a country where such instincts are taken for granted and are not outwardly condemned. There are two or three 'gay' clubs in Istanbul, Ankara and Izmir (there may be more), but these are hardly a feature of the cities as they are in Paris, London, New York or San Francisco. There are no 'gay' movements that I know of, no protest marches for causes in search of a persecution, because there is no real persecution to protest about. There is a particular group of transvestites who carry on outrageously as if they wish to be arrested, and when they are, smiling at the flashlight cameras as they are carted off to court, everyone seems to be happy.

Language

One of Kemal Atatürk's most remarkable accomplishments was the alphabet reform which he supervised personally in the 1930s, travelling to virtually every important town in Turkey, the exemplary teacher with his chalk and blackboard. The Turks flocked to see their national hero and followed his instructions. It was hoped to complete the reform in fifteen years; in fact it took five. Until then, the language was a *meze* of Persian, Arabic, Greek and Turkish ingredients; now it is converted to Roman lettering and literacy has increased.

Even so, it is still hellishly difficult to master, and sounds as if someone is seriously ill. Unless you are a born linguist, you can comfort yourself with the advantages of *not* being fluent, for these exist: you are spared the tedium of talk about the weather, pop music, football or television, while you are forced to establish contact by looking at someone in the face which leads to greater understanding as you resort to sign language. The other person may not be as brilliant and as nice as you believe, but at least there is the benefit of the doubt – on *both* sides.

Of course, I am trying to see the best in a definite handicap, and you would be well advised to take a pocket dictionary and especially such useful phrase books as the Berlitz *Turkish for Travellers* and the American *Say it in Turkish*.

Meanwhile, these are a few basic words and pronunciations. The following are crucial:

Pronunciation

ç	at the start of a word this sounds like *ch* as in church; at the end, more like *ch* as in Dutch, and sharper.
ş	*sh* as in shop.
ğ	is silent.
ö	*ur* as in pure.
ü	difficult to convey, rather like the French *tu*, with a slightly upward inflection.
a	as in care.
c	like j, in jar.
g	hard as in goat.
ı	(i without dot) *er* as in early.
s	as in bus rather than is.

Words and phrases

Please	*lütfen*
Thank you	*teşekkür ederim* (tesh-ekk-ur-ay-derim)
Yes	*evet* (eh-vet)
No	*hayır*

More emphatic than *hayır* is the exclamation *yok!* This is a final, unequivocal, raised-eyes *no*. If used with humorous exasperation, this can send the Turks into fits of laughter. Conversely, *var!* is an equally emphatic yes, there is! conveying triumph.

What?	*ne?*
Good morning	*günaydın* (goon-ay-din)
Hello	*merhaba*
Goodbye	*Allaha ısmarladık* from the person departing; *güle güle* from the person staying

Beautiful, lovely	*güzel* (goo-zelle)
Big	*büyük*
Old	*eski*
New	*yeni*
Today	*bugün*
Tomorrow	*yarın*
Yesterday	*dün*
England	*İngiltere*
Turkey	*Türkiye*
Slow	*yavaş* (yavash)
Towel	*havlu*
Water	*su* (sue)
Mineral water	*maden suyu*
Welcome	*hoş geldiniz*
Glad to be here	*hoş bulduk*
I would like . . .	*istiyorum* . . .
How much?	*kaç lira* (kutch lira)
Where is . . . ?	*nerede . . . ?* (neh-rayday)
When?	*Ne zaman?*
Room	*oda*
Single room	*bir kişilik oda*
Double room	*ıki kişilik oda*
Room with two beds	*ıki yataklı oda*
Double bed	*çift kişilik yatak*
Room with shower	*duşlu oda*
A quiet room, please	*sakin bir oda, lütfen*
Where is the toilet?	*tuvalet nerede?* (too-va-let neh-re-deh)
Men	*erkekler*
Women	*kadınlar*
Mr	*Bay*
Mrs/Miss	*Bayan*
I love you	*seni seviyorum* (seeny sev your room)
So-so	*şoyle böyle* (Shirley Birley)
Cheers!	*serefinize!* (sherry-fay)
Left	*sol*
Right	*sağ*
Straight on	*doğru*
Airport	*havaalanı*
Boulevard	*bulvar*
Bus depot	*otogar*
Caravanserai	*kervansaray*
Castle	*kale*
Great mosque	*ulu cami*
Lake	*göl*
Map	*harita*
Market	*agora* (at ancient sites)

Mosque	*cami*
Mountain	*dağ*
Mountain pass	*geçit*
Narrow street	*sokak*
Palace	*saray*
Police station	*karakol*
Post office	*PTT (postane)*
Pulpit	*mimber*
River	*nehir*
Sea	*deniz*
Street	*cadde (cad.)*
Theological school	*medrese*
Tomb	*türbe*
Tourist office	*turizm bürosu*
Town centre	*şehir merkezi*

Lavatories

Frankly, these are not the most enchanting feature of Turkey and may well come as a shock if you are unfamiliar with the hole in the ground, also used in France. As the Turks use water for cleanliness, this may vex the foreigner (yourself) even further, and if the practice (however hygienic) distresses you be sure to carry tissues with you in case there is no proper lavatory paper. And if there is, do respect the Turkish habit and ask to put the soiled paper in the appropriate basket instead of risking havoc to the plumbing, which has not improved since the Romans.

Do not be alarmed: I am referring to the worst examples. The lavatories in most hotels and all government offices are Western and efficient. At the bus stops, an attendant looks after them and keeps them clean, deserving the small tip which he expects. Some foreigners have a peculiar mental block about this, resenting the need to pay for a crap, but it must be a charmless job for the attendant and this is a good way of disposing of your coins and smallest notes.

Though the Turks do not indulge in such Australian euphemisms as 'Adam's Boudoir', or the 'Romeos' and 'Juliets' seen at one 'Shakespeare' pub in England, they do have pictures of ladies with long hair. Good luck!

Law and order

Surprisingly, you will see no police in Turkey. This does not mean that they don't exist; they do so in plain clothes, but the law is upheld by the *jandarma*, part of the army. Foreigners tend to be disconcerted by the sight of soldiers armed with guns, but this is for their own protection. You may not see guns in such evidence at Heathrow or Kennedy airports, but you can be sure they are there. And though guns are unwelcome they could explain why there is so little sign of trouble.

It cannot be fun to fall foul of Turkish law, especially if your convictions are passionately opposed to the government, but that applies to every nation in the world. It could be argued that stability is preferable to the form of democracy which came perilously close to anarchy before the military took over in 1980. As it is, Muslim traditions and military control make Turkey one of the least crime-ridden countries in the world, one of the few places in the Mediterranean where you are virtually free from pick-pockets and can mislay something valuable and have it returned. Even so, there are the inevitable exceptions, and it is foolish to carry all your money and identification documents with you if you go out on the town, especially in Istanbul.

Drugs   There is one cardinal rule: *do not take drugs* or import them into the country. It is illegal and the Turkish law should be respected, if only for your own safety. Few films have slandered an entire country with such bias as *Midnight Express* and the Turks are hurt by it, even today. Apart from the possibility that the noisy atmosphere of a Turkish prison might be preferable to the colder formality of an English jail, the Turks find it mystifying that they were portrayed as the villains while the drug-pusher emerged as the hero. Yet, ironically, *Midnight Express* was a blessing for it scared the drug-taking hippies and cheapies away who might have descended on the country in force otherwise. Consequently, Turkey does not seem to have much of a drug problem.

Antiquities   Do not try to remove any when you leave the country!

Opening times

It is a good idea always to check on opening times before making a trek. It is infuriating to travel some distance only to find that the place you want to see is closed, and there is often no consistency in the opening and closing times of museums, palaces, churches and so on. The best thing is to check at your hotel or at one of the tourist information centres in any town before your intended visit.

As a general rule, most Turkish museums are open from around 9.30 a.m. to 5 p.m. every day of the week except Mondays. Palaces are usually open every day except Mondays and Thursdays, though the Topkapı Palace Museum in Istanbul is closed on Tuesdays.

Telephone codes

You can make automatic calls to the following cities. Lift the receiver, wait for the dial tone, then dial 9 and wait for a tone change, then continue with the code and number.

Adana	711
Adıyaman	8781
Aksaray	4811
Alanya	3231
Amasya	3781
Ankara	4
Antakya	891
Antalya	311
Artvin	0581
Aydın	631
Ayvalık	6631
Bingöl	8181
Bitlis	8491
Bodrum	6141
Bursa	241
Çanakkale	1961
Çeşme	5492
Datça	6145
Denizli	621
Dıyarbakır	831
Doğubayazıt	0278
Edirne	1811
Edremit	6711
Erzurum	011
Finike	3225
Fethiye	6151
Foça	5431
Gaziantep	851
Gelibolu	1891
Giresun	0511
Hopa	0571
Iskenderun	881
Istanbul	1
Izmir	51
Izmit	211

Iznik	2527
Kars	0211
Kaş	3226
Kemer	3214
Konya	331
Köyceğiz	6114
Kuşadası	6361
Malatya	821
Manavgat	3211
Mardin	8411
Marmaris	6121
Mersin	741
Milas	6131
Muğla	6111
Nevşehir	4851
Rize	054
Samsun	361
Selçuk	5451
Silifke	7591
Sinop	3761
Sivas	477
Tarsus	761
Tatvan	8497
Trabzon	031
Uludağ	2418
Ünye	3731
Ürgüp	4868
Van	0611
Yalova	1931

To telephone home, dial 99 and then the country code as follows:
● United Kingdom and Northern Ireland 44
● United States and Canada 1
● Australia 61
● New Zealand 64
For the international operator, dial 528 23 03.

Time differences

Turkish time is two hours ahead of Greenwich Mean Time.

To calculate the time in the United States, subtract seven to thirteen hours (eastern to western times).
For Australia, add six to eight hours.
New Zealand is ten hours ahead of Turkish time.

Tipping

Restaurants   This is not obligatory as a service charge is usually included in the bill (see p. 47).

Taxis   Tipping is not obligatory but considered advisable. You are not expected to tip *dolmuş* drivers.

Hamam   Distribute about 30 per cent of the total charge among the staff who have attended to you at a Turkish bath.

Others   Hairdressers, barbers and hotel staff can be tipped in accordance with the percentage you would offer at home.

Turkish baths

The famous *hamam* can be invigorating but do not expect the hot steam rooms which are used in the West by people who frequently go to lose weight or cure a hangover. In Turkey the objective is simply to have a good wash. Because a great city like Istanbul tends to be on the grubby side, and until recently few houses boasted bathrooms, the need to wash was very real. Indeed, cleanliness is part of the Muslim tradition, which explains the taps, fountains and basins for ablutions that surround the mosques.

Another reason for going to a *hamam* is purely architectural, for some are spectacular, such as the Galatasaray in İstiklal Caddesi in Istanbul and the Cağaloğlu near the Blue Mosque which is 300 years old. Others, in Kuşadası and Fethiye, are sympathetic; less so in Marmaris.

Be prepared for the following ritual: the *tellak* will give you two thin and totally inadequate striped towels (this applies all over the world) and possibly a pair of wooden clogs known as *nalın* on which you precariously clip-clop into a large, warm, marble room in the larger establishments, or a small washroom with a marble seat and wash-basin. The *tellak* reappears and throws bowls of hot water over you, as if you had done him wrong, and then proceeds with a vengeance as he smothers you in soapsuds, rinses you off with more bowls of water, wipes off the residue with a flannel as if you were the window of a car, and then, suddenly, goes into the attack as he pins you down with a rough hand-pad, scrubbing your skin so violently that weeks of carefully acquired suntan are removed in an instant. After this, the *masaj* finishes you off with a volley of blows. By this time you have surrendered and think only of survival.

I enjoyed (that is hardly the word!) such an experience in a back street *hamam* in Trabzon, but this was the hardest I endured and I am sure there are others from which you emerge more gently refreshed.

Needless to say, there is strict segregation of the sexes, as usual.

Women in Turkey

The role of Turkish women

Women and men are equal in the precepts of the Koran. Even today this is hard to accept, though Kemal Atatürk did his utmost to achieve such equality, declaring: 'We have to believe that everything in the world is the result, directly or indirectly, of the work of women . . . A country which seeks development and modernisation must accept the need for change . . . We must have Turkish women as partners in everything, to share our lives with them, and to value them as friends, helpers and colleagues in our scientific, spiritual, social and economic life.' In 1926 the Turkish Civil Code gave women equal rights with men in family disputes, made polygamy illegal, and ensured equal rights in divorce and inheritance.

In 1934 the law gave Turkish women the right to vote and be elected to Parliament; three months later eighteen women deputies were elected to the Grand National Assembly – a step forward which impressed the outside world. Since then, Turkish women can be found in all professions, especially in universities, receiving the same pay as men. The first woman in the world to be elected to a Supreme Court of Appeal was Turkish.

Even so, it must be admitted that the impression received in less sophisticated parts of Turkey is very different, with women working in the fields yet staying discreetly in the background if you are invited to their houses, refusing to eat with you. I remember a delightful moment in Bodrum when three formidable ladies who run Charter Agencies in the USA complained to my friend, Dursun Mutlu, about the passive role of Turkish wives (though Mrs Mutlu, as it happens, is Dutch). 'It seems to us', declared the spokeswoman, 'that when the husband comes home he does not stay with his wife, or help with the cooking, or say that he loves her, but goes off to be one of the boys.' Dursun blinked: 'One for the boys? Long time ago, perhaps.' He smiled uncomfortably. 'Not so much now, I think.'

Women travelling alone in Turkey

It is often claimed that women travelling alone are likely to be pestered, especially as they travel further east. No such cases have come to my notice, though this could well be true. Conversely, single women have told me that they have received politeness and assistance throughout.

67

Again, much depends on appearances. If a woman dresses provocatively in shorts or short skirts, she may provoke. It is desirable to travel in pairs and, if hitch-hiking, avoid doing so at night and select your lift carefully, preferably with other women in the vehicle.

In some respects the Turks are still old-fashioned and view the sight of topless sunbathing ladies with astonishment. It is so much simpler to respect the traditions of the country by adapting to them instead of expecting the Turks to adapt to you.

Useful addresses

This is not a definitive list in any way but an acknowledgement of people who have offered personal assistance.

Turkish Tourist Office, Egyptian House, 170 Piccadilly, London W1V 9DD, tel.: 01-734 8681.

One of the most helpful tourist offices in London, well known for its consistent and intelligent advice for travellers to Turkey and partly responsible for the popularity of Turkey today as the new place to go to. The excellent and friendly supervision under Mrs Kahraman is maintained by her successor, Mr Düzgünoğlu.

Turkish Airlines, 11 Hanover Street, London W1, tel.: 01-499 9240 (sales), 01-499 9247 (reservations).
In Turkey: Abide-i Hürriyet Caddesi, Vakıf İşhanı, Kat 2, 154–156, Istanbul, tel.: 573.35.25.

Turkish Maritime Shipping Agency, Türkıye Denizcilik İşletmeleri, Denizyollari Ac, Rıhtım Caddesi, Karaköy, Istanbul, tel.: 144.02.07/145.53.66; telex 24810 DZYLTR.

Turkish Touring and Automobile Club, Halaskargazi Caddesi 364, Şişli, Istanbul, tel.: 131.46.31–36.

Agencies   These have a good record and *may* be able to assist you with a flight considerably cheaper than the scheduled flights of national airlines.
Aegean Turkish Holidays, 53a Salusbury Road, London NW6 6NJ, tel.: 01-372 6902/5. Specialising exclusively in Turkey, this agency covers a wide range and caters for the enterprising traveller with Two Centre Holidays, Blue Cruise and Hotel or Villa Combination, Fly Drive and coach tours including the Aegean, with Eastern Turkey for the more discerning adventurer. The service benefits from the expert knowledge of the director, A. B. Kaltakkıran, who takes a strong personal interest.
Celebrity, 18 Frith Street, London W1V 5TS, tel.: 01-734 4386. Good choice of hotels in Istanbul, Izmir and Kuşadası; also northern Cyprus.

Falcon, Astley House, 33 Notting Hill Gate, London W8 3JQ, tel.: 01-221 6298. For flight-only reservations, 01-221 0088. Specialising for 18–30 year olds, 01-221 5018.
Metak, 69 Welbeck Street, London W1M 7HA, tel.: 01-935 6961. Offer clients the facility of a flight-only arrangement.
Sunmed, Sunmed House, 4–5 Manor Mount, London SE23 3PZ, tel.: 01-291 1555. In 1988 Sunmed offer ten resorts served by four Turkish airports from four UK airports.
Sunquest, Aldine House, 9–15 Aldine Street, London W12 8AW, tel.: 01-749 9933. Sunquest holidays have economy flights to Istanbul and Antalya, and are the agency for the Turkish Maritime Lines which operate along the Black Sea and the Mediterranean. First rate.
Turkish Delight, 164B Heath Road, Twickenham, Middlesex TW1 4BN, tel.: 01-891 5901. Specialise in the coastline from Bodrum to Kaş (Dalaman airport) with an exceptionally friendly and efficient service on the spot.
Turquoise, 9 Maddox Street, London W1R 9LE, tel.: 01-491 2448. Imaginative choice of middle-range hotels in Istanbul, along the coast and Cyprus.

Wildlife

The wildlife in Turkey is marvellous, from the turtles at Dalyan to the storks nesting on tops of towers and the wild boar. The most tragic sight of all is the dancing bear, howling as his piratical owner gives a fierce tug on his chain and bangs a tambourine as the noble creature is forced to perform. Fortunately, this encounter is rare.

Climbing over ruins like those at Termessos, keep an eye open for long, black snakes which are poisonous though unlikely to bite unless attacked. The worst menace comes from mosquitoes: eating garlic is one solution, a funny little machine which plugs in is another, and lavender water is alleged to be a deterrent too. If you are bitten, at least the inconvenience and blemish is only temporary.

Gazetteer

Introduction

This guide is not intended for the expert who will have no need for such basic information, nor is it aimed at those whose only wish is to lie prostrate on a beach, returning home with a suntan but little else in terms of knowledge or experience gained of the country visited. It is written with the hope that it might prove useful to those travellers who have a taste for adventure, combining a holiday with exploration and the fun of finding out what lies around the corner.

Independent travellers who wish to avoid being herded around in large groups, preferring to make their own travel and accommodation arrangements, and plan their own excursions and itineraries could find the advice and guidance offered in this gazetteer section invaluable in suggesting routes between major points of interest, places to stay and where to eat. You may, of course, choose not to visit all the points of interest suggested on a route, but from the information given you can decide for yourself whether to bypass a town or site and travel to the next destination which you feel may be of interest along the route.

It is always more rewarding – and in Turkey almost imperative – to move at your own pace rather than trying to stick to a rigid timetable or route, your concentration bent on reaching the next destination in a plan fixed firmly in your mind. Such an attitude is almost impossible to maintain in Turkey anyway because, apart from turning travel into a chore rather than a pleasure, you will inevitably want to pause to savour a location you particularly like for longer than a preconceived timetable would allow, or you may decide to take an unscheduled break, especially if you are driving, for the distances in Turkey can be considerable and the roads and the driving standards of your fellow road-users may leave something to be desired.

It is much more rewarding, in Turkey as elsewhere, both to move inland and venture out to sea occasionally when travelling the coastline: in this way you will learn more about the country, its landscape and its people, as well as varying the type of terrain through which you are travelling. An afternoon swim in the Mediterranean off Antalya is doubly rewarding if you have climbed to the ruins of Termessos in the morning.

For the sake of simplicity, the gazetteer has been divided into seven separate sections, many of which are based on the geographical regions into which the Turks themselves have divided their country for administrative purposes. An exception is the section on the Turkish Riviera which combines parts of both the Aegean and Mediterranean geographical divisions. Since this is the most popular area of the country with holiday-makers, it is probably helpful to treat the area between Bodrum on the Aegean coast and Kemer near Antalya on the Mediterranean as a separate area and consequently it has been allocated a section on its own.

It should be stressed that the suggestions given for routes are exactly that: suggestions, not commands written on tablets of stone. While they have been devised, where possible, to include a variety of places to visit – towns, beaches, ancient sites, buildings of architectural importance and centres of cultural interest, combining a degree of liveliness in the resorts and cities with the solitude of more remote areas – it is you alone who know what you hope to gain from your travels. It is, presumably, why you consider yourself an independent traveller.

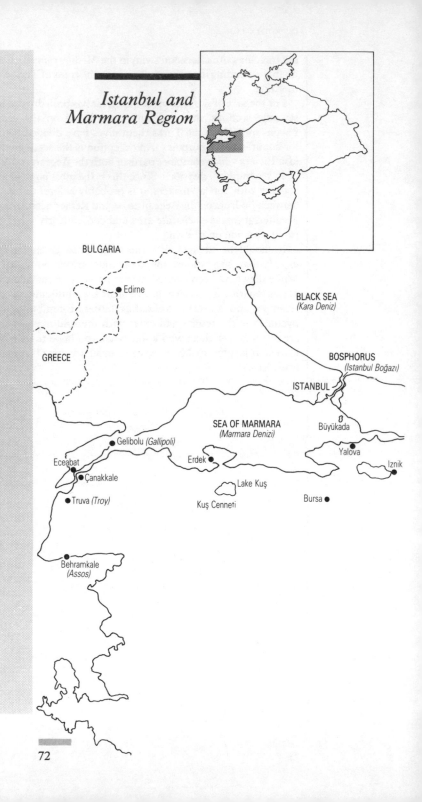

Istanbul and Marmara Region

BULGARIA

● Edirne

BLACK SEA
(Kara Deniz)

GREECE

BOSPHORUS
(Istanbul Boğazı)

ISTANBUL

SEA OF MARMARA
(Marmara Denizi)

Büyükada

Gelibolu (Gallipoli)

Yalova

Eceabat

Erdek ●

İznik

● Çanakkale

Lake Kuş

● Truva (Troy)

Kuş Cenneti

Bursa ●

Behramkale
(Assos)

Istanbul and Marmara Region

Introduction

'Should we be obliged to look but once upon the world, it would be upon this site, with all our feeling.' So said Lamartine (1790–1869), the French poet and historian, about Istanbul: clearly a man who understood a great deal of the charm of the largest and most exciting city in Turkey.

It is a place full of contrasts: nowhere else in the country are you so much aware of the links between old and new, east and west, as in this port city built on two continents on the straits separating Europe from Asia. The Topkapı, Dolmabahçe and Beylerbeyi Palaces are made to seem all the more majestic when compared with the liveliness and good natured racket generated in the Covered Bazaar; and the magnitude and awe-inspiring architectural splendour of the Ayasofia museum contrasts vividly with the fun and entertainment to be found in Flower Sellers' Alley. Art galleries and museums abound which cater to every taste, with treasures from the Hatti, Hittite, Assyrian, Babylonian, Byzantine and Ottoman periods of the city's long history yet, in typical Istanbul fashion, the new is juxtaposed with the old when the international arts festival is held there in June and July each year.

Of course, everyone will take away their own impressions of the city, but probably one of the most memorable aspects of a visit will be the boat trip along the Bosphorus where *yalı*, modern hotels, elegant palaces and parks line a waterway busy with craft of varying sizes.

It would be easy to spend all the time at your disposal in Istanbul itself – and still not see all you wanted to – without travelling to the surrounding Marmara region, yet to do so would be to deny yourself the different pleasure of travelling through lush greenery and along sandy coastline between stops at Yalova, Bursa, Çanakkale, the National Park of Kuş Cenneti and the historical areas – ancient and modern – of Gallipoli and Troy.

73

Istanbul

There is no city like it in the world. Istanbul is not a pretty place but it is exhilarating and glorious to look at. Istanbul is tough, noisy, robust, ruthless and could be overwhelming if it were not for the respite of the waters of the Golden Horn and Bosphorus (Boğazı). These relieve the hardness of the city with the gentle touch of fishermen along Galata Bridge who cast their lines optimistically into that murky water – and frequently pull them up again with a flash of silver at the end.

Then you have the street vendors selling trays containing a single ware: combs, charm bracelets, watches, or cellophane-wrapped objects which could be caramels until a closer look reveals them as sticky-tape. The vendors, and the boys with their weighing machines, stay there for hours shouting to the passer-by and if someone stops and makes a single purchase then their perseverance is rewarded. They typify the resilience of Istanbul which is almost brutal in its strength yet gloriously defiant towards adversity. Just as the Turks are devoid of malice, neither do they have self-pity.

Like truly strong men who can afford to be gentle, the Turks have a tender side as well – exemplified in their love of flowers, their friendliness to strangers, and the sheer exuberance of living. Some people advise you not to go the Princes Islands at the weekend because the ferries are crowded, but this is the time to see Turkish families at their most content, relishing the day's outing, singing and dancing to Turkish music on a cassette player during the journey back.

Remorseless yet welcoming, grimy yet magnificent, the beauty of Istanbul is unique. Once you have crossed the Golden Horn in the early morning and seen a rose-pink sun ascending through the heat-mist over the mosques and minarets, it is a beauty that lingers in the mind. Because of that extraordinary skyline as you cross from Galata to old Stamboul, you know you are somewhere different – you have, in fact, arrived at the gateway to Asia. Things are happening – nothing is soft or static except on Sunday, for Atatürk decreed that this should be respected as a day of rest. Otherwise the power of Istanbul makes other cities seem tame by comparison, and the atmosphere is so stimulating that it revives the most flagging spirit.

Stay several days and start by taking one of the ordinary passenger ferries at a cost of a few pence which is the easiest way of understanding the juxtaposition of the Golden Horn and the great sweep of the Bosphorus heading towards the Sea of Marmara which is visible on one side, leading to the Black Sea on the other. Otherwise, I am sure that many new arrivals believe that the Golden Horn *is* the Bosphorus and that they are crossing into Asia when they walk over Galata

Bridge. A journey to Üsküdar (better known to us as Scutari) on the Asian side of the Bosphorus puts this into perspective and gives you a flavour of Turkey too, with all the bustle involved. Other ferries take you along the Horn and towards the Black Sea where you can stop off at such resorts as Tarabya and make the return journey by bus.

The city itself is rich for exploration. As well as the famous attractions listed below, there are the less well-known pavilions restored by Mr Çelik Gülersoy, Istanbul's most distinguished conservationist and chairman of the powerful Touring Club. He has provided oases of quiet and relaxation where you can escape from the surrounding din, like the Malta Pavilion at the top of Yıldız Park which has been restored superbly, a most attractive building with beautifully painted ceilings, surrounded by Judas trees and a marble terrace where you can have refreshments. Not only do you escape from the dust and noise, but you step back in time as well: a perfect pause in the middle of the morning or the afternoon, with views over the Bosphorus. Mr Gülersoy has also recreated an entire street of traditional wooden houses near Ayasofia, occupied by sweet-shops and restaurants, which have proved hugely popular with the Turks themselves who throng there on a Sunday afternoon. Appalled by the gradual destruction of old buildings due to the demands made by the population explosion after the war, Mr Gülersoy had the foresight to preserve whatever he could, though his efforts did not please the previous régime who warned him confidentially, 'You have absolute freedom to do and say what you please,' – adding 'but you could be killed.' Fortunately, with the backing of the Touring Club, he was able to resist such pressure and has the support of President Evren today.

To go to Istanbul without seeing the main attractions – the Ayasofia and Topkapı – would be a wasted opportunity. Sightseeing is an unattractive phrase implying flocks of sheep-like tourists, but Istanbul is so vast that visitors are easily absorbed and nothing should deter you from seeing the greatest splendours, unique to Istanbul. Equally, there is tremendous satisfaction in visiting lesser known places like Beylerbeyi Palace on the shores of the Bosphorus at Üsküdar, underneath the great bridge which crosses to Asia.

Main areas

In view of the size and layout of the city, divided by the Golden Horn and then split in half by the Bosphorus, this may help you to find your way about.

The Golden Horn (Haliç)

Paradoxically, the side which you reach from Europe is known as the Old City, formerly Byzantium and then Constantinople, while the other side is frequently called 'European' simply because it is more modern. In early days there was little connection between the two, and the crossing was made by ferry. Today the inlet is connected by the Galata (Karaköy) Bridge, the Atatürk Bridge and, still further back, the Istanbul Bridge between Eyüp and Halıcıoğlu.

In the loose terms of Old and New, the old City curves round at

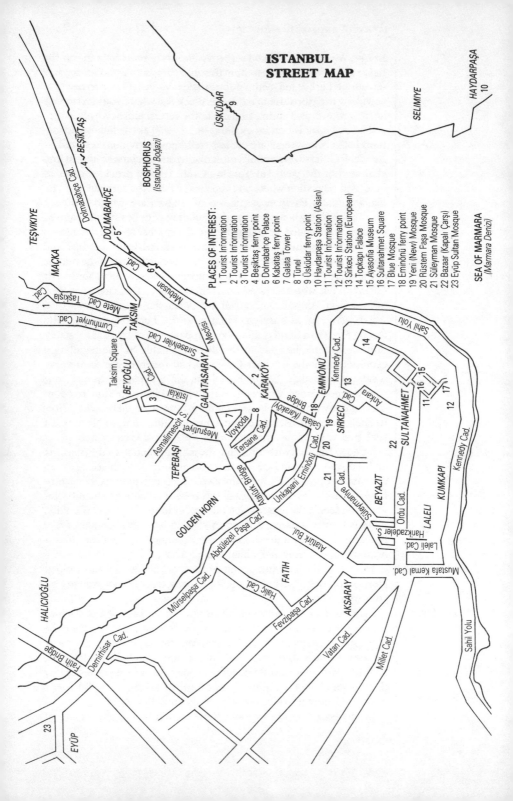

Seraglio Point (site of the Topkapı Palace) to the Sea of Marmara; the New City looks towards the Bosphorus. This, in turn, flows into the Sea of Marmara and continues towards the Dardanelles and the Aegean in one direction, and reaches the Black Sea in the other. A simple ferry journey from the Karaköy stop (on the New side) takes you to the Asian side and the station of Haydarpaşa, which serves the whole of Turkey. If you wish to go to Üsküdar, also on the Asian side, take a ferry from Eminönü, near the bridge on the Old side – an enjoyable trip at a nominal price which will help you to place Istanbul in perspective right away.

Beyoğlu   The New side is always recognisable from the Galata Tower, dating from the time when Galata was a busy port for Genoese merchants. It is astonishing to realise that an estimated 50,000 Italians lived here around the twelfth century, to be replaced later by the Greeks and, more surprisingly, by the French.

Pera was the richer town above Galata and the two are embraced under the name of Beyoğlu, which is also known as the European quarter. Pera is the site of Istanbul's first great hotel, the Pera Palas, just above the terminal for the airport buses. Less than 200 m from the Pera Palas, past the Etap Hotel on the right, then the Londres where the road narrows, you pass one of the helpful Turkish Tourist Offices, before you reach the British Consulate and the flower and vegetable markets in the alleys opposite. Here you join the important main road of İstiklal Caddesi which starts at Galatasaray Square and continues in a straight line to Taksim Square, lined with consulates, banks, post offices and smart, sophisticated shops.

Taksim Square could be described as the heart or pivot of the New district, with numerous small restaurants and bars off it, and the big hotels either in it, like the bigger Etap Marmara, or beyond it, like the Sheraton, Divan and Hilton. These lead down to the Bosphorus and Beşiktaş, an important ferry stop for the Princes Islands (see pp. 107–10) and Yalova, with the Dolmabahçe Palace beyond, the attractive Yıldız Park above with the Malta and Şale Pavilions, and the suspension bridge crossing to Asia in the distance.

The Old City   Sometimes known romantically as Stamboul, the Old City, on the other side of Galata Bridge, is more colourful. Plainly, your explorations and growing familiarity with the city will to some extent depend on your choice of hotel – those on the Pera side tend to be grander, while the Laleli district in the Old City has a large number of smaller and less expensive hotels, though there are first-class, newly restored hotels around Ayasofia as well. Either way, you will be bound to visit the old city in order to see Ayasofia, the Blue Mosque and the Topkapı Palace. Even if you flinch from sightseeing, jostled by tourists, these are landmarks you should see. Another favourite is the Covered Bazaar.

Sultanahmet Square embraces the gardens between Ayasofia

77

and the Blue Mosque, with numerous open-air cafés and a useful Tourist Information Centre. Once this was a grand ceremonial square based on Rome and must have been worthy of a Cecil B. de Mille epic with its golden statue of Justinian, a golden gate, and a golden milestone which measured the distances between the outposts of the Roman Empire. All of this was looted by the Crusaders in 1204.

Continuing down the hill towards the Sea of Marmara from this centre known as Aksaray, you reach the district of Laleli with its smaller hotels, and the numerous restaurants at Yeşilköy. Driving along by the Sea of Marmara, the road is lined by the ancient walls which stretch intermittently for 27 km. Once they enclosed the ancient city, making it impregnable.

You will pass several nightclub–restaurants (lively at night) on your way to the two airports (local and international) which are scarcely half an hour's journey from Galata Bridge, though you should allow ample time to get to them during the rush hour (see p. 79).

The Bosphorus

There are numerous tours of the Bosphorus with such names as 'Bosphorus and Two Continents Vision', but it is more fun to take one of the ordinary passenger ferries which zig-zag from shore to shore. Then stop off for lunch at a place you like the look of, not necessarily as fashionable as Tarabya, such as the modest Domani at Yeniköy, which is just beside the ferry jetty and overlooks the water, with a good selection of seafood. If you prefer to return by bus, the stop is at the end of the street, in Köybaşı Caddesi near the Carlton Hotel. Such a trip will enhance one of your first days in Istanbul and give you an idea of the scope of the city.

Continuing up the Bosphorus, from Yeniköy and Arnavutköy (both famous for their fish restaurants) and Bebek Bay, you pass the ruined fortress of Rumeli Hisari (built 1452) whose walls run down the hill to the water's edge at the narrowest point of the channel, only 650 m wide. The coastline is linked with former villages and *yalıs*, the old wooden houses of the wealthier merchants.

Tarabya has always been fashionable, a summer retreat for foreign embassies, and remains so today. Nicknamed Arabia, it has a waterfront of first-rate fish restaurants and the looming Tarabya Hotel beyond. The next stop is Büyükdere, and then you head towards the Black Sea. It takes two and a half hours one way if you take the Special Tourist Excursion boat from Eminönü (beside Galata Bridge in the Old City) to the end of the Bosphorus, but you must allow limitless time if you take a passenger boat. Exploring Istanbul should always be as leisurely as possible.

The Asian side

Going from the Sea of Marmara towards the Black Sea, this starts with Haydarpaşa station and the smart, modern suburb of Kadıköy, and continues to Üsküdar, with the Selimiye barracks where Florence Nightingale tended the wounded soldiers during the Crimean War (see p. 93). Continuing towards the Black Sea from Üsküdar, you pass the Beylerbeyi Palace (see p. 91), virtually underneath the suspension bridge to Asia. You can continue to Küçüksu (which can also be reached by bus or *dolmuş* on the Üsküdar–Beykoz road), a favourite picnic spot where two streams once flowed into the Bosphorus with a pleasant, shaded grass valley between: they were known as 'The Sweet Waters of Asia'. A hunting lodge was built on the shore in the nineteenth century in the style of a lodge for Sultan Abdülmecit, with an echo of one of Ludwig's castles in Bavaria. In 1983 this baroque masterpiece was opened to the public: hours are 9.30 a.m. to 4 p.m.; closed Monday and Thursday.

The last ferry stop on the Asian side is Anadolu Kavağı, with the ruins of an ancient castle on the hill above; opposite, on the European side, is the last stop of Rumeli Kavağı with several good, quiet fish restaurants near an old fortress – and then you are out before you know it, into the Black Sea.

Beware the rush hour If you are travelling through Istanbul, may Allah protect you, for the rush-hour traffic can be intimidating. Try to avoid Friday afternoon, when the entire city seems in turmoil with cars trying to evacuate soon after midday. Being stuck in an endless jam on a sultry day is boring enough, but when the traffic flows be prepared for an eventful burst of speed as cars jostle for position like dodgems in a fairground, switching lanes at will. If your nerves or brakes are faulty, I really do advise you to steer clear of Friday afternoon.

History Istanbul is such a natural harbour, the obvious door to Asia Minor and easy to defend, that the earlier settlers who chose Üsküdar on the other side of the Bosphorus were nicknamed *kör*, 'blind', for ignoring the safe inlet of the Golden Horn opposite. Originally, this was the site for Byzantium, allegedly named after Byzas who landed a shipload of Greeks when he anchored in the Horn in 600 BC; it rapidly became an important centre for trade.

Occupied by the Persian King Darius, it assumed independence once more and fought off the attack by Philip of Macedonia (Alexander the Great's father) whose troops were detected in the moonlight, which explains the crescent on the Turkish flag today. The city then fell to Rome, but flourished under the *Pax Romana* until it was seized in AD 196 by Septimus Severus. He was born in Africa but took the Imperial Roman Army by force; he died in York.

Byzantium became Constantinople after it was occupied by the Emperor Constantine in AD 330 and became a Christian capital with the first church of St Sophia.

1204 Crusaders, led by the Venetians, stormed and looted the city. A column with the golden statue of Justinian, and a golden milestone, were taken from the Ceremonial Square, based on Rome.

1261 The city recaptured by the Byzantine Emperor of Nicaea, Michael VIII, who formed an alliance with the Genoese.

1449–53	Constantine XI called in vain on the Western church for military support. Mehmet II was able to take the supposedly impregnable city of Constantinople by blockading the Bosphorus after transporting his vessels overland to the Golden Horn. The emperor was killed when the Janissaries stormed the city and Mehmet rode to St Sophia and instructed the priests to return to the Islamic faith. Constantinople became Istanbul, the name apparently derived from the words *stin poli* meaning 'in the city'. Another phrase, 'born to the purple', described the elder sons of Byzantine emperors who were born in special purple chambers which signified primogeniture, the right of succession.
1520–66	Under Süleyman the Magnificent, Istanbul became the capital of the Ottoman Empire and one of the great centres of the civilised world.
1808	Selim III was assassinated in the harem as the Janissaries rebelled.
1838	The first bridge was built across the Golden Horn.
1870	The railway started: the Pera Palas Hotel was built to receive the first passengers off the Orient Express in 1892.
1908	The revolutionary Young Turks occupied the city, and Sultan Abdül Hamit II was deposed the following year.
1912	The Bulgars attempted to invade the city but failed.
1922	Atatürk abolished the sultanate and established the Turkish Republic in Ankara, so the seat of power – the Grand National Assembly – was shifted away from Istanbul which was both more vulnerable to attack and more divided by feuds and rival factions.
1973	The great bridge which stretches across two continents was opened to celebrate the fiftieth anniversary of the Republic; in the first twenty-eight months it was used by more than thirty million cars and the tolls had paid off the entire cost of the construction. Today it seems inconceivable that all such traffic was carried across the Bosphorus by ferry before one of the longest suspension bridges in the world linked Europe and Asia. There are plans for another bridge from the tip of the Golden Horn to Üsküdar, but this would spoil the perfect symmetry which exists today.
What to see *The Topkapı* *Palace*	Occupying the finest point of the city – the tip of the Golden Horn as it turns into the Bosphorus and the Sea of Marmara – the palace was built by Mehmet II between 1459 and 1465. He had found a ruined city after he conquered Constantinople fifteen years earlier (the Genoese had betrayed the Christian faith by allowing him to carry his boats across Galata into the Golden Horn, so avoiding the naval barrier). He built the palace on the overlooking hill, protected by walls to the water's edge, on the site of the Byzantine acropolis, and it became the seat of power for the next 400 years. Later sultans added their own embellishments, creating the labyrinthine puzzle

which surrounds the four courtyards today. Süleyman was the first sultan to live there permanently. When Lady Mary Wortley Montagu looked across from Pera in the eighteenth century, she wrote that the view 'shows us the port, the city and the *seraglio*, and the distant hills of Asia, perhaps, altogether the most beautiful prospect in the world.'

Today you are restricted to only a few of the hundreds of rooms with their corridors and courtyards, once a gilded cage for the women of the harem and an ornate prison for the younger sons who were cruelly confined. The claustrophobia of such an existence must have been suffocating – yet magnificent. With an average population of 5,000, swollen to three times that number on special occasions, the kitchens alone employed 200 cooks: it is now a museum for a formidable collection of Chinese and Japanese porcelain from the fourteenth and fifteenth centuries.

Advice Tour operators reveal a sadistic streak in their over-punishing schedules which whirl you from one historic monument to another with little chance to pause and less to absorb. Allow yourself time to enjoy such a unique experience at leisure – do not attempt to see too many places in one day. An entire morning is needed to appreciate the Topkapı Palace – preferably early on a weekday to avoid the worst of the crowds, but not Tuesday when it is closed – for this is a city within the city. Treat yourself to lunch afterwards, but as the Topkapı restaurant is non-alcoholic you might prefer to relax in the peaceful garden behind the Konak Hotel and then walk across to the Ayasofia. In this way you will have the chance to assimilate the two outstanding features of Istanbul as a pleasure rather than a duty.

After you have bought your ticket, you can wait for a guided tour or wander through the **Gate of Salutation**, built by Süleyman in 1524, which only the sultans could ride through on horseback. It leads to the courtyard with the **Executioner's Fountain** where the head gardener would wash his hands and sword after beheading his prisoners, or strangling them with a silken cord if they were royal. The **Courtyard of the Divan** was where the business of the palace was discussed and the viziers met once a week as a form of cabinet; shaded by cypress trees, it has latticed windows to conceal the sultan as he eavesdropped. It now houses the Archaeological Museum, which contains the sarcophagus of Alexander (closed Mondays).

The Harem You can only visit the Harem if you join a group and pay extra, but it is worth it for the exquisitely decorated main room and a glimpse of the 400 other rooms which formed a forbidden area within the palace. Only a few are open to the public but they convey the oppressive opulence of this rarefied world where the favourites were chosen by the 'black' eunuchs (the ugliest of all to prevent temptation, and the most powerful), who escorted the girls along the Golden Way to the sultan's private rooms. A welcome, lighter touch is provided by the charming frescoes of food in the *Yemiş Odasi* – or Fruit Room – allegedly painted to whet the appetite of a sickly prince.

Ahmet II's Audience Hall This is where foreign potentates and ambassadors were received, if only to be insulted. To impress the foreigners with the omnipotence of the sultan, they were forced to submit to the humiliation of being seized by two eunuchs who pushed them before the sultan where they had to crawl on the floor, touching it with their foreheads in respect. Even if they spoke the language fluently, they were only allowed to address the sultan through an interpreter. As soon as he was bored and gave the signal, the eunuchs dragged them out, backwards.

The Treasury Here is where the loot was kept that was earned in war: the sultans' power was exemplified in a wealth of ornamental thrones, jewellery, armour and swords decorated with diamonds and pearls – including the dagger featured in the film *Topkapi* and the gigantic Spoonmaker diamond, 86 carats and the size of an orange. Two uncut emeralds weighing three and six pounds used to hang from the ceiling like light bulbs. Even so, imagination is needed to conceive of the even greater grandeur when the sultans were in residence, with golden floors and silken draperies, peacocks strutting and screaming in the Tulip Garden (a Turkish flower introduced to Europe by Louis XIV's ambassador) and firework displays illustrating dragons which illuminated the night.

Probably no place in the world was so exotic or so cruel.

Ayasofia   Also known as Hagia Sophia, Saint Sophia and Santa Sophia, this is one of the architectural wonders not just of Istanbul but of all the world, the supreme masterpiece of Byzantine art. For nine hundred years it was the greatest monument in Christendom; for the next five hundred one of the most important mosques; today it is a museum. The atmosphere is slightly forbidding, but anyone who does not feel a sense of awe, inspired by the immense dome which is 56 m high and 31 m in diameter, must be disenchanted with life itself. Severe perhaps, but infinitely serene.

'Solomon, I have surpassed thee!' Justinian exulted when he had it constructed on the site of an earlier church which was destroyed in the Nicaea riots of AD 532. The designs were made by Anthemius of Tralles, a noted mathematician, and Isidorus of Miletus, the last head of the Athens Academy. Consecrated in 537, St Sophia was the largest building in the world, fireproof, with four immense pillars (or piers) held together with molten lead which supported four arches and lesser domes, creating a space so overwhelming that it seems to defy the laws of gravity. Indeed, people were afraid to enter it at first in case the dome collapsed. Gradually they accepted the technical marvel as a symbol of faith suspended from heaven by a golden chain. Colour was provided by stone and marble brought from other parts of the empire: red from the temple of Baalbek and green from Ephesus. Once it was bright with golden ornaments and chandeliers.

With the Turkish occupation in 1453 it became a mosque, with the addition of the corner minarets, and many of the decorations were concealed by whitewash. These were gradually restored with exemplary dedication by Thomas Whittemore, of the Byzantine Museum of America, after the building became a museum on the instructions of Atatürk in 1933. The American restorer completed his work in 1960. Today the building is almost stark, which has the advantage of revealing the architectural splendour without distraction, endorsing the claim by Sir Steven Runciman that it is 'a building which has never been surpassed'. Mosaics to look out for on the Vestibule door show Constantine offering the Virgin Mary a model of the mediaeval town of Constantinople. On the other side of Mary and the infant Jesus, Justinian holds a model of St Sophia itself.

Other magnificent features are the elaborate brass door of the library; the marble slabs laid into the walls under a mosaic cross; and the Şadırvan Fountain (1753) in the courtyard outside, a fine example of Ottoman baroque. Also outside, in the garden beyond the baptistry, you can find the tomb of Selim the Sot who was either murdered or so drunk that he drowned in a *hamam* in 1574. His nickname, however, may have been undeserved for he had a love of poetry as well as of wine and women. He is buried with his favourite wife, five of his murdered sons, and thirty-two of his grandchildren. The tomb was designed by Sinan and decorated with Iznik tiles.

The museum is closed on Mondays.

The Blue Mosque   The Blue Mosque is better known to the Turks as the Sultanahmet after Sultan Ahmet I who had it built at the start of the seventeenth century to rival Justinian's St Sophia a short distance away. With this aim in mind, the mosque boasts six minarets, unique in Turkey, even surpassing the Ka'aba in Mecca to which the sultan added a seventh after protests from the faithful.

The 'Blue' comes from the incomparable Iznik tiles, more the greenish colour of turquoise, with 21,000 examples of this vanished ceramic art. The exterior is equally fine, with tiers of domes rising to a peak supported by four columns inside which make it appear less open than in Ayasofia, but here the decoration is everything.

The Covered Bazaar   The Covered Bazaar, *Kapalı Çarşı*, is overwhelming, so be prepared for an exhausting visit unless you want a cursory look with little intention of buying. It was built by Mehmet the Conqueror to help revive a flagging city in 1461 after he conquered Constantinople, and though it has suffered from constant fires since then, the last in 1954, it remains remarkably unchanged. It is still the largest shopping centre in the world contained under one roof, with 1,000 shops in sixty-seven streets, each devoted to a single product: brass, gold, shoes, pearls, *kilims*, carpets. There is the usual fun of bargaining for those who relish it, and the Bazaar is excellent for such traditional crafts as hand-beaten copper (the circular trays are decorative and useful), patterned plates and embroidered blouses. If you are accompanied by a Turk, prices will drop instantly.

If you need to relax, look for the PTT signs and pause at the Havuzlu restaurant, a name which means 'pool' and boasts a small one today, instead of the former well. It provides an oasis of calm in the surrounding din. The Bazaar ought to be seen, if only once. It is open 9 a.m. to 1 p.m. and from 2 to 7 p.m.; closed on Sundays.

The Yeni or New Mosque

Not all that new for it goes back to 1597, this tends to be overlooked for its architectural qualities yet, ironically, is the landmark which visitors remember due to its position by Galata Bridge in the Old City. Not far away, to the northwest, the **Rüstem Paşa** should not be overlooked – a beautiful, small mosque designed by the architect Sinan who usually worked on a larger scale. However, the best reason for going there is to look inside at the walls which are covered with gloriously vivid blue ceramic tiles with swirling patterns of imaginary flowers: they sing with life.

The Mosque of Süleyman

For many Turks this is the finest mosque of all. The sense it conveys is one of stark, absolute and almost brutal power, yet it is reassuring in its great simplicity. It was built for Süleyman the Magnificent by the architect Sinan who started in 1550 and finished seven years later. The mosque marked the thirtieth year of Süleyman's reign; the four minarets, one at each corner, signify that he was the fourth sultan to reign in Istanbul; and the ten balconies for the *muezzins* indicate that he was the tenth of the Osman dynasty.

The perfection of the mosque lies in the mathematical proportions rather than the decorations, though the stained glass by İbrahim the Drunkard is deservedly famous. The scope is immense: the mosque and inner courtyard could contain more than 25,000 worshippers, including the sultan who was concealed behind a screened box. Women prayed separately at the back. The interior emulates the classical concept of Ayasofia, with a central nave and a dome supported by four massive square columns and arches, with smaller domes on either side buttressed by the mosque walls, creating an uninterrupted space as if the dome were suspended of its own accord. Light is cast by 138 stained glass windows. It is still in active use for worship.

Sinan died nearby and his tomb can be seen in the garden of his house above the mosque. To the east is the tomb of Süleyman in a room decorated with Iznik tiles and stained glass; his favourite daughter, Mihrimah, lies beside him. The smaller tomb of his ambitious wife Roxelana, also decorated with tiles, is alongside.

The café of Pierre Loti

On one of my first visits to Istanbul, I sought out the home of Pierre Loti (1850–1923), the romantic French novelist who fell in love with Turkey and the Golden Horn in particular. In his lifetime, the shore was lined with wooden houses, gardens, cypress trees and marble jetties. The Horn was busy with the traffic of sailing ships and the first vessels driven by steam, while the water was still pure enough for boys to swim in. But even then the industrialists were encroaching. Probably Loti mourned the pristine past in his turn, just as we look back wistfully to the Horn as he knew it, his house surrounded by fields and old tombstones which were carefully looked after.

Sunset would be the best time to see it today, casting an illusion which conceals the filth of the water, the ugly graveyard which has replaced the marble, and the industry which has spoilt the view. The café is still there and has a faded charm, but if you go with great expectations, as I did, you may be disappointed. The good news is the promise by the new mayor that he will cleanse the murky waters until they resemble the blue of his eyes, but I doubt if I shall live that long.

The mosque at Eyüp My reward came with the accidental discovery of the mosque at Eyüp. Lazily, but also because I did not know the way, I had taken a taxi to Pierre Loti's café so I walked down the hill afterwards. Just as the industry of the Horn at this inland point comes as a revelation, the back streets are alive with children playing football among the rubble and Turks returning home from work, far from the tourist track. Eyüp was once a village outside the walls of Istanbul and the atmosphere is less hectic than the centre of the city, almost that of a backwater suffering from neglect. When I reached the bottom, I came across the sacred mosque of the Eyüp Sultan Cami which was all the better for being unexpected. It is sacred to the Muslims as the burial place of Eyüp Ensari (Ayoub in Arabic and Job in English), the standard bearer for the Prophet Mohammed who died during the Arabian siege of Constantinople in 674–78. His tomb is isolated in an inner courtyard and because he carried the banner for Islam it is treated with a reverence comparable to that of Mecca or Medina. The legend has it that Eyüp's grave was lost but rediscovered by Mehmet II during his siege of the city in 1453, a 'miracle' which inspired his soldiers to greater efforts in their holy war. Mehmet built a mosque which was destroyed in the earthquake of 1766; the new one was built as recently as 1800 for Sultan Selim III in baroque style.

The inner courtyards are spacious and surprising with flocks of pigeons rising and falling and even lame storks in the plane trees, unable to continue on their way to Africa. The sultans used to come here for a form of coronation, and flocks of pilgrims still do so today.

The tomb, *türbe*, of the saintly Eyüp is lined with Iznik tiles and the mosque itself is sumptuously decorated. It is well worth a visit though you should be particularly careful in your appearance and behaviour because it is so sacred.

I caught a bus opposite which took an endless though interesting journey back to Galata, but you can also take the ferry from the Eyüp stop nearby, past warehouses and shipyards and the sooty commerce of the Golden Horn.

Voyvoda Caddesi

On the New City side, just by the Galata Bridge, is the district of Karaköy. It contains a point of curiosity: a street named Voyvoda Caddesi after the fifteenth-century Wallachian warrior Vlad the Impaler, who thrust his Turkish prisoners on to spikes and ate his lunch underneath while they screamed and struggled slowly to their deaths. He was also known as Dracul, son of Dracula, who was immortalised by my great-uncle Bram Stoker in his famous novel. It seems odd that the Turks should honour such a bloodthirsty enemy, but they claim they captured him and buried the corpse in this street. The Romanians have a different story: I have seen his tomb at Snagov, near Bucharest, where they buried him, too.

The Tünel

This is a more tangible oddity: a tunnel which takes you up 600 m from Galata Bridge to Istiklal Caddesi. It is allegedly the shortest underground journey in the world.

Flower Sellers' Alley

It is easy to miss the entrance on the left hand side as you walk down Istiklal Caddesi to Taksim Square. At number 51, it is concealed behind an old-fashioned portico with stalls immediately inside selling nuts and raisins, with a beer saloon on the other side. But all you have to do is ask – everyone knows *Çiçek Pasajı*.

The alley takes its name from the adjacent market with lavish displays of flowers, fish and fruit. In Flower Sellers' Alley there is no such colour apart from that provided by the Turks themselves, and they could hardly be more colourful. The alley itself is drab and grey with cats peering down in disapproval from the overhanging corrugated roofs, erected to prevent masonry falling on the customers below. The old houses have known grander and quieter days but are now in a state of decay with shuttered or broken windows where you have the occasional, startling glimpse of someone moving inside, for the first impression is that of a façade without any substance behind.

This sombre setting enhances the gaiety below which hardly needs distraction. It must be one of the most joyful spots on earth, by-passed by progress, with people who go there simply to enjoy themselves. Tourists are the only intrusion though one of the restaurants has been smartened up and the lovely fat violinist, Hasan, who used to play inside with such passion that he might have been auditioning for Carnegie Hall, has died since I first heard him interrupting his performance angrily to push a rival violinist away.

Each side of the alley is lined with restaurants with tables and chairs outside where Turks from various parts of the country come to celebrate. Some are singing or declaiming without musical instruments, others are being serenaded by the strolling players including a hideous but warm-hearted woman with an object that looks like a massive colander and sounds no better. The scene is wonderfully alive and the various singers, acrobats and orators are somehow not in competition but fuse together in a boisterous but friendly cacophony. I have spent many happy hours there absorbing the atmosphere which could be that of a turbulent port in the last century and seldom disappoints. There is ceaseless movement and a constant parade of people who stroll up and down the middle, just a couple of yards between the tables. I have grown to recognise the players on this extraordinary stage: the 'rival' violinist, shooed away by Hasan, who now reigns supreme, a wizened little man with puffed-out cheeks like Popeye; the boy with the plain, expressionless face who perseveres with his sticks of chewing-gum and shames the tourists when they refuse to buy any by presenting them with one for nothing, after which they tip him handsomely and have to do so again to make him leave; he gives me a broad wink as he goes, realising that I have understood his game (I fell for it myself earlier!). A dreadful woman dances dreadfully with lira notes in her mouth stuffed there by herself for no one wants to know her, and a shoe-shine boy pirouettes in parody behind her while the chewing-gum boy assists the waiter in trying to move her on to the next restaurant to annoy someone else.

An acrobat balances precariously on a tiny wooden plank on rollers and swings a hoop around his neck while he stands a bottle of pop on his nose for all of ten seconds. This is capped by a double-somersault – a one-man circus – and the chewing-gum boy watches open-mouthed in admiration. Afterwards, instead of passing round a cap, the acrobat pours a bottle of cologne into your hands so that he can accept his tips with dignity as payment instead of charity.

While his unsmiling father plays the flute, a boy aged six or seven beats a drum with a powerful rhythm: how those small hands must tire. People give the boy notes when he seizes a moment's rest and I notice that the father regards this resentfully, especially when his son gives a sudden solo on the drums with spontaneous pleasure.

Vendors sell crab claws and even skewers of Adana kebabı, which makes me wonder how the waiters react to this encroachment, though they never seem to mind.

A small boy walks past with a weighing-machine – surely one of the sadder sights in a place like this – yet one or two customers give him his living for the night. A sadder sight is a youth who staggers past, so pale and weak from hunger that I follow and thrust L 1,000 into his hand thinking how generous I am; at least I am thankful that he does not look grateful when he turns round, simply dazed. My suspicion that this is hunger rather than any drug is confirmed when some Turks make way for him at their table and push some of their dishes of food towards him which he devours voraciously in silence.

In my philanthropical mood, encouraged by another *rakı*, I buy a rose from a man after some tourists have rejected him haughtily, and then feel rather foolish as I put it in my buttonhole.

The noise increases. Turks interrupt their meals to sing to the accompaniment of one of the strolling musicians, cheered on by their companions. A man from Kars, near the Russian border in the east, starts a wild dance, his feet shooting out with the speed of castanets. At the top of the alley I see the feet of another acrobat standing on his hands on a pyramid of tables.

A tattered man dominates the tables near me, clasping his ear in one hand while striking himself with the other. He shouts a song passionately, receiving rapturous applause at every pause. His act seems to consist of tearing himself apart in sheer fury, but the smiles and laughter confirm that he is a born comic. The tables at the top of the alley are sent flying as a fight breaks out and the waiters rush to our tables to whisk the glasses and bottles away while one man pursues another down the alley and people flee before them like the young bloods in Pamplona running in front of the bulls. I notice that the men, covered in blood, look thankful when they are separated, in spite of sudden, unconvincing, attempts to return to the attack. The glasses, plates and bottles are restored – all in a matter of seconds.

I love this place! It may be tough but it's the toughness which affords generosity as the Turks welcome you to their table if you are looking for a seat, and offer to share their food. Strangers become friends, though it is unlikely that you will ever meet again. Even tourists are welcomed. If Çiçek Pasajı were not already so well known, I would hesitate to recommend it as a place you should not miss for I dread the day when it descends to a mere tourist attraction and the Turks simulate the fun instead of relishing the reality. But that is the curse of the travel writer, that you can kill the place you love.

The Dolmabahçe Palace

After the sanctity of Ayasofia and the claustrophobia of the Topkapı, the antidote is found on the shores of the Bosphorus in the Dolmabahçe Palace. The place could be dismissed as an eccentric folly, yet there is nothing accidental about it. The site, 2 km away from today's Galata Bridge, has a historical significance for this was the harbour where Mehmet II assembled his fleet and pulled his lighter vessels overland to the Golden Horn during the siege of Constantinople. Afterwards, a garden was laid out and the harbour reclaimed. Nor is the style a matter of whim on the part of the architect, Balian, who built it in 1853 for Sultan Abdül Mecit. It could be described as Italian rococo–baroque but it really defies any architectural terminology. Intended to make Westerners feel at home, it was part of the reforming sultan's determination to lead Turkey towards Europe. At the Dolmabahçe he dressed in a frock coat to receive ambassadors and held society balls where he danced the waltz in person. It was here that Kemal Atatürk died, having disposed of the sultanate forever.

Everything is on a gigantic scale, starting with the massive wrought-iron gates topped by the sultan's signature, and the white statues of lionesses cavorting with their cubs in the gardens in front of the wedding-cake exterior. Much of it is out of proportion: the largest chandelier in the world, weighing 4,000 kg (4½ tons); Ali Baba vases which could hide a prison-full of thieves; and a hall which suggests the dome of St Paul's, though this is gaudily painted, with a minstrel gallery that was used for feasts. The Ambassadors' Waiting Room is plush with gilt chairs and scarlet drapes and every piece of furniture seems magnified.

One explanation for this bizarre interior decoration is the gifts from foreign potentates, which resemble the horrors in the attic which are rediscovered, dusted off, and presented as wedding gifts to an unloved and distant relative. The chandelier was given to Abdül Aziz by Queen Victoria, and the guide will assure you in a solemn aside that she was in love with the sultan, though the visual evidence suggests otherwise; elephant tusks came from the Governor of Hejaz in northwest Arabia; the polar-bear rugs from Czar Nicholas of Russia. It's as if size signified power; it is characteristic of Atatürk's lack of ostentation that he chose to sleep in one of the smaller rooms, though even the smallest room in the palace – a white marble bathroom where the sultans made love – is voluptuous and huge. The numerous clocks are all stopped at 9.05 in memory of the President who died at that moment on 10 November 1938.

The Palace and Harem are open from 9.30 a.m. to 4 p.m. every day except Mondays and Thursdays; from 1 November to 28 February, they close early at 3 p.m. You are supposed to join a guided tour in groups of thirty, but you can probably manage not to.

Nearly two-thirds of Dolmabahçe are occupied by the harem and women's quarters, and though these are part of the palace they are isolated in the traditional way, separated by wooden and iron doors at the end of corridors.

The Naval Museum — Nearby, at the busy ferry point known as Beşiktaş, this excellent museum offers further proof of Atatürk's simplicity: a tiny rowing boat designed especially for him and carved in hardwood with the replicas of the sultans' galleys, complete with the figures of the oarsmen, the sultan himself, the sultana and splendid figureheads of lions – it is plainly a work of devotion. It brings to life the numerous prints of Constantinople with great galleys forging through the busy water traffic years ago, and is well worth seeing as a respite from antiquities and architectural magnificence.

Yıldız Park — Stretching up the hill from Beşiktaş above the Dolmabahçe, this is hardly visible as you drive down the main road, yet provides a welcome oasis in the din. Once it was part of the forest which covered the European shore of the Bosphorus; today it has been transformed into parkland, with gardens and a lake, after being badly neglected in the 1950s when it turned into an overgrown jungle. The Touring Club of Turkey started the restoration in 1979 and deserves full credit for its impeccable taste, yet the restoration is more than meticulous: it provides entertainment too, with Turkish families relaxing here on sunny days. Climb the hill to the Malta Pavilion at the top or take a taxi up, and walk *down* to Bcşiktaş.

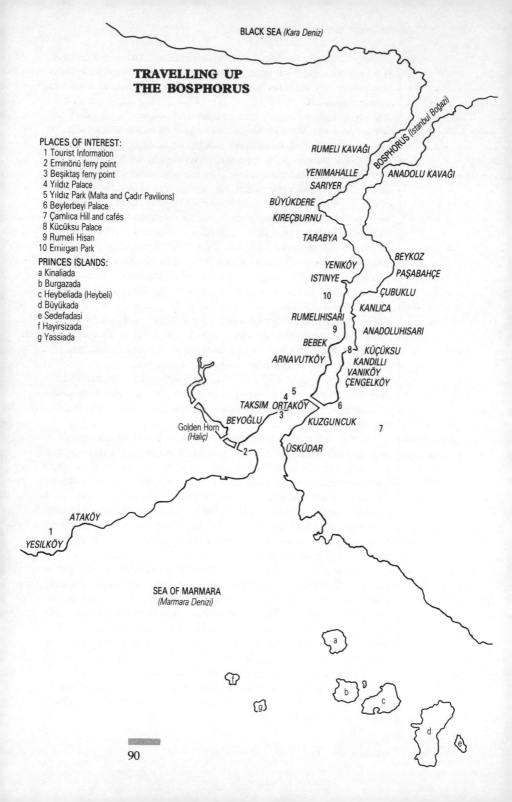

BLACK SEA *(Kara Deniz)*

TRAVELLING UP
THE BOSPHORUS

PLACES OF INTEREST:
1 Tourist Information
2 Eminönü ferry point
3 Beşiktaş ferry point
4 Yıldız Palace
5 Yıldız Park (Malta and Çadır Pavilions)
6 Beylerbeyi Palace
7 Çamlıca Hill and cafés
8 Küçüksu Palace
9 Rumeli Hisarı
10 Emirgan Park

PRINCES ISLANDS:
a Kinaliada
b Burgazada
c Heybeliada (Heybeli)
d Büyükada
e Sedefadasi
f Hayirsizada
g Yassiada

BOSPHORUS *(Istanbul Boğazı)*

RUMELI KAVAĞI
YENIMAHALLE
SARIYER
BÜYÜKDERE
KIREÇBURNU
TARABYA
YENIKÖY
ISTINYE
10
RUMELIHISARI
9
BEBEK
ARNAVUTKÖY

ANADOLU KAVAĞI

BEYKOZ
PAŞABAHÇE
ÇUBUKLU
KANLICA
ANADOLUHISARI
KÜÇÜKSU
KANDILLI
VANIKÖY
ÇENGELKÖY

TAKSIM ORTAKÖY
BEYOĞLU
Golden Horn
(Haliç)
4 5
3
2

6
KUZGUNCUK
7
ÜSKÜDAR

ATAKÖY
1
YESILKÖY

SEA OF MARMARA
(Marmara Denizi)

a
f
b
c
g
d
e

The Malta Pavilion   One of the triumphs of Çelik Gülersoy of the Touring Club, and deserves the 'Europa Nostra' award it won for its restoration. The oldest building in Yıldız Park, set among Judas trees so that the surroundings are filled with purple blossom in the spring, it has a white marble terrace with views over the Bosphorus where you can eat and .drink – excellent for morning coffee or afternoon tea, with a snack if you need one, rather than a full meal. The range is rich: sandwiches; köfte and börek; soup and salads; even steak, to say nothing of the sticky cakes and ice-creams. You can have any drink you wish, and the Pavilion is noted for its cocktails in the early evening.

I basked on the terrace in the early sun of May on a Sunday morning after arriving in Istanbul the night before, and I could feel myself relax, absorbed by the sympathetic atmosphere – even the muzak is romantic. The colours of the Pavilion are exceptionally pleasing – white columns and balconies against a pistachio green background – and somehow convey the former splendour of a Russian *dacha*. In fact it was built in the grounds of the massive stone Çırağan Palace at the beginning of the nineteenth century, and was used as an additional pavilion by one of the last sultans, Abdül Hamit II, who could no longer afford to subsidise buildings on such a massive scale. It was largely destroyed by fire in 1910. With beds of roses outside and beautiful painted ceilings within, it is one of the most peaceful resting places in Istanbul, devoid of the garishness of the Dolmabahçe below, or the Beylerbeyi Palace on the opposite side of the Bosphorus.

Beylerbeyi Palace   The Beylerbeyi Palace is frequently overlooked because of its position on the Asian side of the Bosphorus, eclipsed by the great suspension bridge which crosses the two continents and hangs overhead. In fact it is easy to reach: after all, you simply have to descend on the Asian side of the bridge. But it is far more enjoyable to take the ordinary passenger ferry across the Bosphorus to Üsküdar, and a bus or taxi from there.

Built in 1865 as another extravagance of Abdül Aziz, it became the home – virtually the prison – of Abdül Hamit II, who died here in 1918 after six years' residence. It is easy to imagine its sensational position before this area was developed, with sweeping views of the Bosphorus – it was a natural waterfront retreat for numerous governors. In the time of Mahmut II, it was a wooden palace which was burnt down and rebuilt as we know it today by the architect Serkis Balian who employed 5,000 men, so the resemblance to the Dolmabahçe Palace – designed by his brother Nikoğos Balian – is hardly coincidental. Though the two palaces are not that far away, the crossing by boat must have made the Beylerbeyi seem remote. It was used either as a summer lodge or a special residence for such distinguished visitors as the King of Montenegro, the Shah of Iran, and the Empress Eugenie of France who paused here on the way to open the Suez Canal which was built by her cousin, Ferdinand de Lesseps.

A Dolmabahçe in miniature, with sugar-cake façade and monstrous magnificence within, the Beylerbeyi sports crystal chandeliers that are only slightly less massive, Chinese and Sèvres vases, porcelain from the imperial factory at Yıldız, and overpainted ceilings inset with attractive illustrations of sailing ships. Yet the palace has considerable, if oppressive, charm. A white marble fountain in the central hall, now empty, once freshened the hot-house atmosphere which, one suspects, had the musk of Eastern perfumes, while providing a delightfully soothing sound.

With the conflicting mixture of European and Eastern design, the layout approximates to the basic requirements of a Turkish house, albeit on a colossal scale, with a separate harem and women's quarters, and the *selamlık* which was exclusively male. The decorations resemble a film-set for an Eastern romance by a camp designer who has lost control – even the marble pillars are painted an eccentric blue. The staircase in the main hall in the men's quarters is wide enough for a regiment, flanked by two gigantic gilded candelabra. Altogether, the description 'a pretty little palace' is true only in comparison with the Dolmabahçe, but because it is less well known with fewer visitors there is a much greater intimacy.

The Beylerbeyi is open from 9 a.m. to 5 p.m., closed on Mondays and Thursdays. The entrance fee is L 1,500, with an extra L 2,000 if you want to take photographs.

The Hidiv Kasrı   Afterwards, you can continue further up the Bosphorus to another pavilion which has been restored by the Touring Club, about fifteen minutes' drive away. The summer palace of the last Egyptian viceroy (Khedive) deposed by the British, it was built in the hills above the Bosphorus, opposite Tarabya. It is described as being art nouveau but reminds me more of a Tuscan villa. The house was surrounded by parkland which belonged to the Egyptians until 1937 when the property was occupied by the Municipality of Istanbul and neglected for the next forty-five years until the Touring Club redeemed it in 1982.

The house is used as a hotel today with numerous, well-furnished bedrooms; the gardens have been restored impeccably. Extremely popular with the Turks, it lacks the simpler perfection and zest of the Malta Pavilion partly because the scale is grander. The dining room, dark and overwhelming even in daytime, has an unexciting menu so it is better to sit outside on the white marble terrace, flanked by rose beds, where a glass of beer and a plate of smoked sturgeon are welcome though costly at nearly L 6,000. The rooms inside are used for evening concerts. During the day, spare the time to linger and absorb the atmosphere.

Çamlıca Hill   Above Beylerbeyi, and 4 km from the Üsküdar ferry point (take a taxi or a number 9 bus) you can get marvellous views of Istanbul and the traffic of the Bosphorus, probably at their best at sunset. On a clear day you can see the mountain peak of Uludağ, which rises over Bursa, and the Black Sea to the north.

Çamlıca Hill was a favourite cultural centre in the last century but the area subsided into a morass of mud and shanty dwellings after the last war. The Touring Club came to the rescue yet again in 1980, bringing thousands of tons of fresh soil, grass and hundreds of trees. Now there are two cafés in eighteenth-century style, linked with seven marble kiosks which also offer refreshments.

The Selimiye Barracks

Turning back towards the central part of Üsküdar, just above Haydarpaşa Station you will find the barracks where Florence Nightingale nursed the wounded during the Crimean War: they are well worth a visit. Her famous lamp remains as a memorial there today, while the English cemetery nearby honours the British who gave their lives on behalf of Turkey at various times since then: an Assistant Military Attaché to the British Embassy in Constantinople, who died of typhoid when he served with the Turkish forces in 1870; and a young sailor from the *Ark Royal* who died in 1920, with the poignant inscription, 'His sun had set while it was still day.' The cemetery is dominated by a massive memorial to Florence Nightingale and those killed in the Crimean War.

What to do
Night life

Night life is peculiar, not in the sense that it is bizarre but rather that it is not bizarre enough and it is hard to find. You might expect that Istanbul would be rich in exotic clubs with belly dancers writhing to the drums and flutes of turbaned Turks, but such places around Istiklal and Taksim are clip-joints whose greatest sin is dullness. There is no quarter devoted to entertainment, like the Plaka in Athens or Montmartre in Paris, nor is there the refuge of the great British pub or the New York bar. The closest you will find in this respect is the glorious Flower Sellers' Alley, but this closes down before midnight (see p. 86). Otherwise, choose one of the smaller restaurants with two or three musicians to enhance the atmosphere (there are several in Sıraselviler off Taksim Square). Even with a meal this will be considerably cheaper than the clip-joint. There are several so-called nightclubs but you should not be surprised if you find yourself surrounded by tourists.

Galata Tower Built by the Genoese in 1348 as a fortification, this structure is one of the landmarks of Istanbul with remarkable views over the Golden Horn. There are three 'eating establishments': a restaurant from 9 p.m. to 1 a.m.; a *lokanta* with Turkish music from 7 p.m. to 1 a.m., and – the main attraction – the top-floor nightclub with a special 'show' including oriental dance and folk music. The entertainment is excellent value and the surroundings are unusual. It is claimed that the massive chain which shut off the Golden Horn during emergencies was raised and lowered by a capstan in the tower. It is in Şişhane, in Yüksek Kaldırım, tel.: 145.11.60.

Samdan This is a five-star, deluxe restaurant with a discotheque supposedly popular with 'the beautiful people'. It is very expensive, with French and Turkish specialities: fine for a really special occasion. In the summer you can eat out of doors. It is in Nisbetiye Caddesi, Etiler (tel.: 163.48.98), moving in the summer to Piyasa Caddesi 101, Büyükdere (tel.: 162.03.79), beyond Tarabya and closer to the Black Sea. It is open from 7 p.m. to 1 a.m.

Yirmi Dokuz Nearby in Nisbetiye Caddesi 29 (tel.: 163.54.11), this deluxe restaurant has music with dancing upstairs.

Bakus Fenerbahçe on the Asian side of the Bosphorus is a main avenue leading to the lighthouse with numerous fish restaurants, some of which have entertainment. The Bakus is across from Eski Belvü Gazinosu (tel.: 336.11.20) and it is vital to reserve at weekends. The restaurant is housed in an old villa and the entertainment includes 'the most famous Turkish belly dancers' so it is well worth the expense. You would have the advantage of a romantic ferry crossing to Üsküdar at dusk.

Caddebostan Mini Maksim Also on the Asian side, this is near a ferry stop. Open in the summer only, it has a seaside atmosphere, providing dinner and entertainment with Turkish music. On Mondays there is a disco. Tel.: 358.23.73.

Büyük Maksim An expensive but good nightclub with a Turkish show. Sıraselviler Caddesi (tel.: 144.31.34).

Ziya On the Bosphorus just beyond the bridge, this place will give you outdoor meals in the summer to live music. Muallim Naci Caddesi 109 (tel.: 161.60.05). Open from 12 noon to 1 a.m., with weekend reservations essential.

Kervansaray Near the Hilton, this caters for tourists, but the floor show is excellent and varied. Cumhuriyet Caddesi 30 (tel.: 147.16.30). Also in this district are **Lalezar** (Gümüşsuyu, Askerocağı Caddesi, tel.: 149.52.44), with views over the Horn and the Bosphorus and the promise of 'lively music and dancing' as well as a wide choice of *mezes*; **Kulüp 33** for its floor show; **Sevillanas** (Cumhuriyet Caddesi, tel.: 146.32.11), a restaurant/nightclub which serves paella; and **Günay** (Cumhuriyet Caddesi 349, tel.: 140.46.51), with a disco, show and dinner.

Bars   Bars are found mainly in the reconstructed Pavilions and the big hotels: the Hilton, Sheraton and Etap Marmara have rooftop bars which are worth visiting for their panoramic views over the Golden Horn. The Pera Palas is near to the ground-floor foyer but is richer in atmosphere, if you are lucky.

Along the main road from Taksim Square beyond the bus-stop and close to the park are several bars, one of which seems decidedly gay. These are proper bars with separate cubicles or stools beside the bar itself. A glimpse inside should confirm the atmosphere you're seeking or wish to avoid. **Asper** and **Tequila** are virtually adjacent.

Bars can also be found in Sıraselviler Caddesi, on the left hand side as you walk down from Taksim Square, notably **Valentino's** in a magnificent room at the top of an old and now dingy Turkish mansion. This has an interesting atmosphere, almost conspiratorial as if it was a meeting place for dissidents, and as it is used by Turks it is predominantly male. Such places only start to grow lively after midnight.

Where to stay

As in any big city, hotels come in distinct categories. And as in most cities, you can sometimes find a satisfactory compromise between the unashamedly expensive and the wretchedly cheap.

Top range

The Hilton In Cumhuriyet Caddesi (beyond Taksim Square), tel.: 131.46.46; 410 rooms. The Hilton has the advantage of a superb setting overlooking the Bosphorus. A pleasingly low-lying building instead of the usual skyscraper, it was built when Istanbul was comparatively empty, and has the reputation for being one of the finest Hilton hotels in the world. The facilities are formidable: Turkish baths and Finnish saunas; a beauty salon with solarium; an exercise room; a massage parlour; tennis courts and squash courts; an indoor pool decorated with a miniature cliff-face, greenery and waterfall, and a large outdoor pool – a blessing in Istanbul – in the ten acres of 'lush gardens'.

The rooftop bar has splendid views over the city and there are three restaurants including the Roof Rotisserie, famous for its *mezes* buffet.

Obviously ideal for the businessman on an expense account, there is also a full telex and secretarial service.

There is even the Hilton heliport with flights over the city, which would be an exciting way of putting the various parts of Istanbul into perspective.

And yet, in spite of the jacuzzis and taped music (or because of them), a Hilton is a Hilton is a Hilton, and it is not called Hilton International for nothing. A village inside the city, such hotels are insulated from the bustle of Istanbul, just as the Topkapı must have been several centuries ago.

It is very expensive, though the prices vary drastically according to the type of room, the Bosphorus view being considerably dearer than the garden view. A single room starts around L 107,000, a Bosphorus twin around L 178,500, and a suite over twice that. This includes service and VAT, but if there are two of you, do not expect to stay for less than L 178,500 if you are having breakfast as well. Group rates are cheaper.

The Sheraton, 80174 Taksim Park, tel.: 131.21.21/60; 460 rooms. Another luxurious international hotel, more American than Turkish except when a fair is being held on the ground floor when the atmosphere has the pleasing flavour of a market. Considerable effort is made by the management (though not always by some of the condescending staff) to make your stay comfortable and interesting. The rooms are air-conditioned with their own bathrooms and some have balconies with 'views towards the sea'. Mine overlooked the new gardens of

Taksim Square which was perfectly agreeable; for splendid panoramic views go to the rooftop bar.

The outdoor swimming pool is exceptional, with snacks and drinks from the Aquarius Bar; the Park Café is good for light meals; so is the Mangal restaurant, though more expensive. You can dance in the Sultan to disco music until the early hours, while the Taksim Bar offers live entertainment.

With the usual beauty parlour and similar facilities, the Sheraton is self-contained, which you may welcome as an advantage.

Single rooms range from L 107,000 to L 152,000; doubles from L 143,000 to over L 178,500. Deluxe two bedroom suites are close to L 895,000, but if you are the sort of traveller who contemplates going to the Hilton or the Sheraton in the first place, you may not be daunted by such expense.

The Etap There are two Etaps in Istanbul: one is virtually opposite the Pera Palas; the grander, *Etap Marmara*, is in Taksim Square, though if you have just flown in from Heathrow you may find it disconcertingly familiar, complete with moving walkways (tel.: 151.46.96; 424 rooms). There is the usual choice of bars and restaurants; pool, sauna and nightclub; and panoramic views from Istanbul's tallest building.

Single rooms L 107,000–134,000; twin doubles L 134,000–178,500.

The other Etap is on a more modest scale; in Meşrutiyet Caddesi, tel.: 151.46.46; 200 rooms.

Pera Palas Hotel, Meşrutiyet Caddesi 98, Tepebaşi, Beyoğlu, tel.: 151.45.60; 116 rooms. This is something different altogether, one of the great hotels in the world. Far from being international, the Pera Palas is gloriously Turkish as you realise from the moment you enter and see the sumptuous middle hall beyond, a massive baroque room worthy of the Dolmabahçe, in brown, yellow and gold, with a ceiling inset with domes and windows, and an overwhelming chandelier. Unlike the palaces, the effect is not oppressive but restful. Even if you are not staying here it is worth visiting for coffee, or a drink at the main bar around the corner.

The Pera Palas was built in 1892 for the first passengers off the Orient Express, simply because there was nowhere else for them to stay, and the original china of the *Compagnie Internationale des Wagons-Lits* can be seen in a glass case. Though the hotel may have seemed like a Hilton in its day, it has an old-fashioned grace and Oriental splendour. You realise you have arrived in Istanbul. The elegance of the open wrought-iron lift is a constant delight, the staff are carefully chosen and attentive, and something always seems to be happening in that main hall – a circumcision party; a wedding; or some excuse for celebration – and then the ground floor is vibrant with enjoyment, the tables are laden with food, the orchestra plays and the people applaud. Anyone who thinks that the Turks are a dour people should see them here at such a moment. It's wonderfully infectious. Throughout, the scene is observed with a discerning smile by Hasan Süzer, the manager, who may look impassive but knows exactly what is going on down to the smallest detail. A man of impressive authority, Mr Süzer is a true *hotelier* in the best sense of that old-fashioned accolade.

Yet the Pera Palas has its critics: those to whom the luxury of the large high-ceilinged bathrooms is less important than jacuzzis or the last word in 'sanitisation'; those who fail to appreciate the past, with the room where Kemal Atatürk stayed as a young officer meticulously restored with photographs and memorabilia. It is worth asking if you can see it, if only to realise the reverence felt towards him. The clock is permanently stopped at the hour of his death – 9.05 a.m. – forecast by a fortune teller who was two minutes out. Critics also claim that prices are exorbitant and it is true that they have risen steeply in the last few years, as they have elsewhere. A few have found the food indifferent, but I do not agree. It is necessary to ask for yoghurt or eggs, or whatever you want for breakfast, in addition to the rather spartan choice available, including the traditional white cheese and black olives.

When the hotel opened it was advertised as being 'high up and isolated on all four sides' but with the growth of Istanbul that isolation no longer exists and some of the rooms are as noisy as they would be in any bustling city. In fact, the sounds of activity can be reassuring.

There is no beauty parlour and no pool. The 'Hilton/Sheraton' rules do not apply here. The Pera Palas is not just a place to stay in, but a rare experience. The rival manager of one of the big international hotels told me that he would love to get his hands on the Pera Palas and transform it. May Allah forbid! One can just imagine the converted Sultana Bar with barmen dressed as eunuchs, and the Harem Restaurant with 'genuine Ottoman atmosphere and snacks'. There is nothing quaint about the Pera Palas.

Prices fluctuate: be prepared to pay L 62,500 for a single room; more for a double.

Yeşil Ev, Sultanahmet, tel.: 528.67.64, 511.11.50. This is another hotel which stands alone, one of the last nineteenth-century Istanbul mansions, lovingly restored by the incomparable Mr Çelik Gülersoy and the Turkish Touring and Automobile Association, opened to the public as recently as 1984. As usual, his taste is faultless: on a more intimate scale than the Pera Palas, the furnishings are perfect and old-fashioned – brass bedsteads, carpets over wooden floors, heavy curtains, chandeliers and oil-lamps. Instead of the inevitable 'twins', the double beds are huge and comfortable. The position is convenient for sightseeing, down a side-street between Ayasofia and the Blue Mosque. A skilful blend of old and new, the rooms have baths and showers, and central heating in winter, while the wooden exterior emulates the past. There is a Turkish *hamam*, and no air-conditioning. John Betjeman would have loved it.

The Yeşil Ev possesses one of the most restful gardens in Istanbul, ideal for relaxing in after visiting Ayasofia even if you are not staying there. A pool of pink porphyry (a rock composed of crystals) and a fountain stand in the centre of the garden, taken from the Yıldız Palace and re-erected here. There is a spacious glass summerhouse for breakfast, tea, drinks or snacks – or you can eat outside. This is the restful oasis I searched for on previous visits.

The scrupulous attention throughout has won the Yeşil Ev the Europa Nostra Award. The brochure dares to claim that 'it is a delightful experience to wake up in the morning to the sound of birds in the garden' and that is beyond cost. Even so, it's expensive: L 85,000 for a double room.

Next to the Yeşil Ev was an old *medrese*, or theological school, built in the classical Turkish style but allowed to fall into ruins. Starting work in 1983, the Touring Club have restored this too as part of the Yeşil Ev complex, with stone courtyard, garden and trees, and it functions now as a market for arts and crafts where you can see artists engaged in calligraphy, the painting of miniatures and copperwork.

The Street of Soğukçeşme is probably Mr Gülersoy's most dramatic restoration, an entire row of broken-down wooden houses nearby which have been reconstructed and furnished for practical daily use as coffee-houses, bookshops and sweetshops, with the upper floors providing accommodation as guest houses and views towards Ayasofia opposite. The success of this venture is confirmed by the crowds of Turkish visitors who throng the street especially at the weekends, eager for this nostalgic facsimile of the past.

Ayasofya Pansiyonlari, Soğukçeşme, Sultanahmet, tel.: 512.57.32. The street, which is closed to traffic, starts near the first gate of the Topkapı Palace and continues towards Ayasofia. It is named Soğukçeşme after a fountain (dated 1800) and a Roman cistern. With old wooden houses lining the palace walls, it was one of the features of old Stamboul until it fell into disrepair and was rescued by the Touring Club. Today nine of the houses have been transformed into a row of pensions and the Roman cistern has become a tavern. A receptionist gives you two keys, for the front door and your room, so that you feel at home. The brochure adds 'Only a knave welcomes' which makes my mind boggle a bit but I am sure the explanation is simple.

Houses are painted in the colours of flowers: Jasmin House, Rose Mansion, etc., which sounds slightly twee; there is an undeniable sense of reconstruction. This is largely because the houses *have* been reconstructed and are new. As soon as they are tempered by the weather, and the surrounding trees and climbing vines have grown, the appearance will be less pristine.

As in the Yeşil Ev, the rooms are comfortable with big double beds, armchairs and velvet curtains, with the astonishing view of Ayasofia when you open the window.

Prices range from L 53,600 for a single room on the street side to L 89,500 for a double; suites cost from L 116,000.

Divan Hotel, Cumhuriyet Caddesi, Elmadağ, tel.: 131.41.00; 96 air-conditioned rooms. This is highly recommended as an alternative to the more pretentious and expensive hotels in the deluxe category, though some would claim that the Divan is genuinely more luxurious. Ask specifically for rooms at the back if you want quiet, always a rarity in a big city.

The facilities include the ubiquitous beauty parlour – of which I have no experience – but I can vouch for the outstanding restaurant, discreet and strictly professional, which is known for serving some of the best food in Istanbul and is used by the Turks as well as tourists. I was taken there by the proprietor of a newspaper one lunchtime; you may wish for greater 'atmosphere' in the evening. The Patisserie tea-shop is famous too, especially for its Turkish delight which is unequalled. Try a box of rose-petal *and* another of pistachio. There is also the Divan Pub, more of a snack bar for a light meal and a convenient meeting place. The bar is perfectly adequate if unexciting. It is the no-nonsense professionalism of the place which I admire.

Single rooms are about L 89,500, double L 129,500. Lunch and dinner cost the same – around L 18,000.

Maçka Hotel, Eytem Caddesi 35, Teşvikiye, tel.: 140.10.53; 184 rooms all with bath and television. Situated near the Hilton though closer to the Bosphorus, this is a massive, older-style Turkish hotel, though without the baroque elegance of the Pera Palas. I suspect that the first rather gloomy impression could be replaced by affection in spite of the slot machines hall. There is a sauna bath and cooling room complete with television, and most of the usual facilities. The lengthy ballroom suggests that it is ideal for functions.

A single room costs from L 58,000, doubles from L 83,750.

Mid-range
Dilson Hotel, Sıraselviler Caddesi 49, Taksim, tel.: 143.20.32; 92 rooms with bath. Conveniently situated in a street off Taksim Square, this is a good middle-range hotel with a lounge where you can entertain or the Avlu Bar decorated in Turkish style. Restaurant food is both Turkish and international; the atmosphere cheerful and friendly.

A single room costs from L 31,250, a double from L 44,500.

The Londres, (Büyük Londra Oteli) Meşrutiyet Caddesi 117, Tepebaşı, tel.: 145.06.70; 42 rooms. Recently restored in attractive period style, this hotel is pleasantly unpretentious. The back rooms are quiet and the showers, for once, are vigorous. There are few facilities, which comes as a relief. Close to the Pera Palas and within easy walking distance of Taksim Square, it now has the advantage of an attractive terrace opposite which looks over the Golden Horn and conceals a massive car-park. It is good value for money, at about L 25,000 for two.

Hotel Keban, Sıraselviler Caddesi 51, Taksim, tel.: 143.33.10; 87 rooms with bath or shower and air conditioning. Off Taksim Square, near the Dilson, this is understandably popular, with small refrigerators in some of the rooms. It is good value at approximately L 22,250 for a double room.

Gezi Hotel, Mete Caddesi 42, Taksim, tel.: 145.21.67; 42 rooms with bath. Also off Taksim Square, this is recommended by Aegean Holidays as hard to beat from a budget viewpoint. It has a bar, but is otherwise basic. About L 22,250.

Hotel Alibaba, Meşrutiyet Caddesi 119, tel.: 144.07.81. Close to the Londres, this is at the lower end of this price range, about L 12,000 for a room. You would be wise to see the room beforehand and confirm the price, but it could prove satisfactory on a modest scale.

Most of the above hotels (with the exception of the Yeşil Ev) are situated on the Beyoğlu side of the Golden Horn, around Taksim Square, which tends to be more expensive. The older part of the city on the side with Ayasofia and the Topkapı is more reasonable, especially in districts like Aksaray and Laleli, approaching the sea of Marmara, where there are rooms from L 9,000 to 14,000. Ask for Ordu Caddesi and walk up Harikzadeler for numerous inexpensive hotels. They include:

Akgün Hotel, Hazdenadar Sokak 6, Ordu Caddesi, Aksaray, tel.: 512.02.60; 87 rooms: old-fashioned and comfortable with English-speaking staff. About L 22,250 for a double room.

Hotel Barin, Fevziye Caddesi 7, Şehzadebaşı, tel.: 525.25.67; 30 rooms with showers. This is a new hotel and recommended. Prices are from L 14,000 single, and L 18,000 double, with breakfast included.

Hotel Florida, Fevziye Caddesi 38, Laleli, tel.: 528.10.21; 28 smallish rooms from L 14,000 single.

Hotel Eyfel, Kurultay Sokak 19, Beyazıt, tel.: 520.97.88; 92 rooms with shower. This is in the centre of the old city, a few minutes from the Bazaar and convenient for general sight-seeing. It is friendly, with an American bar and restaurant. Prices are from L 18,000 single, L 22,250 double.

Hotel Koza, Cakirağa Mahallesi Asımbey Sokak 22, Aksaray, tel.: 524.75.06; 35 rooms. Situated in Aksaray, a few minutes from the Topkapı Palace, this is modern and small, with a lounge, breakfast room and bar, though no restaurant. Prices are slightly higher at L 22,250 upwards.

Hotel Oran, Harikzadeler Sokak 40, Laleli, tel.: 528.58.13; 22 rooms with shower from L 9,000 single and L 14,000 double.

Hotel Neşet, opposite at Harikzadeler Sokak 23, tel.: 526.74.12; similar to the Oran.

Hotel Doru, Gençtürk Caddesi 44, Laleli, tel.: 527.69.28; 25 rooms, modern, from L 14,000 single.

Astor Hotel, Laleli Caddesi 12, Aksaray, tel.: 522.44.23; 42 rooms from L 18,000–22,250.

La Miraj, a small hotel in the old city, has showers in all the rooms but bed and breakfast only. There is a small lounge and a breakfast room.

Hotel Keçik, opened only in 1986, is conveniently situated near the centre of the old city. All rooms have showers; bed and breakfast only.

Hotel Gün, a small, basic hotel in the old city, which is good value. All rooms have showers; small lounge, breakfast room and bar.

Bottom range   This is the hardest range of all to find – inexpensive when you need to work on a low budget, yet clean and comfortable so your holiday is not ruined by horrible accommodation.

Hotel Nomad Recommended to me by the professor who arranged for my talk to the students at the Bosphorus University, this should be reliable. It is in the old part of the city – more than a pension, but less than a hotel – and the balcony has views. It is popular with students, teachers, professional people and impoverished writers. I cannot find it listed elsewhere, which suggests that it could be an unspoilt 'discovery'. Tel.: 511.12.96; prices approximately L 10,000 a room.

München Hotel, Gençtürk Caddesi 55, Laleli, tel.: 526.53.43; 22 rooms from L 6,000 for a single and L 7,500 for a double. Every room has a bath and, despite the name, the helpful staff speak English but not German. Alternative hotels can be found in the same street.

Yücelt Hostel, Caferiye Sokak 6, Sultanahmet, tel.: 522.47.90; hostel and cafeteria. Opposite Ayasofia, the situation is ideal; this place is good for the young and used to be associated with the YMCA. Double rooms go from L 9,000; 3-bedded from L 14,000. There are no private baths, but public showers and a Turkish bath.

Universities   In July and August some universities open their dormitories to foreign students: you can get information from one of the tourist information bureaus.

You could also try:

Hotel Klodfarer, Klodfarer Caddesi 22, tel.: 528.48.50; prices from L 4,000 single, L 5,000 double.

IYHF International Youth Hostel, 63 Cerrahpaşa Caddesi, tel.: 543.00.08. Open from July to September, this large hostel in Aksaray offers good value at L 1,000 a bed.

Hotel İpek Palas, Orhaniye Caddesi 9, tel.: 520.97.24. Though near to the Sirkeci railway station, this has the advantage of comparative quiet, spacious rooms, and is good value at about L 14,000 for a double room with bath.

Küçük Karadeniz Hotel, Orhaniye Caddesi 12, tel.: 522.63.00. This is on the same street, but a double room costs only L 10,000.

On the outskirts | **Kalyon Hotel**, Sahil Yolu Selimiye, Sultanahmet, tel.: 520.13.03; 38 rooms. On the main road towards the Sea of Marmara, this is a popular hotel with a smart, terraced restaurant used by non-residents, and the bedrooms are spacious. It is in the mid to top price range, with a single room starting at L 44,500 but reports suggest that the cost is worth while.

Harem Hotel On the Asian side of the Bosphorus at Ambar Sokak, Selimiye, Üsküdar; tel.: 333.20.25; 100 rooms. You need to cross the Bosphorus from the Golden Horn, but that is no hardship. The gain lies in the quiet, the views, and the swimming pool. It is a convenient base for exploring that shoreline, with such places of interest as the Beylerbeyi Palace, and frequent ferries to the Princes Islands, so it would be worth dividing your time between here and one of the hotels either side of the Horn, if your stay in Istanbul is lengthy and if you have the determination to see everything you can. Though some reports are critical, it is good value, with a room and breakfast from L 14,500.

Grand Tarabya Hotel, Kefeliköy Caddesi, Tarabya, tel.: 162.10.00; 215 rooms with baths, balconies, and television. Situated on the Bosphorus in the fashionable resort of Tarabya, nicknamed Arabia, this is 18 km from the centre of Istanbul and a mere twenty minutes' drive – if you are lucky and miss the rush hour. On a Friday or Saturday evening, it would be twice that. The glossy (everything about the hotel is glossy) brochure quotes the French poet Lamartine – 'It is there that God, man, nature and art have conspired together to create the most marvellous vista imaginable.' The following boast of 'a breathtaking skyline of domes and minarets' suggests that neither the poet nor the brochure writer has stayed in the Grand Tarabya, which is in fact tucked around the corner on the way to the Black Sea. But the view of the Bosphorus is splendid enough. However, the brashness of the Grand Hotel, a monstrous modern block, its empty bar and international restaurant made me take against the place on sight. Only after a first-rate breakfast on my balcony the next morning, overlooking the traffic on the water below, did I regard the place in a more kindly fashion. The Grand Tarabya is ideal for parties, wedding receptions and conferences in the hall which contains 200 seats complete with audio system and translation. There is also a shopping centre.

If I sound patronising, this is because the grand hotel is not my kind of hotel. I prefer to be right in the heart of the city, staying somewhere simpler, or more majestically opulent, like the Pera Palas. Others who are less hard to please will relish the service offered and the incomparable situation with the lively restaurants of Tarabya a short walk away for the evening's entertainment – especially if someone else is paying.

It is not as exorbitant as you might expect for such grandeur: starting from L 89,500 for a double room overlooking the garden; and from

L 107,000 overlooking the Bosphorus.

Prices   Do not regard any of the prices given here as final. In the out-of-season months (November to March) you can expect a considerable discount, of as much as 30 per cent. Depending on the type of hotel and your length of visit, you can get reduced terms if the hotel is not fully booked and if you intend to stay an entire week. Do always ask to see your rooms beforehand, to avoid regrets afterwards.

Where to   It should come as no surprise that Istanbul boasts some of the
eat   classiest restaurants in the world. Those along the Bosphorus, at Tarabya and Arnavutköy, serve incomparable seafood; the **Abdullah**, set in the hills above Emirgan, has its own kitchen garden; **Rejans** yields an echo of Tsarist Russia. The hotels are more than just reliable, with first-class cuisine at the **Divan** and exotic surroundings at the **Pera Palas**, while the **Sheraton** specialises in traditional Ottoman dishes in the **Revan**. The **Plaza** has a chic sophistication worthy of Rome or New York.

Yet the greater reward, and fun, lies in making your own discovery among the lesser-known and lesser-priced restaurants which you can find in every part of the city. The modest kebab houses where you can see the pieces of lamb strung together on sticks and cooked over a charcoal grill are both delicious and excellent value.

A guide can be of real use in recommending some of the more interesting restaurants in the mid-priced range and I shall start with some I recommend from personal experience, followed by others according to the district. I should start by explaining the difference between a *lokanta* – which used to be the equivalent of a modest Greek taverna – and a restaurant, which was decidedly grander. There is not much difference any more, as this story indicates: a man used to lunch regularly and cheaply at his favourite *lokanta* until he had to leave for several weeks on business. When he returned he had much the same meal but was startled to find that the bill came to twice the usual price. When he protested, the smiling waiter gave a shrug of explanation: 'When you were here last,' he said, 'we were *lokanta*. Now,' and he spoke with considerable pride, 'we are *restaurant!*'

Hacıbaba, İstiklal Caddesi 49, tel.: 144.18.86; open from 11 a.m. to 11 p.m., though you would be wise to stick to the usual times and to book beforehand at weekends. This is the sort of place I wish I had known on earlier visits: strictly, almost abruptly, professional, serving first-rate food unpretentiously at reasonable prices. I had passed it many times without realising that it existed, for the entrance in the main shopping street of İstiklal is unimpressive. However, if you turn right at the last turning as you go to Taksim Square, you climb some stairs to find a peaceful terrace overlooking the garden of a Greek Orthodox Church.

I called there soon after midday when it was empty and returned in the evening to find it crowded on the Saturday night. Far from being

103

my own 'discovery' (recommended to me by a friend in Bodrum) the Hacıbaba is deservedly popular, if not fashionable. The staff were so busy with their Turkish customers that they seemed indifferent at first, an impression belied when they moved a table for me outside to the terrace and changed an order without fuss or argument when I made a mistake in my translation.

In summer months the terrace is preferable so, if you wish to make certain of a table, book beforehand. I was eating on my own which staff always find irritating, until other customers joined my table and then everyone smiled.

The setting is sympathetic, the food exceptional. It is known for grilled meats and tender baked lamb, served with a spiced wild rice which is so tasty that it is worth having as a dish on its own if you are not ordering lamb but something else like the big prawns. The menu is intelligent in Turkish, English and French. This is a pleasant place to take someone, and inexpensive at L 9,000 for an excellent dinner including wine.

Liman Lokantasi, Yolcu-Salonu Üstü, Karaköy, tel.: 144.10.33; lunch only from noon to 4 p.m., closed on Sundays. At the Pera end of Galata Bridge, turn right from the lower tunnel exit, cross the street and turn left on Kardeşim Sokağı beyond a tall building. Take the first right by the NTN sign and look for a window display of fish. If you get lost, ask for the Maritime Office for it is in the same block.

I find it preferable to Pandeli's on the other side of Galata Bridge, in spite of its being less fashionable – or because of it. The windows overlook the ferries and cargo ships moored below. There is a cafeteria below. I find the Liman relaxing, quiet and friendly, with an imaginative choice of seafood.

Asmalimescit The small alley virtually facing the Pera Palas Hotel, though slightly to the right as you leave, has a number of small, interesting restaurants full of Turks. The most sympathetic are the **Yakup** and **Refih** which have very good, inexpensive food such as cold octopus and stuffed peppers which you can choose from glass cases. The atmosphere is Turkish rather than tourist.

Also recommended, though I have not been there personally, is **Hacı Salih** in one of the streets cutting down to İstiklal (Sakizağaci Sokak) used by Turkish businessmen for lunch.

Rejans Lokantasi In this same area, Galatasaray, in the Lido Pasaji between İstiklal Caddesi 244 and Meşrutiyet Caddesi, tel.: 144.16.10; open from 12 noon to 3 p.m. and from 7 p.m. to 11 p.m. I suggest that a late dinner is best for atmosphere. This is a famous Istanbul restaurant originally started, so the story goes, by two White Russian sisters who fled here after the Revolution. Today it is frankly a faded shadow of its former splendour but is still worth going to for the carefree atmosphere and the Russian food which is first-rate, starting with *piroshki* and a bottle of lemon vodka plonked on your table. *Piroshki* are the traditional Russian pastries filled with meat, a version of the Turkish *börek*. Rejans also serves the classic beetroot soup Borsch, duck and chocolate meringue. The atmosphere is enhanced when the tables are crowded, so this would be a good place to take a party on a Saturday night.

Taksim district **Divan Hotel**, Cumhuriyet Caddesi, tel.: 131.41.00; open from 12 noon to 3 p.m., and 7 to 11 p.m. daily. With exceptional cuisine and music and dancing in the evening, this is suitable for business lunches, or greater relaxation in the evening. Even then it is sufficiently smart and formal to make a tie and jacket advisable.

At **the Sheraton** the **Revan** restaurant specialises in Ottoman dishes though the menu looks surprisingly predictable and familiar. This is expensive, like the Divan, but popular with those who are not preoccupied with the size of the bill.

Maçka district **The Plaza**, close to the Maçka Hotel, is badly signposted and hard to find at Bronz Sokak 4/a, tel.: 141.63.56. Possibly it is the most elegant restaurant in all of Istanbul with glass, greenery and water, reached through a long arcade which makes it invisible from the outside. It is restful on a hot day with impeccable if inscrutable service. The food is international and you will enjoy it all the more if someone else is paying! Undeniably smart, it gives little reminder that you are in Istanbul; there is even the inevitable 'muzak', plus the real advantage of air-conditioning.

Park Şamdan, Mim Kemal Öke Caddesi, tel.: 140.83.68. This is on the edge of the park, hence the name; it is popular, well decorated, with a varied menu. It is also fashionable, and priced accordingly.

Le Terasse or The Terrace, Bayıldım Yokuşu 10, tel.: 160.73.04. One of the newest and smartest restaurants in the city with views over the Bosphorus and Golden Horn, this has the advantage of the terrace where you can eat *al fresco*. You can drink while you wait for your table or postpone your meal at a bar on the second floor. It is open for lunch, and then for special tea parties for women until dinner begins in the evening. The cuisine is international.

Beyoğlu district **The Four Seasons**, Dört Mevsim (near the Swedish Consulate), 509 İstiklal Caddesi, tel.: 145.89.41; open from 12 noon to 3 p.m. and 6 to 11 p.m., not Sunday. Excellent, but expensive, Turkish and French cuisine in an attractive dining-room. Reservations are needed.

Eminönü and Sirkeci district **Pandeli**, on the left-hand side as you enter the Spice Bazaar (Mısır Çarşısı) near the New Mosque, tel.: 527.39.09; lunches only, 11.30 a.m. to 3.30 p.m. This is exceptionally popular with American tourists but, though the food is good, I found the atmosphere a disappointment, probably because I was expecting too much. The prices are touristic.

Konyalı, in the grounds of the Topkapı Palace, tel.: 526.27.27; lunches only, 12 noon to 3 p.m., closed Tuesday. The obvious place

105

	after your visit to the palace, with a fine view. Other people will have the same idea and it may prove difficult finding a table. The food is basic, and beer is the only drink.
Kumkapı district	Down the hill towards the Sea of Marmara, this area is off the tourist track yet noted for a number of small, lively seafood restaurants. It is a favourite place for the Turks.

Kemal, near Kumkapı Square, is good in the evenings. Also look out for the **Minas**.

Üçler, Kumkapı Square, is recommended highly and is known for its version of warm aubergines. However, I was so infuriated by the insolent service that I queried my bill (something I seldom do) which seemed to have a surprising number of items on it considering the small amount I had eaten having decided to try elsewhere. I discovered that I had been charged for the water with my *rakı*, a bit like being charged for the glass with your beer, so I can hardly recommend the Üçler personally though others find it the best of all.

Marmara district

Marmara is on the way to, or from, the airport.

Gelik, Sahilyolu 68, Ataköy, tel.: 571.37.72. A large family restaurant, specialising in lamb and pilav, this is usually crowded with Turks which is always an encouraging sign. You can also eat outside.

Arnavutköy district

An attractive part of the Bosphorus, with old wooden houses, this district can be reached by ferry. It has excellent fish restaurants – for squid, mussels and the blue fish known as *lüfer*. Some have entertainment.

Antik, Birinci Caddesi 47, tel.: 163.66.27. Many Turks recommend this as the best in Arnavutköy; it is described both as 'luxurious' and 'intimate'. On the waterfront with a balcony, it offers dinner with the music of a piano and violin.

Kaptan, near to Antik, is more local and inexpensive, without entertainment (unless it is spontaneous!).

Kuyu, Birinci Caddesi 31, tel.: 163.67.50; from 12 noon to 3 p.m. and 7 to 11 p.m. daily. Popular with the staff of the American Consulate, this is livelier than the Kaptan and is crowded at weekends. It has good seafood.

Emirgan district

Abdullah, Koru Caddesi 11, tel.: 163.64.16; from 12 noon to 3 p.m. and 7 to 11 p.m., closed Tuesday. Set in the hills above the Bosphorus, this has had the reputation of being Istanbul's classiest restaurant, with every ingredient as fresh as possible: fish from the water below; vegetables from its kitchen garden; even milk from its own cows. Certainly the setting is superlative, with attractive buildings resembling an Italian villa set in an appropriate garden. But I fear that years of popularity and praise have diminished the dedication. Though the atmosphere remains sympathetic, the food is good but not superlative, and you would be advised to choose the quail only if you like the idea of eating match-boxes – *full* match-boxes. I would not be so harsh except that the bill is harsher. L 88,000 for a light lunch for three is a lot for Turkey. Even so, it would be worth visiting with Turkish friends.

Tarabya
district

A jolly bay on the Bosphorus, lined with restaurants, Tarabya has plenty of tourists in the evening, but there are many Turks as well and a buzz of enjoyment with music and dancing as well as first-rate seafood.

Palet II, Yeniköy Caddesi 80, tel.: 162.00.20. There are several Palet restaurants, named after the former owner's passion as an amateur painter (palette rather than palate). They are highly professional and very crowded at the weekends. No. II is the most popular, and slightly more expensive than I and III. It provides first-rate smoked sturgeon – indeed, the *mezes* are so good you need little else. Other specialities are mussel soup, grilled shrimps, chocolate soufflé.

Kireçburnu

The Facyo, also on the Bosphorus, Tarabya Caddesi 13, tel.: 162.00.24; from 12 noon, daily. I have already praised my banquet on my first visit (see p. 44). There is music in the evening.

A Trip to the Princes Islands

When the conditions are right, a day's outing to the Princes Islands (known simply to the Turks as *Adalar,* meaning islands) is a jolly occasion and a welcome light relief from the roar of Istanbul. Indeed, I would recommend a visit to the nearest island if only for a restful lunch out of doors.

An 'island' sounds romantic, barren and unspoilt, but the charm of the Princes Islands lies in the nostalgia of the small resorts with their peaceful promenades which suggest a gentler period when people travelled by horse and phaeton as they still do here today.

There are nine islands in the channel which leads to the Sea of Marmara, an hour's sailing away. Departures should be at 9.45 a.m. from Kabataş, near the Dolmabahçe Palace, and returns from Büyükada at 4, 6 and 7.30 p.m., but it is vital to check beforehand. Many of the islanders commute to work in Istanbul, but even if you are going out when they are coming in it makes sense to board the ferry at least ten minutes before sailing time if you want a seat. The ferry charge is virtually nominal (about L 1,000), for which you receive a metal disc which you insert with difficulty in a turnstile: this entitles you to a free return. Do not expect regular sailings on the hour and do not go ashore until you confirm that this is the island you are aiming for. Mind you, with time to spare, try to visit two islands at least, for they are subtly different and you can usually find a boat to take you the short distance to the next one.

Against advice, I sailed on a Sunday morning when the ferry was crowded with cheerful Turkish families though I had the bad luck to find myself pressed against a pert English teacher who put aside her Margaret Drabble novel to recount her entire life history – and how tedious it was! – to an admiring Turkish gentleman who gazed at her with soulful longing. They were starting to make plans to meet again when she gave him an abrupt goodbye – 'Here we are already, good Lord that was quick!' – and promptly stepped ashore on to the *wrong* island, forcing her way through the crowds before he could stop her. I went ashore too, though not in pursuit, for I wanted to see the island of Heybeli as well as Büyükada, the main island and my destination.

Heybeli   There is something immediately attractive about Heybeli, a pleasant waterfront dotted with palms and restaurants with no vehicles apart from the elegant barouches drawn by pairs of horses. Children play football on the quay, muscular young men play it behind a cage, old men water the flower beds, and there is the scent of half-remembered holidays. It would be a nice place to hold a luncheon party, insisting that the ladies wear long dresses and carry parasols, while the gentlemen who take their arms as they alight from the boat should be crisp in white linen suits, topped with straw panamas.

Everyone seemed to be enjoying the holiday atmosphere on my visit; only an overloaded donkey staring with tragic, haunting eyes disconcerted me. But there was a nasty memory which belongs to the past. In the days of Byzantium, the islands were used as a convenient refuge for religious exiles from the mainland, and the remains of monasteries and churches testify to their importance. Centuries later, they were used as a dumping ground in a wretched moment of Istanbul's history, described by Francis Yeats Brown ('The Bengal Lancer') in his book *The Golden Horn*, which is painful to relate. In a sudden, brutal purge, all the stray dogs of Istanbul, and they were legion, were herded up, and as they had been treated affectionately until then, there was no difficulty in catching them. Because it was against the Muslim creed to kill them unnecessarily, they were shipped instead to Köpek Adası (known as Dog Island) and left there to die. In the savage heat of summer the thousands of dogs grew mad with thirst, ripping the new arrivals apart in order to drink their blood, until finally all were destroyed.

In the last century, the islands were used as an escape in the summer heat by Istanbul's more prosperous businessmen, especially the Greeks and Jews, which explains the prevalence of attractive wooden houses, decorated externally in Victorian 'gingerbread' style, which you can see today. This is a welcome contrast to the shock of the shoreline opposite, stretching from Üsküdar to Kartal, of uninterrupted towers and industrialisation, a visible and alarming proof of Istanbul's population explosion since the last war.

You can stay in Heybeli at the Panorama Hotel and there are numerous restaurants of which the best is supposed to be the Gazino in the pine woods a short ride out of town. I ate a late breakfast at Fıçı

108

on the quayside – an omelette and beer which cost me L 1,000 – and strolled towards the dashing white Naval Academy near the ferry stage, passing the English schoolteacher immersed again in Drabble, waiting for her friends, presumably still unaware that they were waiting for her on another island. I thought of explaining this but thought again: for all I knew, her escape from her Turkish admirer was calculated. At the gates of the Academy I was turned away crossly by the naval police who patrol these peaceful streets in pairs.

Büyükada   From Heybeli, I took a small ferry across to Büyükada, a larger and more bustling island of considerable charm, where the residents as well as the visitors use the horse-drawn carriages for transport. Taking one of the barouches, I realised for the first time how satisfying this form of travel must have been unless you were in a hurry, with the chance to absorb the details of the wooden houses and their gardens and to sniff the scent of the pines. Half-way across there is a mandatory stop for twenty minutes where your carriage draws up beside a score of others and the horses rest while you sit down in a garden for some refreshment. Afterwards, I persuaded my driver to ride down the path to the sea where I was told there was a beach. There is, beyond a complex of buildings, and several people were sunbathing on a patch of sand, with the sea cordoned off beyond. People refer to lovely coves and bathing but, though I am a compulsive swimmer, I did not swim here: the thought of the sewage pouring out of Istanbul and the industrial sewers opposite dampened my enthusiasm.

Fix a price with your driver beforehand. As I was travelling alone and made him take a detour, I paid L 6,000.

Back in the town, I walked up to the Hotel Splendid which lives up to its name – a white wedding-cake with twin breast-like shapes on the roof, reminiscent of Cannes, with large rooms, old-fashioned furniture, and an immense inner courtyard with a fountain. The hotel costs from L 20,000 a room regardless of the view, so insist that you overlook the sea, which is what the Splendid is all about.

All of Büyükada has the feel of a Mediterranean resort, with cafés called Monte Carlo and Capri. I ate a late lunch on the waterfront and absorbed the scene which was pleasantly merry. Children ran everywhere: a chubby boy in a yellow gauze bonnet tottered forward recklessly while his youthful father followed with outstretched arms ready to catch him if he fell. One of the insistent shoe-blacks revealed a softer side as he pushed an old man in a wheelchair who smiled at me as their progress was blocked by a man photographing his family.

The ferries make life more difficult by displaying no visible time-tables or destinations, so make certain you are on the right one and not continuing to Yalova or Kartal opposite, though at least you could take a bus back to Üsküdar from there. But then you would miss the gaiety of the return journey.

First there is the panic stampede down the wooden planks as the siren announces the ferry's immediate departure, followed by bitter frustration as the gates are slammed against the last arrivals, changing to relief when they discover it was not their ferry after all. Then the scramble when the right one arrives in order to find a seat, especially for the open area at the stern with separate wooden chairs instead of benches. I joined the rush, and was rewarded with a chair of my own; when a ferry hoots it means 'run for all you're worth'.

As the boat slipped out, a group of young men and women clapped hands in time to their transistor and started to dance on a patch of deck, plainly enjoying themselves hugely. The man in particular preened like a peacock though he was scrawny and balding; his vanity was delightful to watch because he was so happy. He danced with two girls at once, one of whom was a beauty. Despite the narcissism, everyone enjoyed the performance, with cries and laughter from the crowd which gathered round as the man indulged in a particularly bold display with the beautiful girl in the silk dress, his teeth exposed and his hands twirling in a sort of courtship. We passed a small island with one private house, a wood, and a colourful carpet of wild flowers; then we stopped at Burgazada (Burgaz Island) which sports a jolly harbour with a few painted fishing boats at one end and a crowd below waiting to board. People started to slump in their chairs, exhausted by the fun. A handsome young couple beside me fussed over their baby daughter with foolish endearments, and gave me sly bashful looks as if to apologise for such an excess of adoration, which turned to smiles as I admired the child. Istanbul approached – the sky was now a dull rose pink as dusk descended over that incomparable skyline of mosques and minarets as we turned towards the Golden Horn. It was a good day out.

Thrace

European Turkey is only 3 per cent of the whole and seems detached, quite apart from its geographical position on the borders of Greece and Bulgaria. Yet it is important for four reasons.

It is the main route to Istanbul from Yugoslavia and Greece, carrying the main road for both cars and buses from Salonika, Kavala and Xanthi to the Turkish border. It is also a useful alternative route down to the Turkish Aegean coast, on which you can bypass Istanbul completely by cutting south from Kesan and taking the car-ferry across the Dardanelles to Çanakkale. The Dardanelles itself is steeped in history: it is the route to Asia taken by Xerxes and the legions of Alexander, was crossed by Lord Byron when he swam the Hellespont, and was the setting for the abortive Allied landings in 1915.

Edirne, originally Adrianople, is a worth-while stop, especially if you are driving independently, in order to see the great mosque of Selimiye Cami which many believe is the finest in Turkey.

Otherwise, Thrace is not of especial excitement in itself, but more the promise of delights to come.

Edirne

History

Founded by the Roman Emperor Hadrian in AD 125, the town was named Hadrianopolis, later shortened to Adrianople, and finally, by the Turks, to Edirne. The Ottomans, who captured it in 1363, made it their capital and a launching point for their invasions of Europe. Finally, Mehmet the Conqueror advanced from Edirne on Constantinople which he captured in 1453 after a fifty-day siege. Edirne then reverted to its role as a military outpost on the Balkan Peninsula.

After the First World War Thrace was handed to the Greeks, while Istanbul was declared an international port. Meanwhile, the Greek army advanced towards Ankara in 1920–21, until they were defeated at the Battle of the Sakarya River and retreated to Izmir from where they were forced to evacuate. The tide then turned in Kemal Atatürk's favour: the Soviet–Turkish Treaty restored the Eastern territory, including Kars; Italy withdrew and so did the French; and the Allies agreed to the reoccupation of Thrace. Edirne returned to its role as the first stop on the way to Istanbul.

Situated on a slope, surrounded by the River Tunca which gave protection to the city when it was a military base for the Ottoman armies as they marched into Europe, Edirne is an agreeable place to pause in today, with the great mosque and numerous Ottoman monuments, a lively bazaar, and narrow streets with overhanging, wooden houses where men and women once lived in separate quarters. The main square has the usual statue of Atatürk, and also one of champion wrestlers – for Edirne is famous for the annual tournament of greased wrestlers in late May and early June, held on the island of Sarayiçi on the River Tunca, once a hunting reserve for the sultans.

What to see

Eski Cami

The Old Mosque was built in 1403 with one minaret for the *muezzin* to call the people to prayer, though this tradition is usually replaced by a loudspeaker today. Calligraphy is an essential part of Ottoman decoration and this mosque is noted for the Arabic lettering of the Koran.

Üçşerefeli Cami

Near the main square, this mosque was completed for Murat II in 1447 and has three balconies around one of the four minarets, once the tallest in Turkey at 66.5 m. The Turkish bath (*hamam*) next to it was designed by Sinan and has been restored.

Muradiye

An earlier and smaller mosque for Murat, this was built on a hill to the north-east; and should be seen for its tiles. They once belonged to the Whirling Dervishes for whom the building was intended as a hospice before Murat transformed it into a mosque and placed the Whirlers in a separate monastery in the gardens. The *mihrab* (prayer niche) has fine examples of fifteenth-century Iznik tiles.

The Mosque of Beyazıt II

A twenty-minute walk to the far side of the River Tunca beyond Sarayiçi, reached by crossing the Bridge of the Conqueror, this mosque dates from 1488 and was the site of the first lunatic asylum, part of an early religious complex which was perfectly restored in the 1970s. The forerunner of the kitchens, schools and baths which surrounded the most important mosques at a later date, it was also an expression of the Islamic belief that the mad 'are touched by God'. The patients were afforded humane treatment: a fountain to add to the sense of peace, a stage of ten musicians to help calm broken nerves, and pheasants and partridges as part of the diet. It sounds a far cry from London's Bedlam Hospital which was founded as a madhouse some fifty years later in 1547.

Selimiye Cami

The great mosque built by the architect Sinan for Selim II was started in 1569 and finished six years later when Sinan was eighty-five years old; he regarded it as his 'crowning glory'.

Of all the mosques in Turkey, its genius is immediately apparent. Its vast dome is surrounded by four immensely tall and slender minarets, always a combination which delights the eye. Sinan, the greatest Turkish architect, declared that an early mosque was his apprenticeship, the Süleyman Mosque in Istanbul his 'journeyman's work, and the Selimiye at Edirne, my masterpiece'. This was a declaration of truth rather than vanity. The scope is tremendous with a splendid dome 45 m high, while the minarets are 80 m, supported by eight pillars and external buttresses which allow the weight of an abundance of windows on every level. It is said that Sinan wanted 1,000 windows, but Selim II protested, gently and wisely, that 999 might be better as 'a figure that people will remember'.

Sinan's individuality is seen everywhere in this culminate work – the bold use of space, the overall simplicity with ornate detail such as the marble *mimber* (pulpit) to the right of the entrance, and the *mihrab* on the left, lined with the famous turquoise Iznik tiles. The *mihrab* in the imperial lodge is noted for the two wooden shutters in the middle which open to reveal a view overlooking the town and countryside in the direction, as always, of Mecca. The exterior has the rare advantage of a clear view which reveals the mathematical proportions with horizontal levels and vertical towers stretching towards the sky.

Even a glimpse as you pass by on a bus is magnificent, but time is needed to absorb the details and the symmetry of this unique example of Turkish culture of the sixteenth century.

Where to stay

The **Kervan Hotel**, Talatpaşa Caddesi 134, tel.: 1355; comfortable rooms from L 6,000.

The **Sultan Hotel**, on the same street, tel.: 1372, is more expensive, with double rooms from L 9,000.

The tourist office on Hürriyet Meydanı, tel.: 1518, will help with cheaper lodgings.

Bear in mind that Edirne is still a main stop on the route from western Europe to Istanbul, so lodgings are often full of Turks returning home or going to Germany, or long-distance lorry drivers.

Where to eat The smaller restaurants in the old town are the best; also the **Meriç**, at Karaağaç.

Istanbul to Çanakkale

You can start from Istanbul, and explore the southern shore of the Sea of Marmara until you reach Çanakkale in the west, or go there directly from Thrace. A passenger ferry leaves Kabataş (near Dolmabahçe) in Istanbul at around 9.45 a.m. but, as usual, it is wise to check beforehand and arrive early to make sure of a seat. The car-ferry to Yalova leaves from the outskirts of town, a two-hour journey which is often full in summer, and not quite as tempting as it sounds. Once you are on it, the Sea of Marmara is not particularly exciting, and the shore is industrialised to begin with, but the trip is very cheap and an agreeable way of passing time although the bar does not sell beer or spirits.

Buses direct to Bursa leave from the Asian side of the Bosphorus, a fifteen-minute walk from the railway station of Haydarpaşa.

Yalova Yalova is pleasant enough, though not perhaps worth stopping at. Better to continue to Iznik 60 km away, driving through green, fertile countryside with orchards of peaches, cultivated fields and cypress trees, until you reach the large lake which bears the same name as the town of Iznik.

Iznik Founded in 1000 BC, the town was of considerable importance. It was occupied by one of Alexander's feuding generals, Lysimachus, in 316 BC who named it after his wife, Nikaea – hence Nicaea.

A capital of Bithynia until the arrival of the Romans, Nicaea acquired its prominence when Constantine brought Christianity to Constantinople and Nicaea shared in the new faith. In 325, the First Ecumenical Council took place in St Sophia and the Councils continued to meet here until the Seventh Council in 786, when the Fathers of the Church stopped the vandalism of icons and codified rules which are still observed by the Greek Orthodox Church today. In 1078, the town was occupied by the Seljuks, and in 1331 by Orhan (1326–61) son of Osman who founded the Ottoman Empire.

The museum Iznik is noted for its famous ceramic tiles whose colours and designs were unequalled, especially the turquoise green, made from roots, which cannot be emulated today. The art died out in the eighteenth century, but fine examples may be seen in the excellent fourteenth-century museum, while good modern china is sold outside. This museum is also well worth seeing for its setting as well as its contents. Opposite is the decorated minaret of the Green Mosque, *Yeşil Cami*, built in the late fourteenth century and one of the loveliest in Turkey.

Otherwise, there is little hint of Iznik's historic significance in the charming lakeside town of today. And how curious it is that a waterfront on a lake is so totally different from one on the sea, as if it lived in exile, half-forgotten by the outside world. There are broad streets with an abundance of flowers; the restaurants, which serve freshwater fish, have gardens rich with roses, and you are greeted by cheerful faces and giggling girls who ask, in good English, 'Do you like Iznik?', and seem delighted when you assure them that you do.

The bus for Bursa leaves hourly (not in the evening) and takes one and a half hours.

Bursa Because of its size – the population is 850,000 – you might expect an oppressive city; if so, you should be pleasantly surprised. If a city can have a personality, and of course it can, Bursa's is one of bustling good humour, with the pleasant sensation of its being a mountain town with the winter resort of Uludağ, at 2,543 m, only 36 km away, reached by road or cable-car.

Because of Bursa's former importance as the capital of the Ottoman Empire in the fourteenth century, there is plenty to see. The name, incidentally, was derived from Prusias, the King of Bithynia. After a siege of ten years commenced by his father, the city fell to Orhan in 1336 who used it as a base for his expanding empire.

What to see Of the many monuments to be seen, the Green Mosque (*Yeşil Cami*)
Yeşil Cami is the most religious, decorated with the incomparable Iznik tiles, built in 1413–21 for the Sultan Mehmet I. The interior is equally splendid, restored after an earthquake in 1855 so that it looks fresh though timeless, with a fountain carved from a single block of marble, and a tiled *mihrab* 15 m high with carved stonework around the windows.

The mosque is one of the first in a truly Turkish style, free from the former Seljuk and Persian influences, and many consider it the most beautiful in Turkey in spite of its modest size. The setting, among cypress trees, enhances the fine proportions of the entrance. Should a caretaker offer to take you to the sultan's apartment above, seize the opportunity and tip him accordingly, for it is lavishly decorated.

Yeşil Türbe Opposite is the Green Tomb, or *Yeşil Türbe*, where the sultan was buried with his family, a domed building with a blaze of blue and green tiles inside and out, as if it was steeped in colour. The sultan's own coffin is mounted on a spectacular inlaid pedestal. As you are beginning to appreciate, green is the dominant colour in Bursa, which is not wholly accidental for it is also the holy colour of Islam.

Ulu Cami In the centre of Bursa is the city's largest mosque, completed at the end of the fourteenth century in Seljuk style, with an immense square

114

space inside, almost 100 m long, with twenty rounded domes supported by rows of columns. The architectural details, such as a carved walnut *mimber*, are remarkable, but the overriding impression is one of ineffable serenity, largely due to the fountains in the centre. These provide a coolness and calm in contrast to the business of the market outside, further enhanced by the sunlit dome directly above and the light reflected from the windows which illuminate the great swirls of Arabic calligraphy of sayings from the Koran. You emerge refreshed, with a greater understanding of the therapeutic nature of such holy places, pompous though that sounds.

The baths   Apart from architectural and historic interest, Bursa is noted for its curative baths and the healing properties of the thermal springs which are supposed to cure rheumatism and 'skin ailments'. The old baths are in the suburb of Çekirge, and are known as *Eski Kaplıca*; the new, *Yeni Kaplıca*, built on Süleyman's instructions, are near the Çelik Palas Hotel. The hotel has an astonishing, ancient domed pool inside, and from personal experience I can assure you that the mineral water – which is almost boiling when it erupts from the ground – is still extremely hot. After a cold shower, you are ready for the fray.

Where to   Many people come to Bursa from Istanbul if only for the fresh air.
stay   There and back in one day is too exhausting, so there are numerous places to stay overnight. Most of the hotels at Çekirge are there because of the mineral water, either straight from the tap or in special pools; while those at Uludağ cater for winter sports. Uludağ ('The Great Mountain') was known symbolically as Olympos; *çekirge* means locust.

Çelik Palas Hotel, Çekirge Caddesi 79, tel.: 61900; on the way to Çekirge. Apart from its sumptuous mineral baths with the fresh spring water at 47°C containing steel (*çelik*), where the late King of Libya was relaxing when he learnt the news of the coup by Colonel Gaddafi, the Çelik Palas is known as the best hotel in Bursa with a pleasing old-world atmosphere. Though the rooms have modern facilities, the hotel was built after the First World War, becoming one of Kemal Atatürk's favourite stops on his travels. It is one of the few hotels where the dance music in the evening is a real asset: fun to listen to and watch. This could explain why my bar bill was so presumptuous, yet worth it for the atmosphere of a Grand Hotel in the 1930s.

It overlooks the town, is set in attractive gardens, and boasts that it is far from 'urban noise'. But if you really wish for peace and quiet, insist on rooms at the back and forfeit the view.

Equally, if you don't care about the noise, you might prefer one of the hotels right in the centre of the town with the feeling that you are more involved.

A double room costs from L 53,600, and dinner from L 8,000.

Anatolia Hotel, Çekirge Meydanı, tel.: 67110, is another luxurious hotel.

The Akdoğan, 1 Murat Caddesi, tel.: 60610, which is in a lower price range, is excellent value with *hamam*, television and pool, from L 12,000 for a double room.

Artıç Hotel, Fevzi Çakmak Caddesi 123, tel.: 19500, 63 rooms, is in the centre, and prices are reasonable, from L 8,000 for a double.

Diyar Hotel, Çekirge Caddesi 47, tel.: 65130, 35 rooms, opposite the Kültür Park, is reasonable, with showers in all the double rooms.

Panorama Oberj, at Uludağ, tel.: 1237, is open all year with swimming and winter sports.

There are numerous smaller hotels around the covered market in the centre.

Where to eat

Try the town's speciality, *Bursa kebap*, slices of döner laid on fresh bread, with spiced tomato sauce very different from our own. This was invented at the **Kebabçı Iskenderoğlu** (Alexander's Son) in the main Atatürk Caddesi.

The Nazar, Iç Koza Han, near the market, has been highly recommended and is inexpensive.

The Özkent is an open-air restaurant in the Kültür Park.

Kuş Cenneti

Allow the entire day for the drive from Bursa to Çanakkale, especially if you wish to pause on the way at the restful bird sanctuary in the National Park of Kuş Cenneti beside Lake Kuş. There are benches and tables for picnics, towers which enable you to see the various birds below, and a museum with taxidermists' examples of the 200 species of bird who come here. The overall effect is sympathetic, with a large wooden sign bearing the wistful inscription: 'What kind of smallness of a human being it is, to reach for its arms for its morsel of meat. Especial it is the worst kind of prides to kill a bird without defence.' And, one might add, to kill an animal just for the fun of it.

Erdek

The road runs close to the Sea of Marmara but seldom alongside and is uneventful unless you make a detour to Erdek, which is rapidly becoming one of the major resorts for domestic Turkish tourism, especially for those escaping from the population explosion of Istanbul. When you see the new hotels sprouting along the promenade it is easy to appreciate that Erdek and the rest of the island-like bulge called Kapıdağı will become a huge holiday area in the future, and the fact that it will be predominantly Turkish could make it an interesting base for visitors too. Alexander the Great passed through when this *was* an island, and built a causeway to the mainland. Boats go from Erdek to the island of **Marmara Adası** and, again, this would give the chance of seeing beaches popular with Turks rather than tourists.

Returning to the main road, you continue inland until you reach the Dardanelles, named after Dardanos, a former King of Troy, with Gelibolu (Gallipoli) opposite, then continue for approximately 25 km to Çanakkale at the far end, near to the Aegean.

Çanakkale

Çanakkale has a jolly atmosphere in spite of the tragic events of the First World War which scar it visibly to this day, with the constant reminder of a colossal Big Bertha type gun in the main street and a tiny one beside it as if Bertha has given birth. The effect is slightly comic opera, though alarming to realise that such weapons fired across the Straits with considerable devastation.

The water traffic is dominated by gigantic Russian tankers, frequently painted a jaunty red, which have sailed all the way from the Black Sea to the Bosphorus and now seem to be bristling with the excitement of entering the Aegean at last. There is always something to watch at this narrow point of the Straits, only 1.25 km across.

Gelibolu   The road south to Çannakale, across the narrow straits at Gelibolu, formerly Gallipoli, is convenient if you wish to bypass Istanbul and head straight for the coast, but is fascinating too for a greater understanding of the campaign in 1915 when the British ships failed to press forward to Istanbul where their arrival could have tipped the scales in favour of the Allies. This failure was largely due to a lack of nerve following the chance sinking of a British warship after which the Admiral of the Fleet suffered a nervous breakdown.

The campaign   Far from being a wilful ogre as he is usually depicted, Churchill's
of Gallipoli   intentions were bold but correct and his plan could have achieved success if his generals had shown greater initiative. Instead, the British troops, joined by the Anzacs, suffered terrible losses as they tried to storm the cliffs at Helles – probably the wrong place to have chosen in the first place – and later at Suvla Bay, where a fatal hesitation lost them the chance to seize the heights within easy reach a couple of kilometres away, so crucial for those who held them.

While the Commander-in-Chief, Sir Ian Hamilton, was incommunicado on a nearby Greek island, his officers went calling on the dugouts of friends for whisky and soda while their men frolicked in the sea. Meanwhile, for the second time, Kemal Atatürk was the right man in the right place at the right moment. When the British commanders came to their senses it was too late.

There were moments when victory was a matter of metres and minutes away, but Mustafa Kemal showed the greater audacity as he ordered his men not to fight, but to *die* – 'and while you are dying our reinforcements will arrive'. He won the day. Years later, when his enemy Winston Churchill urged his countrymen to 'fight on the beaches' offering nothing but 'blood, toil, tears and sweat', he may have remembered that brilliant Turkish general who had once opposed him.

Lone Pine   Ironically, the only triumph in the entire Allied campaign was the
Cemetery   evacuation, after nine months, under cover of darkness, from Suvla Bay with hardly a man lost compared to the estimated 20,000 casualties expected. Otherwise, the human sacrifice was tragic and this can be realised today if you visit the cemeteries, beautifully tended by their Turkish caretakers. The Anzac Memorial at Lone Pine Cemetery is hauntingly beautiful, lined with cypress trees and

117

pines, with wallflowers and snapdragons between the rows of grave-stones with their poignant inscriptions – 'Dear is the spot to me where my beloved son rests. My Anzac Hero, Mother.' Her son, from the 7th BN Australian Infantry, had been killed on 25 April 1915, the first day of the attack, aged nineteen. It is hard not to be moved by such memories in such surroundings. Further on you can see the Turkish trenches where Atatürk's men dug themselves in, and look down on Suvla Bay below with the flat salt lake that dries out in summer, and appreciate what a close-run thing it was. Maps and photographs do not begin to convey the perspective of such a scene. Visiting Australians must be overcome by the tragic yet noble sense of loss.

The museum   The circular museum is full of weaponry but is far more interesting for such details as the small china bottles of 'rich preserved cream' (!) sent from England to the British officers, and the latest tins against 'vermin in the trenches' from Boots in London. Since the officers enlisted, aching to be part of the war with its classical allusions, and wandered around in uniforms supplied by themselves often run up by their wives from canary-coloured curtain material, maybe the bottles of cream were not so odd after all. The men fared less well: one old soldier from North Devon, now in his nineties, remembers the rock-hard biscuit – 'It was like what the gentry gave their dogs,' he told me, 'but the bully beef went rancid so we were glad to get it.' A nastier feature of the museum is the cabinet with false teeth and a skull with a bullet embedded at the top.

The Hellespont   Near Cape Helles you can swim in the sea – though you would be ill advised to cross – as Byron did on 3 May 1810. It is 6.5 km from Sestos to Asia, and Byron took 1 hour and 10 minutes. There are two great war memorials on the cliffs above – an obelisk cut in stone and shipped from England, which forms the British War Memorial to the 40,000 British and Commonwealth dead, with the Turkish memorial opposite.

From the car ferry port of **Eceabat**, on the Gelibolu Peninsula, you can cross to Çanakkale, leaving Thrace and entering Asia Minor with Çanakkale as the natural stop (see previous p.). On the other side, Turkish slogans carved in the cliffs commemorate the bitter campaign after the British, French, Indian and Anzac forces landed at Helles on 25 April 1915:

STOP 0 PASSER BY   THIS EARTH YOU THUS TREAD UNAWARES   IS WHERE
AN AGE WAS LOST   BOW AND LISTEN FOR THIS QUIET PLACE IS WHERE THE
HEART OF A NATION THROBS

Considering their victory, the Turks seem surprisingly indifferent and totally devoid of boastfulness, recognising the loss of life as a tragedy for both sides.

Daily tours from Çanakkale go to the Gallipoli battlefields and war cemeteries, organised by the *Troyanzac Travel Agency* near the clock tower.

Where to stay in Çanakkale

Hotel Truva (Troy), Yalıbolu, tel.: 1024, is an attractive hotel on the waterfront, though not right in the centre, with comfortable rooms overlooking the passing parade along the Dardanelles. It has a first-rate restaurant and is nicely furnished. From L 25,000 for a double room.

Bakir Hotel, Yalı Caddesi 12, tel.: 4088. A modern hotel with front views of the Dardanelles. Only thirty-five rooms, which helps to explain the attention and friendliness of the staff. Very good reports.

Anafartalar Hotel, Kayserili A., Paşa Caddesi, tel.: 4451.

The Gönül Pension, Inönü Caddesi 21, tel.: 1503, only has eleven rooms and is inexpensive, but is officially recommended.

There are more hotels behind the clock tower, such as the **Konak**, which are inexpensive, but always ask to see your rooms beforehand.

A number of lively restaurants are in the same area, with more atmosphere than the hotels.

Troy

What's in a name? In this case – everything. As related in Homer's *Iliad*, this is the stuff of high romance, of the war which began between the Greeks and the Trojans when Paris, the son of King Priam of Troy, abducted Helen, the wife of King Menelaus who launched a thousand ships to bring her back.

The Trojan Wars lasted ten years and created such heroes as Achilles, Hector and Agamemnon, until Odysseus brought them to an end with the construction of the Trojan Horse. Made of wood, its hollow belly was filled with Greek soldiers who took the city once they were inside it, hence the warning, 'Beware of Greeks bearing gifts'.

Separating the legend from the fact is as complicated as unravelling the layers of civilisation unearthed, literally, by recent excavations. The most notable are those of the German Heinrich Schliemann in the last century, which revealed *nine* cities built on top of each other during a period of 5,000 years.

Finding a treasure trove of jewels, which he believed were those of King Priam, Schliemann was accused of smuggling them out of Turkey in the luggage of his wife who was then seen wearing them in Athens. Ultimately, like so much concerning Troy, the jewels disappeared – possibly they were stolen by the Russians when they entered Berlin at the end of the last war.

The site

Visiting the mound of Hisarlık today, you are advised to do so early or late in the day (shortly after eight in the morning or before eight at night) when the site might offer more romance. Otherwise it has the curiosity value of a mystery – true or false? – for there is little else, apart from the trenches and piles of earth and stones and the undeniable vantage point of Troy's elevated position, which overlooks the plain towards the Aegean now that the waters have receded.

Heretical though it may seem, the clever reconstruction of the wooden Trojan Horse at the entrance, immense yet positively frisky, is more fun than the rubble unless you listen to your guide very, very closely, and stretch your imagination to snapping point. But I must add that my scepticism is not shared by most people who go there, one of whom wrote to me: 'It was not invisible, and one can well imagine the Greeks camped below and Trojans walking the city walls and looking down on them. I found Troy impressive and fascinating.'

The imagination of any visitor to Troy is likely to be enhanced by reading the account of events in Homer's *Iliad*:

The Trojan squadrons flanked by officers
drew up and sortied, in a din of arms
and shouting voices – wave on wave, like cranes
in clamorous lines before the face of heaven,
beating away from winter's gloom and storms,
over the streams of Ocean, hoarsely calling,
to bring a slaughter on the Pygmy warriors –
cranes at dawn descending, beaked in cruel attack.
The Akhaians for their part came on in silence,
raging under their breath, shoulder to shoulder sworn.

Imagine mist the south wind rolls on hills,
a blowing bane for shepherds, but for thieves
better than nightfall – mist where a man can see
a stone's throw and no more: so dense the dust
that clouded up from these advancing hosts
as they devoured the plain.

And near and nearer
the front ranks came, till one from the Trojan front
detached himself to be the first in battle –
vivid and beautiful, Aléxandros,
wearing a cowl of leopard skin, a bow
hung on his back, a longsword at his hip,
with two spears capped in pointed bronze. He shook them
and called out to the best men of the Argives
to meet him in the mêlée face to face.

The Iliad (Bk III, lines 1–12), transl.
Robert Fitzgerald

Assos More rewarding in its reality is Assos (Behramkale) to the south, a shortish detour to the northern shores of the Edremit Peninsula. Aristotle is supposed to have spent three years here and the remains and the setting indicate why as you drive the 19 km to the sea and approach the former walls of the city.

A climb finally reveals an unpretentious Turkish village much as it must have been for the last hundred years, though it is starting to change. You leave your car and walk a short distance to the top of the hill to be rewarded by sensational views of the coastline meandering below and the Greek island of Lesbos. This is what gave Assos such importance: it was an observation point from which every ship could be scrutinised and recognised as friend or foe. Little remains of the Temple of Athena which stood above the acropolis, except for the platform and stumps of columns, and you need to exercise your imagination again to picture the narrow entrance where the statue of Athena was caressed with olive oil so that it would glisten in the first rays of sunlight after the doors were opened. Gradually, you become aware of the extent of an ancient city below, dating from the fourth century BC, with the outlines clearly visible of a gymnasium, walls which stretched for 3 km, and an old harbour dating back to 1000 BC before it was replaced by the new.

With an interesting, though more recent, mosque, this summit is an enchanted place, with the bonus of an easy drive down a cobbled road to a cluster of excellent restaurants on the water's edge (you can stay there if you wish) and the chance of a pebbly, but refreshing, swim around the corner where there is a small area for tents.

Ironically, Assos is visually more rewarding than the greater Troy.

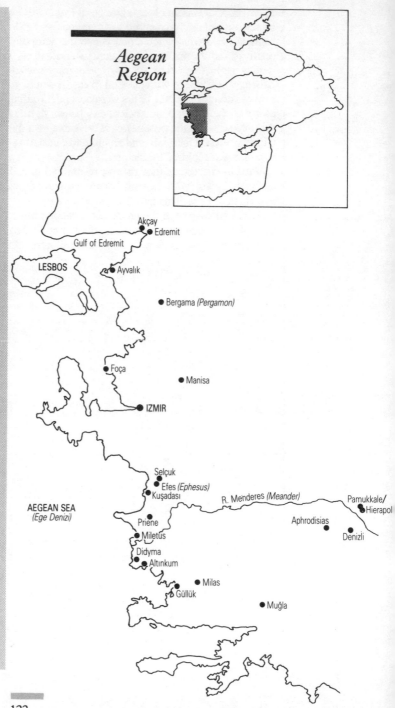

Aegean Region

Akçay
● Edremit
Gulf of Edremit
LESBOS
Ayvalık

● Bergama *(Pergamon)*

Foça
● Manisa

IZMIR

Selçuk
Efes *(Ephesus)*
Kuşadası

R. Menderes *(Meander)*

Pamukkale/
Hierapol

AEGEAN SEA
(Ege Denizi)
Priene
Miletus
Didyma
Altınkum

Aphrodisias
Denizli

● Milas
Güllük
● Muğla

Aegean Region

Introduction

This splendid area is relatively unspoilt when considered in relation to the highly popular stretches of coastline along the Mediterranean south of Bodrum. However, beaches such as those outside Ayvalık are already favourite holiday resorts for the Turks themselves and will undoubtedly become a tourist attraction in the near future.

It is a region which invites you to vary the pace and content of your travels – to spend as much time as you choose in the modern sophisticated city of Izmir; at the ancient sites of Ephesus, Selçuk, Aphrodisias, Priene, Miletus and Didyma; in the coastal resort areas of Edremit, Ayvalık or Kuşadası; or travelling as far inland as Pamukkale ('cotton castle') near Denizli to see the natural wonder of the calcified waterfall surrounded by stalactites and backed by the ruins of Hierapolis. There is, of course, nothing to prevent you travelling further south to Bodrum and beyond to savour yet another change of scenery and pace.

Although climates the world over can never be guaranteed, the Aegean region generally benefits from a mild and sunny climate, avoiding the aridity of the interior.

Edremit to Izmir

Edremit

The Gulf of Edremit is a beautiful area, offering a pleasing combination of visual contrasts to consider – sandy beaches, blue seas, forests and mountain scenery – with Mount Ida (*Kaz Dağı*) in the north rising to 1,767 m. The town of Edremit, as the site of Adramyttium, promises a great deal in terms of historical background, yet the promise is not fulfilled: disappointingly, nothing of the ancient city remains.

Where to stay

The Turban Holiday Village in Akçay is one of the best in Turkey. Turban is usually a name you can rely on, with gentler standards and a more sympathetic Turkish atmosphere than the brash complexes further south subsidised by German investment, but no less professional – as one can see here.

Turban Akçay Vacation Village, Akçay, Edremit, tel.: 204. Under the supervision of Ibrahim Doğan, the service is both efficient and friendly, and though you should not expect the spectacular, this holiday village seems exemplary in many ways: buildings deliberately kept low, flanked by a profusion of pine trees, palms, mulberries and magnolias, beds of luxuriously scented lilies, roses and geraniums, and honeysuckle probably climbing round your chalet door. The food and service were exceptional on my visit, and there is the usual spacious, obligatory swimming pool beside the sea. Perhaps it succeeds because it is more modest than most, with sixty-four beach houses, eight suites and four bungalows but, even so, that adds up to 400 beds. There are showers and lavatories in every room; self-service and à la carte restaurants; bar and disco; tennis court; children's playground, and water sports which could be an advantage for a large family who wish to stay with occasional explorations. These could easily include Assos and Pergamon, though there are more antiquities to be seen still further south.

The main office for up-to-date information and prices is in Istanbul: Inönü Caddesi, Vakif Işhani 3, Taksim, tel.: 145.82.98/149.21.25.

Ayvalık   This is a lively, cheerful, bustling little port, two hours' drive south from Akçay, through an exhilarating countryside of orchards and groves of shimmering olive trees. Ayvalık has been described as 'sprawled out languidly', but this is far from the truth; instead, it is compact and so businesslike that there is a factory in the middle of the harbour front. The whole place is intensely alive, with boys selling ice-creams in traditional costume, shoppers examining boxes of fish laid out on the edge of the harbour, and two excellent restaurants at the end of the curved harbour next to the beautiful old building which used to be the customs house.

The coastline is indented with twenty-three islands of various sizes, and boat trips go to the island of Alibey for a fish lunch. Above all, drive to the top of **Seytan Sofrası**, the Devil's Table, with its circular café, for views at sunset over the vast panorama of islands which seem to shift in the changing light. There are no buses, so if you have no car you will have to take a taxi.

You can go further abroad (literally!) to the Greek island of Lesbos (Mytilene), take a bus to the marvellous hillside town of Molivos in the north, stay overnight and return the following day, but clear this beforehand in Ayvalık. At the very least, try to visit one of the great Turkish sites such as Pergamon.

Where to   Surprisingly, there are few recommendable hotels, though a couple
stay   of possibles as you drive out of town on your left. The main accommodation, and the sprawling resort, lie outside the town at **Sarımsaklı**, on an 11-km stretch of sand which any resort would envy. Obviously, this is going to become one of the popular holiday centres on the Turkish coast; already there are numerous hotels on the edge of the sand.

The Baskent Motel, Sarımsaklı Plajları, Sarımsaklı, Ayvalik, tel.: 116; thirty beds, is one of the most sympathetic. All rooms have a sea view from their balconies, bathrooms and constant hot water, there is good food in the restaurant and snacks in the open-air.

Yet what makes such places so attractive is the friendliness, in this case of the young owner, who is anxious to make you feel welcome. Unlike in Britain, where landlords are liable to eject you if you are caught laughing, the Turks genuinely like to see you enjoy yourselves and are baffled and equally miserable if you do not. The Director of the Tourism Office in Ayvalık, Mr Ercan Koçelli, goes out of his way to help you (tel.: 6631/2122) and his advice could be useful in recommending places to visit. The one objection to resorts like Sarımsaklı, or the holiday village at Akçay, is that they are out of town, and it is vital to explore if you wish to gain the real flavour of Turkey. The town of Ayvalık is quite close and should be visited for an evening meal.

Pergamon   If this is the first ancient site which you see in Turkey, you will be overwhelmed. If you have had a surfeit of antiquities, you may still be overwhelmed, in a different sense, by its sheer magnitude. Unless you have your own transport it is a good idea to negotiate with a taxi-driver in the town of **Bergama** to take you to the acropolis at the top, where you can absorb the perspective and stay for half-an-hour, drive down to the Asclepion, and return to Bergama for about L 13,500, after bargaining. It helps to visit the Archaeological Museum in Bergama before you go, in order to see the model of the famous Altar of Zeus known for its outstanding beauty.

Even though the remains of the original have been taken to Berlin and reconstructed in the Pergamum Museum, the model and the other exhibits will help to place the ancient city in perspective. As usual, the setting is delightful, with a garden of yellow pansies, red roses and purple shrubs, and unexpected pieces of statuary such as an upside-down dolphin, a magnificent torso clad in finely carved armour, and the famous Nikke, Goddess of Triumph. It helps to know a bit of the history too.

History   The death of Alexander the Great was followed by a feud between his claimant generals. Lysimachus left his considerable fortune, acquired as the spoils of war, to the care of Pergamon when he was killed in battle against his rival Seleucus. It was promptly appropriated by his eunuch commander Philitarus, who switched sides, confirming suspicions about a eunuch's fidelity. But he used the fortune to expand the city, which his nephew Eumenes, and adopted son Attalus, brought to fruition. There is a nice, if unlikely, legend that Attalus, realising that his army was composed of cowards, prepared a human sacrifice and wrote 'Victory for the King' backwards on his hand which he pressed against the liver or the lung as he pulled it out of the victim's body. The words, discernible on the entrails, were regarded by his soldiers as such an omen for success that they charged into battle inspired and did indeed win victory for their king over the Gauls.

His successor, Eumenes II, played along with the Romans and benefited from their defeat of Antiochus of Syria. When Pergamon was granted his land in reward, the city controlled an area as far south as Antalya.

What to see

Of interest to visitors today is the library which Eumenes II cultivated until it held 200,000 books, competing with that in Alexandria so that the Egyptians stopped their supply of papyrus in revenge. Flat parchment was then used instead, the forerunner of the modern book rather than the scroll. Finally, when the Alexandrian library was damaged by fire, Mark Antony creamed the best of the collection from Pergamon and gave it as a present to Cleopatra, but by then Attalus III had died without an heir and Pergamon was already in decline.

The greatest period was due to the thirty-eight years of Eumenes II's reign, with the construction of the gymnasium and, above all, of the Altar to Zeus in celebration of his predecessor's victory. More than a thousand figures, half animal and half human, were represented in a series of reliefs, celebrating the triumph of good over evil, or Pergamon over the barbarous Gauls. Part of the most extensive Greek remains in existence, they were removed to Germany by permission of the reigning sultan, and can now be seen (or not, as the case may be) in the Pergamum Museum in East Berlin, a curious destination for such a sunny and liberated origin.

If you start at the top, the view from the acropolis will help you absorb the scene and explain what is going on where, with the German restoration of the library nearby, and the foundations of the Temple to Athena and Altar to Zeus which are all that remain. The theatre is remarkable, Hellenistic, yet pressed steeply against the hillside as if by some gigantic hand, with eighty tiers of seats holding 10,000 people.

One of the most interesting sites today is the Asclepion, the ancient hospital named after the God of Medicine, Asclepius, according to legend the grandfather of Hygeia and Panaceas whose names are recognisable today. They were the daughters of Telesphorus, whose temple was reached by an underground tunnel nearly 90 m long where patients either slept in the hope of a cure, or ran or hobbled through while priests shouted encouragement from the holes in the roof above. More than a hospital in today's sense, the Asclepion was a centre experimenting in the healing powers of herbs and sacred water. The well is still used by optimistic pilgrims today, who bottle the sacred water in the hope of its miraculous power. The atmosphere of the Asclepion really does suggest peacefulness.

Where to eat

Restaurants in Bergama include the **Kardeşler**, near the taxi rank, basic but good, and the **Savın**, smarter, with an outdoor terrace, which could be preferable on a hot day.

Returning to the main road and continuing south to Izmir, there are two more detours should you wish to explore further.

Foça To the west, Foça was the ancient port of Phocaea and the northernmost Ionian settlement, noted for its harbour and seafaring men. Indeed, the Phoceans were such audacious seamen that they colonised other parts of the Mediterranean including Marsalla, now Marseilles, in 546 BC. Today, a French Club Méditerranée returns the compliment. It is even claimed that the Phoceans brought the art of cultivating vines to France; if so, we owe them immeasurably.

Manisa A larger town to the east, formerly Magnesia and a western outpost for the Hittites, Manisa more recently became a country residence for the sultans. The town reflects the courteous formality of such distinction. This somnolent atmosphere – games of backgammon played interminably under the shade of plane trees – is shattered at the end of every May with the Mesir Festival. *Mesir*, a paste with forty-one spices, is supposed to be the ultimate kill-or-cure for illness. During the festival it is thrown in paper wrappers from the top of the Sultan Mosque, built by Süleyman the Magnificent's mother, which has an exquisitely painted balcony you should look out for, dated 1572.

The town is surrounded by poppy fields as far as you can see, once a favourite source of opium. An overhanging rock with a human face suggests the weeping Niobe turned to stone, the daughter of Tantalus who was condemned to crave for food and water which the gods placed out of reach, thus giving us the word 'tantalise'.

From Manisa, you can continue straight to Izmir on the coast.

Izmir Izmir is vast. It is the third largest city, the second port (after Istan-
History bul), with a population of two million, and a harsh approach through long stretches of tough industrial dockland. Little remains of the old city apart from an area of busy streets around the bazaar at Konak, yet this was the foremost Greek colony after Troy, originally built on the suburb of Bayraklı where people lived 3,000 years ago, and rebuilt as Smyrna by Alexander's general, Lysimachus. This meant that it came under the jurisdiction of Pergamon, benefiting equally when the district was ruled from Rome.

The Romans were followed by the musical chairs: Arabs, Seljuks and Crusaders. When Tamerlane occupied the city in 1402 he destroyed most of it, but when the Ottomans succeeded in 1415 their tolerance brought a new prosperity. The Greek population was joined by Jews escaping from persecution in Spain, and the treaty with France arranged by Süleyman the Magnificent turned Smyrna into an international commercial port, trading throughout Europe and acquiring some of the western veneer. All nationalities and faiths were welcome.

This happy relationship endured for centuries until it was shattered after the First World War when the Greeks seized Smyrna as part of their reward for supporting the Allies, and even advanced on Ankara. This was the crucial turning-point for the new Turkish leader, Kemal Atatürk, but his strength was shown again as his army forced the Greeks back to Smyrna where they were defeated in a battle on 9 September 1922 which left the population decimated and the old city in flames. 'This is the end of an era,' said Atatürk, and Smyrna was reborn under the Turkish name of Izmir. This is why so little of the former city remains to be seen today. It explains, also, those curious ghost cities further south where the Greek population was evacuated following the agreement ratified at the Lausanne Conference in 1922–3, when 1,300,000 Greeks (as against 400,000 Turks) were exchanged.

What to do

The Kültür Park in the centre of the city is a useful point to work from. In the summer, from mid-August to mid-September, this is the site of the annual international trade fair, otherwise it is worth visiting for the outside garden restaurants when the weather is oppressive.

Horse-drawn carriages are a surprising feature of such a modern, industrial city and they enable you to drive alongside the sea, a curved waterfront just a minute's walk from the famous Büyük Efes Hotel, with the Atatürk monument in the middle, the smarter shops and restaurants to the right, and the colourful, less expensive *lokantas* to the left. Continuing along this dockside you reach the clock-tower at Konak, built in the nineteenth century. Konak can also be reached by horse and carriage from the Kültür Park. Indeed, a round trip would reveal the heart of the city or, at least, its most interesting features for Izmir can hardly be recommended as either beautiful or a place to linger in.

The clock tower provides a useful landmark with the older, narrow streets of the bazaar nearby and restaurants in the fish market specialising in the local catch. The splendid Archaeological Museum is a short distance away, continuing south, in the Turgutreis Park near the sea, from where, if you feel extraordinarily energetic, you can walk and climb to the Velvet Fortress at the top of the ancient Mount Pagos which was built in the third century BC. An exhausting climb could bring a sense of disappointment, but if you take a taxi you will be rewarded by splendid panoramic views of Izmir below, placing the city in perspective.

Where to stay

Büyük Efes Hotel, Gaziosmanpaşa Bulvarı 1, tel.: 144.300; 296 rooms. This is the biggest and the best hotel in Izmir and merits recommendation. I should add that a notebook I left on a previous visit was looked after scrupulously and handed back as a matter of course. The hotel has the reputation for being prohibitively expensive, but this is only by Turkish standards. In no single way is it inexpensive, but the charge is not unreasonable for the comfort you receive. The outside terraced restaurant may not have the louche atmosphere of the docks around the corner, but it does possess a definite atmosphere of its own – the Deputy Prime Minister dining at the next table contrasting with a group of Turkish students in their best white suits celebrating the end of their college years, gleaming with all the optimism of youth, beautifully behaved with sly smiles to begin with, replaced by greater relaxation and then flashes of solemnity as they realise this is a moment for goodbye as well, before they start out in the world. Delightful to watch. The food is outstandingly good: try the smoked sturgeon.

There is the surprising bonus of the swimming pool in the gardens beyond, which has glass sides so that you can see the swimmers underneath the water after they have dived in, which does something to your own appetite. There are also, of course, all the usual facilities of a large Turkish hotel: tennis courts, sauna and Turkish baths. Prices are from L 89,000 for a double room.

Etap Izmir Hotel, part of the French group, is around the corner at Cumhuriyet Bulvarı 138, tel.: 144.290; 128 rooms. This is smaller and slightly cheaper.

Anba Hotel, Cumhuriyet Bulvarı 124, tel.: 144.380; fifty-three rooms, is in a more moderate price range, and recommended as good value. Rooms cost from L 25,000.

Babadan Hotel, Gaziosmanpaşa Bulvarı 50, Çankaya, tel.: 139.640; thirty-seven rooms, is highly recommended as a down-to-earth professional hotel with large bathrooms in the centre of town, from L 20,000 for a double. Others are nearby, should this be booked.

Billur Hotel, Basmane Meydanı 783, tel.: 136.250; sixty rooms, good value but near the station and slightly noisy. Doubles from L 22,000.

Pansiyon Fa, Kızılay Caddesi 1375, Sokak 24, tel.: 215.178. A small pension run by the Eronat family near the Efes Hotel, so it is conveniently situated. It is inexpensive, so often full up as well. Telephone and book if possible.

All such places have cheaper rates in the out-of-season months in winter.

Where to eat   Take your pick from those on the left hand side on the waterfront. The **Deniz** is one of the better of the smarter ones on the right (facing the sea). The **Alsancak**, inside the city, has been recommended for genuine Turkish atmosphere.

Kuşadası to Pamukkale

Kuşadası   On my first visit fifteen years ago, Kuşadası, 90 km from Izmir, was hardly an enthralling town but there was a slight charm in the back streets which were just beginning to wake up. Now it is a restless, expanding centre and the slight charm has been killed, a willing victim to the prosperity brought by the cruise ships and the international tourists who pour ashore to raid Ephesus and return contented and complacent with a curious collection of misconceptions, before they descend on the next Mediterranean 'antiquity' and acquire new ones. If this sounds condescending, that is the way it is.

Yet, if you are in the right frame of mind, Kuşadası can still be enjoyed, especially when the cruise ships have departed. Also, *because* of the tourists, there is an abundance of shops, restaurants and discos, and a massive marina holding 550 yachts. If you welcome brashness, Kuşadası is the place for you. Thousands do and it is now one of the most popular destinations for British travel agencies.

Also, there is the undeniable attraction of Kuşadası as a base, within easy reach of Ephesus and Selçuk; Aphrodisias and Pamukkale in the interior; and Priene, Miletus and Didyma to the south. If you wish to explore ancient sites, this is a perfect vantage point, and it is in easy reach also of the Greek island of Samos.

Where to stay   **Kısmet Hotel**, İslet Mecilik ve Ticaret. A.S, tel.: 2005. This is recommended as a deluxe refuge on the headland about 3 km from the centre of the hectic town. Even if you prefer to be at the heart of things it is within easy reach, unlike the vast complexes which are 10 or 12 km away (in spite of claiming half this distance in their brochures) where you might be anywhere.

Much of the charm of the Kısmet lies in the beautifully laid-out gardens, with tall palm trees which always enhance such a setting, with the surrounding water below and a view over the marina.

As the restaurant is excellent for lunch, half-board makes sense, with dinner at one of the fish restaurants near the jetty for the cruise ships. Swimming is *not* the reason for staying here, either off the rocks below or from the tiny man-made beach. A double room with breakfast costs from L 35,750; half-board from L 49,000. The Kısmet is open from 1 April to 31 October.

Club Caravanserai, Öküz Mehmet Paşa Kervansarayı, tel.: 036.14.15. Near the harbour and unmistakable with high, crenellated walls, this magnificent caravanserai, built in 1618, is recognised as one of the masterpieces of Ottoman architecture, strong enough to be still standing. Until a few years ago, this was the unusual setting for a Club Méditerranée; now it has been transformed by Turkish tourism into one of the most exotic hotels in the world. It is worth crossing those formidable doors for a drink in the tree-lined courtyard, or simply a stare. Even if you are not staying there, you are made to feel welcome. It is good for a touristy and very expensive dinner, due to the music and entertainment – again there is that incomparable sense of enjoyment.

The rooms are simply furnished with attractive *kilims*, and the unique atmosphere helps to justify the cost. The price for a double room and breakfast is from L 40,000, half-board from L 49,000.

Hotel Akman, İstiklal Caddesi 13, tel.: 1501; forty rooms. This is an excellent example of a middle-range hotel, 800 m from the centre and 100 m from the beach, though swimming here is not really recommended. With room for parking, it is a practical base with a convenient lobby and bar nearby, a restaurant, and terrace, with space for sunbathing on the roof. The rooms all have bathrooms, hot water and balconies. A double room costs from L 25,000.

Bahar, also in the centre, in a back street – family-run and basic, but with a roof terrace. Prices from L 14,750 for a double room with breakfast.

Kalyon Hotel, new, small and friendly in the centre of town, is pleasantly shaded, creating a fresh atmosphere which is welcome. It has attractive decorations and is in the mid-range.

Where to eat

There are many excellent fish restaurants along the waterfront, but these tend to be expensive. Prices drop proportionately as you move away from the sea, yet the quality generally remains high.

On the outskirts

Outside Kuşadası there are several vast, impersonal complexes like the **Imbat** which has the advantage of a good, if narrow, sandy beach as well as a pool, but there have been criticisms of box-like rooms (220 altogether) so check first. The **Tusan** is similar, with better reports of more spacious rooms.

Club Akdeniz, tel.: 521, is most attractively laid out with gardens and trees, every possible facility, and entertainment. Also it has its own beach, but it is an admitted fifteen minutes' drive from town.

Ephesus

Ephesus (present-day Efes) is so splendid that you should allow time to see it in a leisurely fashion, preferably in the early morning light or dusk. This applies to all ancient sites, but to Ephesus and Selçuk in particular because of their scope and the crowds that descend from their charabancs in the middle of the day. You can reach it easily by *dolmuş* from Kuşadası or by bus from Izmir.

History

Originally founded by the Carians in the thirteenth century BC, the site became an Ionian settlement in the eleventh century BC, and was later caught between the Persians and the Greeks, though the Ephesians perfected a skilful balancing act, remaining friends with both sides. After the death of Alexander, Lysimachus acquired the city along with Pergamon and Kuşadası and moved the port, silted by now with deposits from the River Cayster, to its present position. The great age had begun. Continuing the parallel with Pergamon, Ephesus was given to Rome by Attalus III and became the provincial capital.

Ephesus also achieved importance as an early Christian centre. St Paul preached here, and though he left after local opposition from the merchants, he had laid the foundations for Christianity, and wrote his famous epistles to the Ephesians afterwards.

Ephesus was the most important commercial port in the Mediterranean in the second century AD with a population estimated at 300,000; it was the provincial capital of Rome; the Temple to Artemis (Diana) near Selçuk was considered one of the Seven Wonders of the Ancient

131

World; and the Virgin Mary is supposed to have lived, and possibly died, on a site 7 km above Selçuk, now occupied by a small chapel.

Consequently, it is hardly surprising that the city housed a Hellenistic theatre which held 25,000 people, surely the largest in Asia Minor; temples; gymnasiums, and a famous library, apart from such earthier but no less necessary additions as brothels, shops and public lavatories, the remains of which can also be seen today. Several of the buildings have been brilliantly restored, or are still in the process with even greater promise to come.

What to see   The paved **Arcadian Way** (AD 550) was the main street, once lined with shops under covered arcades on either side with colonnades, leading towards the harbour before it was silted up. Imagining the sea ahead, now replaced by a fertile plain, helps to place Ephesus in even more astonishing perspective.

The great **Theatre** is still in use today for festivals, such as the Festival of Culture and Art in the first week of May, though it is disconcerting to see folk-dancing beside a gigantic plastic bottle advertising some soft drink. The commercialism and souvenir touts at Ephesus are a considerable drawback.

The Theatre was originally built in the third century BC but was considerably altered and extended during Roman times. St Paul allegedly preached here during his stay in Ephesus.

From the Theatre you walk along the Sacred Way, passing what was once the busy *agora*. Just beyond is the celebrated **Celcus Library**. The façade has two tiers, with four columned porticoes on ground level and three above. Its decorations are of extraordinary delicacy though the ultimate effect is majestic.

Opposite the Library, the **Street of Curetes**, named after an order of priests, leads uphill. At the beginning, on the left, stand the **Baths of Scholastica** (AD 200), which included public baths, a dining hall and, on the first floor, a dormitory. The building was rebuilt in the fourth century by a Christian lady, Scholastica, whose headless statue you can still see in the entrance hall. It may once have been a brothel; a secret passageway ran under the street to the Library.

Beyond the Baths is the **Temple of Hadrian** (AD 138) which is little more than a Corinthian façade, but it is an ample indication of the sumptuous simplicity and grace that must once have been. Opposite the Temple are the remains of ancient shops and several large houses which probably belonged to prosperous merchants, as many were decorated with frescoes and mosaics.

Further along there are many columns, statues and fountains and then, in a street branching off to the right, you come to the **Temple of Domitian**. Opposite was once the state *agora* and, walking up the hill to the north are ruins of the **Prytaneion**, once the municipal hall and, finally, next door, the **Odeion**, a small theatre used for senate meetings and musical performances.

Selçuk | A forty-five minute walk from Ephesus, though it is better to start the other way round, or better still use a car or *dolmuş* to save time, Selçuk should not be missed. Dominated by a Byzantine fortress above, this is a peaceful incline with St John's Basilica below, built by the Emperor Justinian; the İsa Bey Mosque; and the site of the Temple of Artemis, off the road to Kuşadası, though only a solitary standing column of it can be seen today.

History | Once the temple was the largest in Asia Minor, four times the size of the one at the Parthenon in Athens, surrounded by 129 marble columns – the first temple ever to be constructed out of marble, apart from its wooden roof that was burnt to ashes on the day that Alexander the Great was born, which is why he came to Ephesus in 334 BC on his historic journey south: he wanted to offer to rebuild it. With exquisite tact, the Ephesians refused, explaining that one god could not erect a temple to another. Then they restored it themselves, exactly as it was before.

A greater enemy than fire was water, for the site was so badly waterlogged that the area had to be drained and elaborate foundations laid using trees and the skins of animals. In spite of such precautions, the temple was gradually destroyed and the ruins were covered by silt, so that only the solitary column with a stork occasionally perched on top remains to signify the Wonder of the World today.

What to see | The museum at Selçuk should not be missed on any account. It is well laid out, as always in Turkey, and full of interesting objects from Ephesus (it is frequently, and confusingly, called the Ephesus Museum), including a life-size figure of Artemis, with a row of eggs to represent fertility (not multiple breasts as some people wistfully assume), and the small but perfect boy on a dolphin.

Such museums are well worth seeing. They are not as stuffy as their European counterparts, and they enhance the places you are going to with a much greater understanding.

Aphrodisias | You can visit Aphrodisias from Izmir – in this case, take a bus direct
Getting there | to Karacasu, and a *dolmuş* or taxi from there; or to Nazilli, and a *dolmuş* to Geyre close to the ruins. Be advised that it is a considerable detour, 39 km off the main road to Denizli, but worth while.

Even more than Ephesus, Aphrodisias conveys the day-to-day life of an ancient city and its people. Set in a plain with a tributary of the great River Meander (*Menderes*), the landscape looks deceptively flat until you find yourself beside the monuments which have been restored so brilliantly by Professor Kenan Erim over the last twenty-five years with assistance from the National Geographic Society and the Friends of Aphrodisias. Once you are inside the former city, there are streams, inclines and dips, copses of wild figs and pomegranates, which offer constant interest. This is much as the centre of Aphrodisias must have been, with the poorer quarters kept separate on the outside, catering to the richer élite within.

Yet, in spite of this natural setting, the question arises immediately – why here? Why did such a civilised community decide to live here, as they have done since the third century BC when it was referred to as 'the great city of Caria named after Aphrodite'? The cult of the Goddess of Love (hence aphrodisiac) made the city famous as a shrine.

History   The position of Aphrodisias becomes more understandable as a distant outpost for Greek and Roman civilisation. Alexander the Great passed through here when he crossed the Menderes Valley on his way to India; Caesar gave the city freedom from taxation; Augustus, at the end of the first century BC, declared 'I have selected this one city from all Asia as my own'; while the Emperor Trajan honoured the Aphrodisian ambassadors with special treatment when they arrived in Rome.

What to see   At a time when time itself seemed limitless compared to the acceleration of today, it was logical that such an outpost should enjoy every advantage of civilisation – a better home than home. That the Aphrodisians achieved this can be seen in the monuments they left behind: the stadium seating 30,000 spectators, 300 m long which makes it one of the largest in the world, where gladiators and wild animals performed. Then, in delightful contrast, the small odeon with sculpted marble chairs and the shade of trees, for the more exclusive use of philosophers and orators declaiming their latest works.

Quarrying marble from the hills beyond the valley, Aphrodisian sculptors were famous for their skill. Their damaged legacy can be seen in the museum today as proof that their reputation was deserved. The figures have tremendous strength yet the drapery enclosing a woman is delicate and free, almost rustling with life, while that of Aphrodite herself actually seems to be in motion. A seated philosopher, twice the size of life, dating from around the first century AD, is magnificently calm and composed, though headless now, and the representation of Leda and the Swan reflects the cult of Aphrodite in a powerful, swirling, sensual entanglement.

The influence of Aphrodisian sculpture on Rome, at a time when the use of marble was just beginning, has yet to be confirmed, but the sculptors could have altered the face of the capital, quite literally, with their advanced knowledge.

Visiting the exemplary museum, now overflowing, walking through the city, passing the Temple, the six baths of Hadrian, and the market place, it is astounding to realise that all this has been excavated so recently that only a few years ago the theatre was covered by a ramshackle village, since removed.

The restoration   The story of this recovery (or rather uncovery) is romantic. His curiosity aroused by a reference to the Aphrodisias School of Sculpture when he was studying in America, Professor Erim visited the site in 1959 and noticed chunks of marble all around him – 'delicately fluted columns doubled as hitching posts': even in 1982 I witnessed an echo of this with a white marble column used as a strut to support a wooden shack. Excavating two years later, he struck lucky with a marble head which fitted a torso already recovered from an irrigation ditch, one of the figures which decorated the massive Zoilos Relief (first century BC) which shows the priest greeting the people. Since then, the professor has laboured with love. 'Why do I keep returning here?' he asked, supplying his answer: 'To bring a once great city back to the light of day is a privilege given but to a few.'

With a population of 50,000, larger than that of Pompeii, Aphrodisias rivalled even Rome itself, a thousand miles away. This is what makes it so extraordinary today. The Christians smashed the heads off the statues, broke up the workshops of the sculptors, and converted the temple into a church, all in the dubious name of God. The Seljuk/Turk invaders under Tamerlane the Mongol Conqueror, invaded Asia Minor, defeating the Ottomans at Angora in 1402, and put an end to Aphrodisias as well. Almost single-handedly Professor Erim has restored it.

Denizli Although there's nothing particularly remarkable about this city itself, it is the place from which you take a *dolmuş* to Pamukkale, and it's on the main bus route between the Capadoccia region, Konya and the Aegean coastline. Denizli might also prove useful if you find yourself in Pamukkale without a bed for the night.

Pamukkale Pamukkale (pronounced Pam-ooo-kuller) is so extraordinary (for once one can use that word literally) that it deserves an overnight stop. And if that curious, static white waterfall is the icing on the cake, a visit to Aphrodisias will offer you something more substantial: an ancient city in mid-excavation which promises to rival Ephesus.

Pamukkale is a freak of nature, a constant fall of thermal spring water which petrifies as it cascades down the hill, with tiers of apparent ice and snow, overhanging the brooding plateau below. In the posters, the illusion is sensational. As you approach from the heavy industrial town of Denizli, the effect is disappointing, a whiteish stain on the distant heights. But once you are there, it is irresistible and slightly mad, a mountain resort without snow which deceives the photographic and almost the human eye, for it seems as if snow is all around you.

The lodges at the top are furnished in appropriate alpine style, and the whole place has a cheerful mountain atmosphere. Someone yodelling would not be out of place. At the lower lodge (the **Tusan Motel**) you can swim in the open hot sulphur pool on the very edge of the cliff, a most bizarre experience with the plains stretching below. Above (at the **Pamukkale Motel**) it is equally surprising, with marble statuary scattered on the bed of a spring-water pool as you swim above.

Far from all this being exploited as a shoddy gimmick, it is pres-

135

ented with extreme professionalism, apart from the garish souvenir shops which have sprouted up recently. The food is unexpectedly good and when I was staying there the **Koru Motel** was one of the rare places which had the traditional dish of Circassian chicken on the menu, and it could not have been bettered (see p. 41).

Several kilometres higher up, and worth the effort if you have the time, are more cascading pools with astonishingly vivid changing colours.

Hierapolis   In between there is the additional interest of Hierapolis, founded in 190 BC by Eumenes II, King of Pergamon. It became famous because of its thermal baths which had healing properties for curing heart disease, rheumatism and nervous disorders (or so it was believed), so that the place was known as *Hiera-polis*, 'the Sacred City'. On the death of Attalus III, Eumenes II's great nephew, the city reverted to Roman rule along with Pergamon.

Even with the usual theatre and temple, Hierapolis is not particularly exciting (how blasé one becomes!) but there is one unique point of interest – the Sanctuary of Pluto, or the Plutonium, marked with the sign 'DANGER'. This refers to the poisonous gases supposed to escape from the cave below (hence Pluto, lord of the underworld). As eunuch priests were alleged to be immune while mere mortals collapsed and died from the fumes, the rumour persists that the cave contains a treasure trove and there is even an adventurous Turk prepared to test the story by descending in full diving kit to claim the gold and crystals (better than diamonds) should they be there. A likely story! Yet I have come across a description by the Greek historian Strabo, who came here over 2,000 years ago (he was born in 63 BC) and referred to the fresh air outside where a man may approach safely, 'but for any living creature which enters inside, death is instantaneous. Bulls, for example, which are taken in, collapse and are brought out dead; we ourselves sent in small birds which at once fell lifeless. The eunuchs of Cybele, however, are immune to the extent that they can approach the orifice and look in, and even penetrate for some distance, though not normally without holding their breath.'

This means that the Plutonium has exuded poisonous gases for more than two thousand years, and continues to do so today. And this is not romance. There are no eunuchs to push into the hole today, and an iron gate bars the entrance anyway, but as I looked at it suspiciously I became aware that the ground was scattered with small dead birds who had flown inside and fallen lifeless as they struggled out, exactly as Strabo claimed.

Hierapolis was finally extinguished by an earthquake in 1334. Possibly because they were ill in the first place, the pilgrims to the Sacred City died like flies. There is a vast necropolis, looted by local graverobbers over the centuries, but the coins and artefacts you may be offered are probably counterfeit.

Where
to stay

As Pamukkale is frequently fully booked in the summer months, you would be advised to make a reservation in advance.

Tusan, tel.: 21432; forty-seven rooms, overlooks the plain below and charges from L 26,800 for a double room.

Koru, tel.: 11323; 120 rooms, also overlooks the Denizli plain, but is bigger. It is well designed, with pine trees, oleanders and the usual abundance of flower beds and white marble paths. One indoor pool and two uncovered are filled with the natural spring water which steams slightly in the early morning sun. The chalets make good use of natural materials: wood, stone and marble. Prices are from L 17,800.

Pamukkale, tel.: 10 (local), is simpler, operated by the regional government with basic rooms in contrast to that amazing pool scattered with Roman columns. It is sympathetic and cheaper than the others, with prices from L 13,500.

Konak, tel.: 7 (local), at the foot of the cliff, is a typical Turkish village house run by Mehmet Semerci, and very simple with shared washing, but excellent, genuine Turkish food and even a small pool with the same thermal water as above. Prices are from L 9,000.

Where
to eat

As already mentioned, the Koru Motel is excellent. If Pamukkale seems expensive or full, you could drive into Denizli for genuine Turkish *lokantas* like the Çinar.

Kuşadası to Altınkum

With Kuşadası as your base you can drive south to Didyma and back in one day, though this is only recommended if you are a passionate sightseer of antiquity. It is easily done if you are, and can share a taxi, fixing a definite price beforehand. Otherwise, if you are driving south to Milas, branching off to Bodrum, or to Muğla for Marmaris and the southern coastline, you can take detours to see the following, which are well worth while.

Priene

Years ago, crossing to Kuşadası from the Greek island of Samos, I took a taxi as far as Didyma and returned that evening to stop at Priene, the first of the ancient sites. I had waited to see Priene at the enchanted hour of dusk, when the texture of stone can be absorbed in the honeyed, golden light free from the intercepting glare of the sun, and I was spellbound by the beauty of the simple row of five Ionic columns. I found the peacefulness more satisfying than my ill-timed, midday visit to Ephesus the day before.

I have not returned, but I think of Priene with pleasure even now. So if you are making a similar round trip, save Priene for the last, like Victorian children with the choicest morsel on their plate.

The parallel-line lay-out of the small Hellenistic city (fourth century BC) is well preserved but what makes Priene remarkable is your own imagination as you look over the valley where the River Meander meandered. The outlook was largely that of water, unlike the flat plain today, for the sea reached the city and made Priene one of the busiest ports of the Ionian federation.

Priene was originally based further inland, and the inhabitants were forced to move the site of their city westwards to its present location as silt from the Meander blocked the harbour. The original site of Priene has never been found.

Of the present site, the most important monument is the Temple of Athena, designed by Pytheos, who was also architect of the Mausoleum of Halicarnassus. The temple was still under construction when Alexander the Great and his army arrived in 334 BC, and Alexander offered to finance its completion, provided that he was acknowledged as being its founder. When the city was excavated in the nineteenth century, the inscribed dedication reading 'King Alexander presented this temple to Athena Polias' was discovered.

Should you feel in need of refreshment when viewing the other ruins of the site, which include the House of Alexander, the Sanctuary of Demeter and Kore, a gymnasium and theatre, there is a resting place beside a small waterfall which is reputed to have an excellent restaurant.

Miletus   Another leading Greek city, 22 km further on, was famous for the Hellenistic theatre which held 15,000 people and is still well-preserved though little else remains. Miletus is supposed to have inspired the geometric, grid-iron planning, copied by Priene, though Cnidus at the end of the Datça Peninsula used it too. Again, it is suprising to realise that Miletus was one of the biggest ports in the ancient world, sporting four harbours. The silt that eventually choked them proved a force more corroding than the Persians who destroyed Miletus when the people dared to revolt. They rebuilt it later.

Didyma   Right in the town, 14 km on, is an apparent backyard of tumbled statuary looking as if the pieces are waiting for a giant to collect them. The large, cracked Medusa's head is the most famous, but all these segments are overwhelmed by the Temple of Apollo which remains impressive. The original temple was destroyed by the Persians in 494 BC and remained in ruins for 200 years until Seleucus I of Syria began restoration and development of the temple in the form which can be seen today. The new sanctuary was planned on such a huge scale that rebuilding work took five centuries to accomplish and even then the temple was never completed. Statues lined the road to a small harbour, but they are now in the British Museum in London along with the other loot.

Altınkum   Reactions to Altınkum could hardly be more different. One acquaintance was distinctly discouraging, saying it was a popular resort with a feeling of Costa Turkey: discos, ice-cream parlours and cafés sprouting like the youthful line of recently planted palm trees, all

138

part of Altınkum's explosion as a new popular resort. Conversely, a later report is reassuring: 'There are several hotels and restaurants along and behind the seafront of this pleasant little resort – we found one at the end for L 16,000 a night, including breakfast. There is a sandy beach close to the road and it is possible to hire umbrellas and beds etc. for sunbathing. From eight o'clock in the evening the seafront road is closed to traffic and fills with people taking their evening stroll, choosing restaurants, buying snacks. An unassuming town with a very pleasant atmosphere and many Turkish on holiday.'

When I went there myself it was some years ago, in the middle of the day, and hard to assess, but it is plainly great fun today, especially for young people who are not too demanding, not obsessed by the past, and who create their own good-humoured nightlife in bars like the Summer Garden.

If you stay overnight at Altınkum it is three and a half hours' drive to Bodrum with the chance for a stop for lunch at Güllük, a small harbour with fishing boats and ships taking on cargo.

Otherwise, with the slight anti-climax of Miletus, it would make sense to take the short detour to Priene (at the right time of day) then press on to Bodrum if you wish to visit at least one town in the most exhilarating part of the Turkish Riviera.

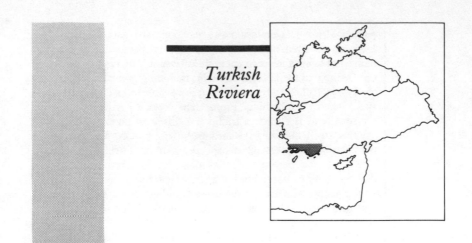

Turkish Riviera

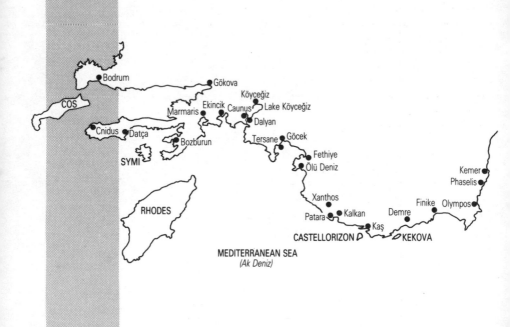

Bodrum

Gökova

COS

Köyceğiz

Ekincik Caunus Lake Köyceğiz

Marmaris

Dalyan

Cnidus Datça

Tersane Göcek

Bozburun

Fethiye

SYMI

Ölü Deniz

Kemer

Phaselis

Xanthos

Finike Olympos

RHODES

Patara Kalkan Demre

Kaş

CASTELLORIZON KEKOVA

MEDITERRANEAN SEA
(Ak Deniz)

Turkish Riviera

Introduction

The part of the Turkish coastline stretching between Bodrum on the Aegean coast and Kemer on the Mediterranean can usefully be considered the new Riviera. Since it is the most rewarding and popular area of the country for both independent traveller and holiday-maker alike, this section describes the region in considerable detail.

It is one of the most glorious coastlines in Europe, though some centres are developing rapidly: perhaps too rapidly. Bodrum, Marmaris, Kaş and other resorts may be increasingly popular with holiday-makers, but they still offer a great deal for the discerning traveller. They could be considered the shock-absorbers of the area, for in between are long stretches of unspoilt coastline with pine forests running down to the shore. You can walk out of town and revel in solitude in a matter of minutes. The Datça Peninsula, in particular, remains untarnished; if you travel by boat, you will see Turkey as it used to be – once you leave the marinas.

Undeniably the coastline is where you will spend much of a visit to this region, but as ever you will find it much more rewarding to use the coastal towns as a starting point for explorations further afield – whether travelling inland to places such as Köyceğiz, and the Gömbe Retreat in the mountains behind Kaş, or putting to sea to sail the Gulf of Gökova, the offshore waters of Kekova, or visiting Castellorizon.

An exploration of this area could be enhanced by undertaking The Blue Cruise around the coast between Bodrum and Fethiye. To do this not only enables you to visit several of the towns along the shoreline, but provides the sense of adventure that a sailing trip entails, and gives you the opportunity to enjoy a holiday away from a hotel environment.

There are ruins to be seen in the area, too: although not as spectacular as those in the Aegean region, Caunus and Patara are of considerable importance if you wish to enrich your travels by trying to see as much as possible of the various landscapes and places of interest in the area. The entire region, in fact, can be seen as a happy and unusual combination of tranquillity, sophistication and boisterous good humour: the degree to which you seek any or all of these qualities is your own choice.

Bodrum to Marmaris

Bodrum Bodrum, once known by the resounding name of Halicarnassus, is my
favourite town along this coast. Each time I return I am aghast at the
development, which looks as if it has doubled in size, yet the jaunty
charm of the little town remains intact and though it is especially popular with British package tours I am seldom aware of the tourism. The
town's basic population of around 15,000 increases to nearly 100,000
in the summer, and the new invasion of the eighteen to thirty age
group is alarming.

The comparison is frequently made to St Tropez, the fashionable
resort in the south of France, and equally to a 'little Greek town'. It
does not remind me of either. Bodrum has a personality all its own and
the abundance of pensions, restaurants and bars is fitting for a place
which seems dedicated to enjoyment. Difficult to get to, even now,
Bodrum has an independent flavour and has always been popular
with artists and writers, many of whom lived here in a sort of exile,
after their opinions had caused offence. The most important of these
was the writer Cevat Şakir Kabaağaclı, known as the Fisherman of
Halicarnassus, who immortalised the town with his stories based on
the lives of the local people, in particular the fishermen. The Greek
writer, Herodotus, known as the 'father of history', was born here in
about 484 BC.

The affection for Bodrum felt by the Turks prevents the town from
becoming a tourist trap. They descend in their thousands at the end of
Ramazan in order to celebrate and, though one has to squeeze
through the narrow streets, the fun is infectious and offsets any inconvenience, such as the impossibility of finding a room to sleep in unless
you have booked in advance.

Always, there is the constant reward of the Castle of St Peter which
offers such a tremendous view on the first approach that it is hard not
to feel exhilarated. This is what a castle should look like: powerful,
inviolate, immensely beautiful with the soft colours of the stones,
some of which were taken from the famous tomb of Mausolus, one of
the seven Wonders of the World. This was built in the form of a
pyramid, 46 m high, with friezes and figures sculpted by the leading
artists of the time, surrounded by thirty-six columns, and what a monumental first impression it must have made. Today, the great Crusader Castle can hardly be less impressive.

Originally, the castle was built on an island which is now connected
to the shore and divides Bodrum into two twin bays. On one side you
have the harbour and marina, Yat Limanı, lined with fishing boats
and yachts; on the other, most of the small hotels and pensions. The
Tourist Office is found in between, close to the castle walls: 12 Eylül
Meydanı, tel.: 1091 (6141 for Bodrum). It is open 8 a.m. to 8 p.m. on

weekdays; 9 a.m. to 12 noon and 3.30 to 7.30 p.m. on Saturdays; closed on Sundays.

Getting there   **By air:** There is now a small, local airfield, Mumcular, running flights to and from Istanbul. The nearest international airports are at Izmir and Dalaman.

By bus: It cannot be denied that Bodrum is a formidable journey from and to Izmir. The stops provide a welcome relief, but prolong the journey accordingly – a distance of 270 km which takes four and a half hours. However, the road is good and the scenery attractive. Try to travel early or late in the day, armed with a book which 'you can't put down', and some fruit if the weather is hot. Not all the buses have air-conditioning and there is frequently someone who objects when the skylights in the roof are opened and a welcome gust of fresh air sweeps in. To Ankara it is fourteen hours, and fifteen to Istanbul. Three hours to Marmaris with a greatly improved service: if you can find a proper bus, seize it. Otherwise the minibus or *dolmuş* service can take an eternity as the driver tries to entice possible passengers on the way, with countless stops.

As usual, the cost of the bus journey is nominal by most standards: L 2,500 to Izmir.

By ferry: A possible route is the ferry boat from the Greek island of Cos, but this must be avoided if you have flown to Greece on a charter flight. Though the Turks could not care less, the Greeks are apt to threaten you with the full cost of a scheduled return flight if they find a Turkish stamp in your passport. However, if you have entered Greece by bus or scheduled air service, this should not apply. The Greek ferry from Cos to Bodrum leaves most mornings in summer, but you are advised to check; the Turkish ferry leaves in mid-afternoon, and the journey takes little more than an hour and a half. Do not be put off if the Greeks assure you that no such Turkish service exists, for it does so most efficiently.

The car ferry to the Datça Peninsula is a new innovation and a boon, leaving in the morning and late afternoon. The attraction of Datça is described later (p. 154), but such a detour will reveal another, lesser-known part of the Turkish coast and spare you the drive to Marmaris which is unrewarding until you reach the splendid avenue of eucalyptus trees.

History   The Greek city of Halicarnassus was founded in the fifth century BC as one of the first Greek colonies in Asia. While the northern cities of the Aegean formed the Ionian Union, those further south joined the Dorian Federation which included Cos, Rhodes, Cnidus, Lalysos, Lindos and Camiros. Though Halicarnassus assumed such power that it was expelled, the city took part in the abortive revolt by the Ionians and Dorians which was quickly put down.

The greatest period in Bodrum's history coincided with the rule of Mausolus, 377–53 BC, who was the Persian *satrap* or governor of

Caria. He made Halicarnassus his capital and virtually an independent state. On his death, his formidable wife, Artemesia II, who also happened to be his sister, was so grief-stricken that she drank wine mixed with his ashes and built the great tomb in his honour, which gives us the word mausoleum. The Rhodians saw their chance to seize Halicarnassus now that it was ruled by a woman: their fleet set sail and met no opposition as it entered the bay. In fact, Artemesia had concealed her own ships in a channel behind the castle and quickly surrounded her enemy. Afterwards she led the captured fleet back to Rhodes where the Greeks were waiting to celebrate a victory, and took them by surprise as well – proving that she was as tough an adversary as any man.

Like many ports along this coast, Bodrum endured a musical-chairs sequence of occupation: Seljuks, Byzantines, Persians, Greeks and Romans, all of them anxious to secure such a natural harbour. Mausolus had fortified his Carian capital so successfully that Alexander the Great met with gallant resistance when he attacked the city. He destroyed it in consequence, though he spared the tomb of his predecessor. Halicarnassus failed to recover, and endured further occupation by the Mentese and the Ottomans until the Knights of St John of Rhodes seized the town in 1402 and established a Christian foothold on the mainland. Dismantling the mausoleum, which had been damaged already by earthquake in the twelfth century, they used many of the stones for their own castle in 1415, which became the new fortress to defend Bodrum. Süleyman the Magnificent captured St Peter's Castle after his conquest of the equivalent Crusader castle on Rhodes in 1523, when the Knights moved to Malta.

What to see   **St Peter's Castle** Inside the castle is one of the finest museums in the Mediterranean, with interest for all the family. The Crusaders, originally divided into separate nationalities and languages, were responsible for the finance of their own particular part of the castle – hence the German, Italian, English and French Towers. The French is the highest and a good starting point with the best views over the bay. The English Tower has a relief of a marble lion with the coat of arms of Edward Plantagenet. The Turks inside are dressed up as Knights of St John and their damsels serve you goblets of wine to the sound of medieval music. This sounds quaint, and it is – but welcoming, too.

The greatest interest comes from the underwater archaeology and the extraordinary finds in recent years, some of which date back, astonishingly, to the fifteenth century BC. Many of these treasures were taken from wrecks along this coastline. The *amphorae*, Greek and Roman two-handled urns for water, are so numerous they are almost commonplace, and an entire room is devoted to them. More exotic are the perfume containers, razors, mirrors and the bronze ingots taken from the wreck of a boat near Antalya which may have been crossing from Cyprus an astounding 3,400 years ago.

The recoveries come from four main wrecks, with pottery, glass and ivory, but the two-handled Mycenaean Greek pottery cup is probably the rarest of all. Sadly, the splendid bronze figure of Demeter, the earth-goddess of fertility, has been removed to the museum in Izmir.

The castle is full of surprises, with a Byzantine hall showing models of underwater exploration which is particularly popular with children; courtyards; gardens with peacocks and doves, and a café where you can rest.

Opening times of the castle are 8.30 a.m. to 12 noon and 1.30 to 5 p.m. daily. There is a small entrance fee, but if you have enjoyed your visit, or been shown around, it would be a courteous gesture to contribute some more to the box as you leave, next to the grain for the doves and peacocks.

The mausoleum Unfortunately, this is little more than a hole in the ground by contrast. If you wish to see the last excavated statues – possibly of Mausolus himself, and his wife Artemesia – you need to go to the British Museum where they were removed along with other British loot.

The theatre This is the oldest surviving monument in Bodrum, sited on the hillside close to the original mausoleum and capable of seating an audience of 10,000.

Where to stay

Accommodation is hard to find in the height of the season. You are advised to book in advance, or search for yourself – allowing ample time to do so in a leisurely way – on your arrival. Though there are few hotels, there are many small pensions and a few self-catering apartments. If you are desperate, go to the Tourist Bureau for advice. Most of the pensions are found in, and off, the main road running beside the sea: Cumhuriyet Caddesi.

Halikarnas Motel, Cumhuriyet Caddesi 128, tel.: 1073, twenty-eight rooms; towards the end of the bay, allegedly lively and good for the disco set with a beach nearby.

Baraz Hotel, Cumhuriyet Caddesi 62, tel.: 1857, twenty-four rooms; on the right-hand side, half-way down, in a good position. This can prove an invaluable standby when other places are full; it is not particularly Turkish, but it is comfortable and efficient, with private showers and telephones. It grows on me every time, but it is vital to insist on a room overlooking the sea with the sensational view of the castle which should lift the most drooping spirits. There is a bar and dining-room. L 15,000 for a single room; from L 21,000 for a double.

Artemis Pansiyon, Cumhuriyet Caddesi 117, tel.: 2530, twenty-three twin-bedded rooms; also on this same street, unpretentious and comfortable with private showers and telephone. There is a lounge, bar, breakfast room, a sun terrace and snack bar beside the sea. L 22,000 for a double room, including breakfast.

Mylasa Pension, Cumhuriyet Caddesi 34, tel.: 1846. This describes itself as 'English-run' although Cynthia and Barry are in fact Australian. The reports are excellent, of exceptional friendliness and welcome. All rooms have shower and toilet; you can breakfast on the roof; there is a comfortable lounge and cool drinks at the bar. The only possible drawback is the noise at night from energetic revellers, unless you happen to be one yourself. L 24,000, including breakfast.

Mercan Hotel, Cumhuriyet Caddesi 88, tel.: 1111; good value at L 9,000 for a single, L 15,000 for a double and L 18,000 for three.

Evin Pansiyon, Kumbahçe Mahallesi, Ortanca Sokak 7, tel.: 1312. At the far end of the street, this is associated with the Burcu Restaurant on the water's edge. L 12,000 for a double room.

Dinç Pansiyon, Cumhuriyet Caddesi 123, tel.: 1141; twenty twin-bedded rooms. This is highly thought of but was fully booked when I tried for a room, and there was a fairly indifferent reception-desk. However, once you are in, the furnishings are excellent, with lounge, bar, television room, breakfast room, and a terrace overlooking the beach. L 20,000 for a double room, including breakfast.

Karya Hotel, Cumhuriyet Caddesi 121, tel.: 1535; similar to the Dinç next door, but new. L 22,400 for a double room.

Umut Motel, Cumhuriyet Caddesi 23, tel.: 164; bungalows set in gardens, a double, including shower and breakfast, is good value at L 9,000.

Herodot Pansiyon, Neyzen Tevfik Caddesi 178, tel.: 1093; seven rooms; on the Marina side of the castle. Consistently recommended over the years, though it is hard to get in. L 9,000 for a single room, L 14,000 for a double.

Seçkin Konaklar, Neyzen Tevfik Caddesi 228, tel.: 1351. In the same area as the Herodot, but more on the apartment basis with several beds at L 14,400 – good value for families.

Manzara Hotel, Kumbahçe Mahallesi, Meteoroloji Yanı, tel.: 1719. A terraced hotel on the hill above Bodrum with excellent views and a small swimming pool with bar and restaurant. The rooms are more like small apartments, with self-contained kitchens. Prices are from L 19,800 for a single room and L 27,000 for a double.

The Maya Studios, Turkkuyusu Keles Cik. 5, tel.: 1637; self-contained rooms. These are four attractive new rooms, well-furnished with big double beds and kitchen units, in a typical side street behind the marina. Because this is hard to find, you would be wise to telephone beforehand to be shown the way or take a taxi. These flats have been built by Dursun Mutlu and his Dutch wife Lon, next to their home. Both speak English and could hardly be more helpful. Dursun is one of the true characters of Bodrum, a famous sponge-diver in his day, and usually to be found in the Hadigari Bar in the early evening before returning to his family. Though he is not an agent, Dursun is aware of what is going on in Bodrum and would prove invaluable if you wanted to hire a Turkish caique or *gulet* for a couple of nights to explore the coastline. He is an exceptional man with a mischievous sense of humour, worthy of respect.

Where to stay outside Bodrum

Many people prefer to stay outside the town in hotels and pensions which are cheaper and quieter.

Torba: Sanat Evi. A smart and very new hotel, this opened in 1987, a few minutes beyond the holiday village of Torba, 3 km from Bodrum. Prices are from L 54,000 for two, for full pension; L 33,300 for half-pension.

Kemer Pansiyon, Uslu Çikmazi 36, Kumbahçe Mahallesi, tel.: 1473; inland from the town, this is cheap as it should be with no plumbing in the rooms. Approximately L 2,750 for a single room.

Gümbet: Ayaz Hotel, tel.: 1174; 155 beds in seventy rooms, each with balcony and sea view. Many people prefer Gümbet to all the surrounding resorts and this hotel is highly recommended. It is run by a Turkish couple, Hüseyin and Birsen, who take a personal interest in all their guests. It is quiet, good for swimming and wind-surfing, with boat trips from the hotel for only L 8,850, including dinner in one of the coves. It is open all year, with central heating in winter. There is a seaside restaurant and bar; a children's playground; a large, new swimming pool and English-speaking staff.

Where to eat

There are numerous restaurants which you can judge on sight, though you would be advised to avoid those which obviously cater for tourists rather than Turks. There are several good places for fish in the alleys opposite the Hadigari Bar (see Bars, p. 148), such as Number 7. Always ask the price if you are selecting by weight.

Körfez in Neyzen Tevfik Caddesi is noted for its tuna kebabs (*trança şiş*); **Balıkçı**, outside Bodrum at the village of Gümüşlük, for its fresh seafood. **Balık**, Çarşı İçi, Bodrum, tel.: 1454, offers Turkish and French cuisine. **Fora**, Hilmi Uran Meydanı 20, tel.: 2244, beside the sea with a view of the castle, is noted for its *mezes* and friendly service. **Kortan**, at the start of Cumhuriyet Caddesi, is extremely smart and is on the expensive side with grilled prawns at L 4,000 and casserole of octopus at L 3,000. **Burcu**, towards the end of Cumhuriyet Caddesi, is also known as *Bursa Inegöl Köfte* after its speciality of spicy meatballs. The food is good and unpretentious and, though the surroundings are not the height of luxury, it is pleasant to have lunch here beside the sea. **Eylal**, beyond the bridge at the end of the street, is authentically Turkish and reasonably priced. **Meryem Ana**, near the marina, has live Turkish music and dancing.

Bodrum's Chinese Restaurant, easy to find and known to taxis, makes a welcome break from Turkish food and is certainly a good place to take Turkish friends if you wish to reciprocate their hospitality. The food is excellent – I still remember the prawns in garlic – and the atmosphere busy and cheerful. It is very popular, but well worth waiting for if it is full. It is not cheap: my bill for five people came to L 40,600, but we had the works.

147

Torba: **Dalli Motel Restaurant**, tel.: 1668, run by Kemal and Zeki, is just beyond the Holiday Village – an excellent restaurant for enjoying a leisurely lunch in the early afternoon.

Bars   **The Hadigari**, tel.: 2962, is by far the most sympathetic bar, with a continental and artistic atmosphere and pleasant music instead of the usual Mediterranean-disco blare. In the street which connects the two parts of the town, it is easy to find if you ask the way. However, you should be warned that it becomes very noisy and crowded in the summer: even the teenagers object!

The Yacht Club Bar is slightly posh: you may be refused if you don't come up to scratch. Cumhuriyet Caddesi 98, tel.: 2631, it is near the Baraz Hotel and Mylasa Pension and open from 6 p.m. to 2 a.m. It is newly established and the conversion of the building into something resembling a yacht club is first-rate and most attractive. Drinks are club prices: L 1,500 for *rakı*, L 2,500 for imported drinks, and I resented paying extra for my plate of nuts, but it is well worth it for the sophisticated surroundings and the usual, yet always surprising, view.

A Greek bar nearby has live bazouki music at night, with another breathtaking view of the sea over a miniature skyline of bottles above the bar. **The Baraz Hotel**, Cumhuriyet Caddesi 62, also has a bar in its 'wine garden'.

The Jazz Café, near the marina, is highly spoken of. Neyzen Tevfik Caddesi 108, tel.: 1533.

The disco at the **Halikarnas Hotel**, Cumhuriyet Caddesi 128, tel.: 1073, proudly boasts that it is 'the best open-air disco in Turkey'.

Guides   Anyone spending time in Bodrum would find it useful to buy the excellent guide, *Bodrum and Environs*, edited by Russell Anderson, George Simpson and Kim Gould.

The Bodrum   During the day you would be well advised to leave Bodrum to
Peninsula   explore the peninsula by boat or by one of the jeeps or mini-buses that go from the *garaj* or bus depot – they have the names of their destinations written on a card on the windscreen. Because the countryside is mountainous, allow ample time if you are driving independently and take advice from Turks who know the best routes.

Gümbet   Two km on the far side of Bodrum's bay, Gümbet is a very popular resort, good for swimming and wind-surfing though, personally, I find the sea too calm and shallow.

Bitez   In the next bay, Bitez is lively with bars, small hotels and restaurants. To me it has a fresher and more continental atmosphere. One km away there is a new holiday village, a complex of two hundred identical white boxes which would be an eyesore elsewhere, yet almost fit the dark shape of the hill as they cascade to the water. Only a few thousand lira per day for a family of six, they are intended mainly for Turkish families.

Karaincir is another pleasant resort village with restaurants and motels.

Akyarlar   Further around the corner, and the closest point to the Greek island
of Cos only 5 km away, Akyarlar was a Greek summer resort until
Turkey became a republic in 1923. The remains of Greek houses and
an abandoned church can be seen, but this is basically a fishing village
and the modest restaurants serve fresh, local catch. The population is
only 270 so the atmosphere is relaxed.

Turgutreis   Continuing around the peninsula, Turgutreis is named after the
famous Turkish admiral and so-called sea wolf, Turgut Reis, whose
early, sixteenth-century map of the world can be seen in relief outside
the Naval Museum in Istanbul. It is now a town rather than a village.
Boats are available for daily tours if you wish to stay overnight at one
of the thirty pensions and eat at one of the dozen restaurants while you
watch the spectacular colours as the sun sinks behind the islands
opposite. The tables are next to the water and the **Batık Sehir** is
recommended.

Gümüşlük   One of the oldest settlements on the peninsula, 25 km from
Bodrum, this remains unspoilt due to protection as an official archaeological site. The ruins of the original city of Mindos can be seen under
the water nearby.

Driving inland, you can reach the northern coastline of the peninsula, stopping at *Yalıkavak*, a popular harbour for yachtsmen, quiet
with a few restaurants, and *Türkbükü*, spread over the hills, spacious
and relaxed with good swimming, camping and yacht facilities, restaurants and pensions.

So finally back to Torba, at the north-eastern point of the Gulf of
Güllük. Bodrum is only a short distance away, by frequent *dolmuş*
service.

Gulf of   The waters in the Gulf of Gökova are among the purest in the Med-
Gökova: iterranean, which makes it so tragic that a power station is even con-
The Blue   templated on the northern coast, not all that far from Abkuk, which is
Cruise   now a pleasant overnight anchorage with a good restaurant. Meanwhile, I can imagine no finer cruising than to start from Bodrum and
either go north along the peninsula, or explore the Gulf of Gökova
(not to be confused with Kekova further south), sail round the Datça
Peninsula, moor at Marmaris and finish at Fethiye. Once this was a
rare privilege enjoyed only by the adventurous few who blazed the
way; now it is available to everyone. This is largely due to the Turks
who encourage yachtsmen, in contrast to the Greeks who seem to relish putting obstacles in their way. Inevitably, the yachting companies
are shifting to Turkey where they are made so welcome.

The Blue Cruise is enchanted, and it is hard not to describe these
waters without using the clichés of the travel brochure. Admittedly,
any coastline looks much the same from a distance, and you have to
appreciate the sensual sensation of drifting across a sea which changes
constantly with the light. There is the incomparable satisfaction of
waking early in your own caique or *gulet* to swim in the cool, clear

149

water before the sun is up, and eat a hearty breakfast afterwards. Seldom does food taste so good, even if you have blunted your appetite with too much *rakı* the night before – a temptation which is hard to resist when the night slides down the mountains opposite and conversation is enhanced by the intimacy of darkness. But a cooling swim, a bowl of yoghurt and honey, and a cup of bitter Turkish coffee works wonders for a hangover!

You can devote an entire visit to sailing, but I hired a pinewood *gulet*, built in Bodrum's boatyards, for three nights only, leaving it at the ferry stop on the Datça Peninsula. On our second morning we moored in Mersinçik Bay, with a first impression of a curved shore lined with trees. As we drew closer the truth was more extraordinary – a carefully cultivated farm with a grove of olives to one side, stretching towards the towering mountains behind, and orchards on the other with lemon, orange, grapefruit and tangerine. Nearly a hundred beehives were dotted on the slopes beyond. A low wall edged the shore, heightened with brushwood as a windbreak for the trees which proved surprisingly varied: mimosa, fig, pine and tall birch. Behind the trees, I could see fields with corn, potatoes, tomatoes and tall yellow sunflowers, suggesting that the land had been cultivated for centuries. This was confirmed by the ruined outlines of old buildings. The boat's engine needed repairs, a delay which I blessed silently and, as the water around the jetty was too shallow for mooring, we swam ashore.

This place was close to paradise, with a small white house covered with pink roses on the promontory in the middle of the bay, and a look-out which could have been there, in some form or other, for thousands of years. I was welcomed by a weather-beaten man, presumably the owner, whose family was busy watering a magical garden of plants, shrubs and trees, recently planted, which will form a copse one day and provide extra shade. Below us, there was a pink patch of long-established oleander, possibly planted there for the honey-bees and the ubiquitous tamarisk. It was the new garden which was so startling, for it had been planted with considerable imagination and skill: young palms and fine, healthy pines, mimosa in flower and arbutus, the strawberry tree. Hibiscus provided garish splashes of colour, a scarlet morning-glory trailed the ground, while the tiny roses which climbed over the roof of the house indicated that it was protected from the wind though there was a welcome, light breeze at this perfect moment of the morning – ten o'clock. Beside the house, also newly planted though flourishing already, was an Australian bottle-brush which I identified from a visit several years ago to the tropical garden of Tresco in the Scilly Isles.

Plainly this garden was a labour of love and it moved me as I realised that this tough-looking Turkish peasant had gone to so much trouble. As he displayed his garden proudly, stepping precisely on the flag-stones, he plucked white lilies and scarlet geraniums from the flowerbeds, handing them to me until I followed him with a positive posy and might have felt bashful if I had not been in Turkey. Two boys, his son and nephew, clutched similar bouquets and beamed with happiness.

On the edge of the cliff was the look-out. 'Roman,' declared the man and I could see that the ancient slabs of stone had been strengthened with jig-saw lines of modern white cement which formed an arresting pattern, adding to the surprising sophistication of this entire settlement. The door was new and expensive, and though I was not allowed to see inside he led me into a small courtyard covered with a rough rush mat which he lifted up to reveal – a dusty mosaic floor! As he brushed the dirt away, a definite pattern emerged. 'Roman!' he exclaimed again, with satisfaction.

While our handsome young captain, Kemal, swam back to the boat for bottles of wine, the 'farmer' invited me to sit at a trellis table outside the house where I was served tea by the women. Otherwise they stayed in the background, while the children watched me, grinning, still clutching their flowers.

As we struggled to understand each other's language, I gathered that the plants and saplings had been brought across the water from Bodrum (there is no road inland), and I marvelled yet again at this simple man's dedication. Though the mountains behind us started to brood in the heat of mid-morning, water was evidently no problem in this lush oasis. I could hear the clacking of a mill in the middle of the olive grove and caught a glimpse of a shimmering stream. How wise he was to live here! How sensible such dedication in planting his garden.

Later, I learnt that the land is owned by several professors in Istanbul. The 'farmer' is employed only as their caretaker. Even so, one sensed that he was blessed to live in such a place and, what is more, he knew it.

I have written on Mersinçik at length because I discovered it by chance. For me, the place is unique, yet I suspect that you could find your own equivalent along this coast. I should advise you that Mersinçik is private, though I should not be surprised to find a perfect restaurant there before long.

Sailing close to the coastline of the Datça Peninsula provides constant interest, with tempting glimpses of sandy inlets, and the sudden rise of a dozen cormorants and their fall below the surface at your approach. It is possible to sail extremely close to the shore so that you can savour the details.

There are several places to stop at, such as *İngiliz Limanı*, the English Harbour, an anchorage so invisible from the sea that it hid British torpedo boats in the last war. Cleopatra's Island is famous for the fine white sand in the small bay, allegedly brought especially from North Africa for her meeting with Mark Antony. I find this an absurd claim, considering the number of galleys that would be needed to transport such a quantity, and even though this is a tideless sea, it is remarkable that such sand should remain here for two thousand years! It makes no sense, yet people swear that it is true, and scientific tests have proved that no such sand is found anywhere else along this Turkish coastline, yet it is known in North Africa. Certainly, it makes for an excellent swim. I would have found the island more romantic if I had not sailed there on a small boat on a dull day from the mainland of Cedir, half an hour's drive from Marmaris, and if I had not been alone. Otherwise, I can imagine that this would be an ideal place to moor your boat and go ashore for a picnic (there is no restaurant) with ample time to search for the ruined castle of Kedreai in the undergrowth. As for Cleopatra, as a Turkish cynic remarked to me: 'If she went everywhere that's claimed, she must have used a speedboat!'

However, my own cynicism is fading as I learn of the astonishing speeds of the Greek galleys which sped across the Aegean at a pace almost equal to the ferries of today. If they could race from Piraeus to Lesbos with a last-minute reprieve for political prisoners, and arrive shortly before their intended execution twenty-four hours later, it is not impossible that the monumental vanity of an omnipotent Egyptian queen should not have been fulfilled in this extraordinary way. Anyhow, the notion of her personal sandy beach makes a good story.

If you decide on a short voyage it could cost you as much as L 146,500 for each day and night on board which sounds exorbitant until you realise that you only pay a quarter of this if there are four of you. This was the price in May but of course it rises in the peak season. Food is extra, to be arranged with the captain's crew. Dursun Mutlu will prove invaluable if you wish to make your own arrangements (see p. 146). Though his own magnificent vessel *The Maya* (named after his daughter) has now been bought by a publishing tycoon in Istanbul, Dursun will know who to contact.

Many tours offer first-rate Blue Cruises to suit every taste and pocket.

Turquoise Holidays offer seven nights with an extra week's stay in Bodrum; depending on your numbers, you can hire a boat of your own or join a group.

Small World can provide an eleven-day cruise from approximately £329 (L 485,250) each, or one week on land and one week's cruise from £279 (L 411,500). Their UK address is the same as that for the Yacht Cruising Association (see p. 154) and their telephone number 0342 27272.

Motif & Yesil Marmaris, the foremost charter company in Marmaris, offers complete voyages with your own group or you can join one of their regular tours. Week-long programmes go from Bodrum to Mersinçik, the English Harbour, Cleopatra's Island, Söğüt, Oraklar and back to Bodrum. Alternative programmes are

Marmaris to Fethiye and back, and round the Datça Peninsula, including Cnidus. There are daily diving tours and courses for beginners. The boats and prices vary drastically, and of course they are highest in August. They start at L 180,000 a day, rising to over L 1,350,000 and these prices are subject to 12 per cent VAT and do not always include meals. This seems a very great deal to pay, but in the case of the Kuğu in the cheaper range, there is accommodation for eight people in four double-bed cabins, a crew of three, a saloon, kitchen, two showers, tender and windsurfer. So it isn't quite so bad for two families.

The best time of the year for sailing is May and June, or September when the water is warmest, and October. July and August are insufferably hot, in spite of the afternoon wind (*meltemi*) coming from the north-west, which can be a mixed blessing in unfamiliar waters. Otherwise, the heat is unpleasant, even at sea, unless you are unusually resistant.

Addresses Yacht Marina at Bodrum, tel.: 1860/1/2. Harbourmaster's office: VHF Channel 11/12/16.

Motif & Yesil Marmaris (Bodrum office), Neyzen Tevfik Caddesi 72, (near Marina), tel.: 2309, 1328.

Sunmed Holidays, 4–6 Manor Mount, London SE23 3PZ, tel.: 01-291 5000; 699 7666.

Admiral Tours, Hilmi Ncbioğlu, Neyzen Tevfik Caddesi 68, Bodrum, tel.: 1781.

Turquoise Holidays, 9 Maddox Street, London W1R 9LE, tel.: 01-491 2448.

YCA The Yacht Cruising Association is unequalled for bareboat sailing on your own. Now in its tenth year, it pioneered flotilla sailing under the skilful direction of Eric Richardson who plainly knows and loves the Lycian coast. The yachts are from thirty to forty-five feet long, many built especially at Eastbourne and transported overland to Brindisi where they sail to join their separate fleets. They prove surprisingly roomy and comfortable, even for three YCA crew and my own ample self when I joined the pilot boat from Marmaris and sailed to Ekincik where the flotilla assembled for a beach barbecue and obligatory sing-song.

Expanding over the years, their well-illustrated brochure lists a wide range of cruises down the coast to choose from – Bodrum to Marmaris; Fethiye to Datça; Marmaris to Kaş. A typical voyage starts on Wednesday at Fethiye, a one-and-a-half hour coach drive from Dalaman Airport to the town where you are welcomed by the staff, shown your yacht, and get to know the other sailors over dinner at a restaurant. On Thursday morning you can shop for provisions and sail for glorious Göcek Bay, exploring these islands over the next couple of days. On Sunday to Ekincik; Monday to the Dalyan Delta; Tuesday to Marmaris. By the following Tuesday you reach Datça, flying back from Dalaman (a three-and-a-half hour coach drive) on the Wednesday, after a fortnight's sailing. Conversely, you can start from Datça and do it the other way round. The new cruise to Kaş takes you through the astonishing waters of Kekova.

Only a limited knowledge of sailing is necessary (you can have a weekend course at Hamble beforehand) and the pilot boat is at hand to help those in need of assistance. Far from the regimented crocodile of boats which you might fear, you can sail for several days independently and only join the others on shore if you feel sociable. All types and ages seem to enjoy it and many friendships are made. The prices are fair, depending on the type of boat, cruise and time of year: ranging from £425 in May to £700 in August, which includes the return flight from London. It is excellent value. You are advised to ask for a brochure if you wish to make your choice from the cruises offered.

Yacht Cruising Association, Old Stone House, Judge's Terrace, Ship Street, East Grinstead, Sussex RH19 1AQ, tel.: 0342 311366/7/8.

Datça

The Datça Peninsula is one of the lesser-known parts of Turkey. It is sufficiently developed to make it possible to drive to the ruins of Cnidus at the end, where the Aegean meets the Mediterranean, yet still off the tourist track so that many of the villages you pass through remain as innocent as they were a hundred years ago.

Datça itself used to be a simple fishing village, rarely visited because it involved a special detour away from the main coast, unless you did so by boat. When I went there first, around ten years ago, there was the modern Dorya Hotel and a couple of decent restaurants, but also some horrible rooms where neither the linen nor the bugs had been changed since the previous occupant. One made me so squeamish that I moved out.

Today, Datça is rapidly becoming a popular resort due to the yachts that call there, and especially the YCA who use the harbour as a starting and finishing point for their flotillas (see previous page).

The little town has considerable charm with a cosmopolitan atmosphere due to the yachts which is probably closer to St Tropez before it was discovered than the inevitable comparisons with Bodrum and Marmaris. Yet it remains so free from the invasion of package tours that several guide books do not even mention it. The setting is superb and a gentle walk or short drive will take you somewhere pleasant to swim, apart from the open mineral pool where I advise you not to swim underwater with your eyes open because the sulphur from the springs will make them smart.

How to get there

To reach Datça you take the main road from Marmaris, a sensationally beautiful drive of under two hours (see p. 158), or the evening car-ferry from Bodrum. This leaves at 5 p.m., takes two and a half hours, and costs L 17,000 for the car and driver, with L 3,000 for each additional person. It arrives on the other side of the peninsula at Körmen with a twenty-minute drive across to Datça on the southern side. There are regular buses, straight to Izmir (a long six-hour journey) and to Dalaman Airport, a distance of 170 km.

Shopping As you enter the town, you will see the bank and post office on the right-hand side, then the bus depot, with the Tourist Bureau nearly opposite, and if you walk down the hill towards the Dorya Hotel on the point you pass several upstairs restaurants overlooking the sea. These are sympathetic, with covered terraces for food, and a string of bars along the quayside below. Because of the number of foreign yachts, these bars can be lively. There are two marinas: Kormen, tel.: 1149, on the northern side at the ferry-stage, and Datça Marina, tel.: 1013.

Though I have heard them described as 'indifferent', I have found the antique shops exceptional, with a wide range of above-average jewellery at reasonable prices, such as silver bracelets. Though persistent in his determination to offer you tea or coffee, M. Sait Kaya at the Anatolia, tel.: 1454, has an interesting selection of old carpets, *kilims* and silver, and is so friendly and trusting that it is almost alarming.

Where to Just before the Dorya Hotel on the point, there is a simple and
stay reasonably priced pension on the left-hand side, slightly inset before the gardens. I found this perfectly adequate myself, though my companion objected to mosquito bites and we moved to the Dorya.

Dorya Hotel, İskele Mahallesi, tel.: 3536; thirty-two rooms. This is in a superb position on the edge of the point, surrounded by beautifully kept gardens with pleasant if not exactly elegant separate blocks of rooms. Because of the slight breeze, this has the advantage of no mosquitoes. You can sunbathe on a terrace beside the sea, but you swim from a ladder and beware of spiky, black sea-urchins. It is a wonderfully restful place to relax in if you have been travelling hard, with a pleasant outside dining-room for breakfast or a light lunch. Yet, on my last two visits, there was an odd atmosphere as if the staff were waiting for a new manager to arrive and spring the place to life. This should have happened by 1988. It is expensive, but only by Turkish standards. A double room for two people, including breakfast, costs around L 25,000.

Club Datça Tatil Köyü, İskele Mahallesi, tel.: 1170; 108 rooms in bungalows; pool and beach. This is a Holiday Village: pool, disco, sauna, tennis courts, water sports and jetty. All rooms have a shower and toilet, and half-board is available.

Fuda Yalı Hotel, İskele Mahallesi, tel.: 1042, has only fourteen rooms but is awarded one star by the official guide to hotels.

Mare Hotel, İskele Mahallesi, tel.: 1211, with fifty rooms, surprisingly has three stars in the same guide, but I have no personal experience of it.

Where to **The Akdeniz** (meaning Mediterranean) overlooks the harbour.
eat The young owner is Doğan Ömer Yalçınkaya, and I urge you to seek

155

him out. Formerly the manager of both the Datça Kitchen (a snack bar, and very good too) and the Sandal Restaurant, he has just opened the Akdeniz. He is ambitious and enthusiastic, speaks English and will arrange for you to have the specialities you want. He is a superb cook himself with a natural instinct for good food and a happy atmosphere. Tel.: 1392.

Kargi   If you wish to avoid the bright lights on your arrival at the Datça Peninsula, and are travelling independently by car, you might enjoy continuing directly to the small bay of Kargi on a road which soon resembles a dirt track and finally gives up altogether. After parking, you walk along a pebble beach to the two pensions in the bay, one with the use of kitchen facilities, the other with a restaurant – both clean and simple. The rooms in the latter are more colourful and individual, costing L 4,000 for the room with a simple supper for L 3,800. The other pension costs L 1,500 per bed.

In contrast to the cosmopolitan atmosphere of Datça, the restaurant looks over the water into blackness, unless there is a moon, and the peace is wonderful. In the morning, as you collect your car, you may be confronted by a line of goats coming to drink at the stream before it enters the sea.

Cnidus   Apart from the attraction of Datça, the reward of travelling here lies in the continuation to Cnidus (Knidos). This is one of the magical spots in Turkey, for the atmosphere and the setting, with its stupendous cliffs nearby, as much as for the extravagant extent of the ruins. These have been allowed to decay, but the remains indicate the importance of this huge city which was founded in 400 BC and served as a natural refuge for sailors at the crucial point where the Aegean flows into the Mediterranean Sea. That was the only way to reach Cnidus, yet the population has been estimated as high as 70,000 at its peak as the headquarters of the Greek Dorian Hexapolis. If it was half this, or even a quarter, such a figure is astonishing when you consider that it would be more than the entire population of the Datça Peninsula today. It reminds ignorant visitors like myself that this was one of the busiest waterways in the world, explaining the chain of ports along the coastline, for ships bound for Rhodes, Crete and Egypt, ports like Ephesus and Priene, where the sea has long since receded; Halicarnassus and Cnidus; Caunus; Patara; Phaselis and Side. And there were many more than these.

Getting there   Today, Cnidus is still reached most easily by sea, either by motorboat from Bodrum or Gümbet, or a day-trip from Datça with the chance of lunch on board or at one of the simple *lokantas* at the landing stage. Better still, make a deal with a local fisherman, and sail at dawn to catch the magic of Cnidus at sunrise before the others descend.

If you are sailing independently, try to judge the time of your arrival, for it makes all the difference if your first impression is that of the clean early morning light or that romantic moment in the evening as

156

the sun starts to fall. To moor overnight and see the ruins by moonlight would be incomparable, but it would be wise to clear this beforehand with the authorities, such as the Datça marinas. The distance from Datça by sea is 38 km. By road it is 34 km along a rough road but the countryside is unspoilt, the villages unchanged, and the final approach exhilarating.

History   It helps to learn as much as you can about such a place before you go there, even to braving the British Museum to see the splendid lion which graced the top of a nearby mausoleum and was looted by Sir Charles Newton in 1857 along with the seated figure of the goddess Demeter. Is such pillage justified? This is a vexed topic with reason on both sides, but there is no denying that the lion in London looks forlorn in its captivity, with a dark surface and deep sockets which suggest that the animal saw and still sees the grandeur of those early times. But the experts at the British Museum assure me that the tomb was in ruins when Newton landed and there was considerable difficulty in hauling the lion down the cliff, so it is probable that he saved this fine antiquity for posterity, preventing its eventual collapse into the sea. Even so, with all the miracles – and horrors – of modern materials like plastic and polystyrene which seldom disintegrate, surely a cast could be made of such treasures in order to resurrect them in their original settings. How gratifying it would be to see this lion in its original position, waiting to greet you on your approach.

Statuary was a feature of Cnidus, the birthplace of Eudoxus who designed the first observatory, and Sostratos who built the lighthouse at Alexandria, one of the Seven Wonders of the Ancient World. Above all, Cnidus was famous for the statue of Aphrodite by Praxiteles. Built in 360 BC, it was based on his mistress, Phyrne, an Athenian courtesan who was famous for her beauty and her daring in showing her breasts to the judges in a court case, though why she felt this gesture was necessary I do not know. Originally the figure was commissioned by his patrons on Cos, but they were so shocked by her nudity that he made them another, discreetly draped. The first was bought by the Cnidians who had no such scruples, and how wise they were. The controversial statue became an early tourist attraction with mariners entering the harbour especially to see it. Not only sexy but superb – Pliny called it the finest statue in the world – the figure was displayed in a temple and was so realistic, especially from behind, that it was locked up for safety at night. One love-struck admirer locked himself in as well, embracing her so passionately that her marble thighs were stained forever afterwards. That was the legend: nothing was left to prove its existence until the excavation by the American Dr Iris Love, which revealed the circular foundations of the temple and a block of marble nearby with the initials PRA and APH. Further proof was provided by coins with the statue on one side and the sculptor on the other; indeed, Dr Love claims that a marble head which she discovered in the vaults of the British Museum is that of the statue itself, but this is denied by the Museum's experts though their ruling is open to argument.

Nowadays it is the lie of the land at Cnidus and the extent of the ruins, especially the massive theatre, which remain to impress. Even these do so gradually, as you start to absorb what they represent: a city contained within a circular wall, built on an innovative system of parallel lines, like a grid-iron of streets and houses, with a causeway joining the island opposite (a perfect site for the resurrected lion) creating two harbours which can be seen today – one for commerce, the other naval and military – both now unuseable because of silt.

Cnidus has been stolen from over the years – some of the marble was taken for the Dolmabahçe Palace in Istanbul – yet pieces of ceramics can still be found as you walk around the ruins today (you would be prevented if you tried to take them away, and it would be ungrateful to do so). Cnidus needs restoration and the removal of the plastic flotsam which disfigures the shore. But the place should not be prettified nor made too available for tourists with such 'facilities' as souvenir shops. At present the two primitive *lokantas* with their signs advertising lobster, and the small army garrison, confirm how unspoilt this former centre of Greek civilisation remains, and it would be a shame to corrupt such innocence.

The road to Marmaris

The road from Datça to Marmaris is spectacular with steep bends and turns, but the surface is good and the journey takes less than two hours. About three-quarters of the way, you need to turn right if you wish to continue to Bozburun at the end of a lower peninsula which hangs like a claw. After leaving the pine forests you enter a fierce landscape where hillsides resemble an avalanche of stones with rare patches of soil ploughed by cows instead of the usual oxen. The road soon becomes terrible, though you are rewarded by the pleasing villages you pass through: **Orhaniye**, perched on a tranquil bay; **Söğüt**, noted for its almonds; and **Bayir**, famous for honey.

At one point the road peters out altogether in the rainier months and I found it necessary to walk down the hill to **Selimiye** which is so isolated that the postal service is a matter of chance, depending on someone's visit to **Bozburun**. When the villagers leave they go by boat to **Cubucak** on the main peninsula and take a bus from there into Marmaris.

This remoteness is a welcome rarity but already foreigners are putting up grander houses on the hill. Meanwhile, the peace can be almost eerie as men play interminable backgammon in a room near the water which sells no food but did produce a bottle of beer, while the women struggle barefoot down the hill, bent double under the weight of bundles of firewood. Understandably, they look disenchanted, though the young men and women are strikingly handsome. Selimiye reminded me of a waterfront village on the Volga visited by my father and a friend when they travelled south to climb the Caucasus. 'Nothing', declared the friend emphatically, as he looked at the empty street suffocating in the oppressive heat of the afternoon, 'could make life bearable in such a place, except for sheer, unmitigated vice!' I doubt if vice exists in Selimiye, but one seldom knows. It was late in November, a bright day with a chill in the midday air, and this might have added to my sense of limbo. Yet on a glorious day in summer this could be one of the most enchanted places on earth.

Around the corner, bustling by comparison, is **Bozburun**, famous for its boatyard and one of the destinations for the flotillas of the YCA. There is a pleasing 'wild west' atmosphere, and the minaret which dominates the town has a bright blue point, but the quayside is strewn with abandoned machinery, concrete-mixers and iron bars, while dredgers extend the harbour raucously with giant boulders. The range of mountains behind enclose the village, making it airless even in late November and I imagine that it must be overwhelmingly hot in summer. It has a certain jauntiness, and the Liman restaurant prepared a special lamb sauté for me in minutes which proved delicious. But I cannot really recommend a detour by road unless you have ample time to spare and wish to explore this lesser-known part of the Datça Peninsula.

Marmaris Marmaris, 100 km from Dalaman Airport and served by hourly buses to Izmir, is one of the brightest, liveliest resorts along the coast. Some people prefer it to Bodrum, but though these two leading resorts share sophistication, they have different personalities. Not so pretty as Bodrum with its low whitewashed houses covered in purple bougainvillea, Marmaris is more of an active town. A long, curved waterfront ends with a cheerful quayside lined with restaurants on one side and yachts on the other, with the YCA flotillas moored around the corner.

The long stretch of beach is more shingle than sand, and the water none too encouraging for me, but this does not deter holiday-makers from basking there happily. Indeed, Marmaris has an atmosphere which induces happiness.

The military camp on the opposite side of Bodrum's bay is laid out so discreetly that the white villa-like blocks are inoffensive; equal care has been taken with the large Turban Holiday Village in Marmaris, skilfully designed among the existing trees so that it is invisible as you sail in, apart from the plinth which marks an open-air disco at night. This arrival as you approach the town has the surprising appearance and exhilaration of a pine-clad Norwegian or New Zealand fjord.

History Once the ancient port of Physkus, the town dates back to 3400 BC when it was another Carian town like Halicarnassus though further south on the borders of Lycia, before it was Hellenised by the Dorians. Then there was the usual musical-chairs sequence with the succession of Roman, Byzantine, Seljuk and Ottoman occupiers. Its situation, so

159

close to Rhodes, was strategic. Alexander attacked in 334 BC, when the people virtually destroyed their town rather than surrender; and Süleyman used the port as an obvious base for his invasion of Rhodes in 1522. Nelson anchored his fleet here in 1798.

Shaken by an earthquake in 1958, the ancient town has little remaining apart from the small sixteenth-century Ottoman fortress on the hill behind the quayside. Due to tourism over the last ten years, Marmaris has now exploded out of all recognition. The Tourist Bureau is at Iskele Meydanı 39, tel.: 1035, situated conveniently between the beach and the quayside, just a few metres from the jetty which houses the immigration and customs.

What to do   Marmaris Bay affords sailors the protection of more than 50 square km of sheltered yachting, with numerous coves and island anchorages. The town is the natural destination where the crew can tie up and go ashore to join the evening promenade and watch that romantic moment when the sun goes down and the crescent moon comes up in imitation of the Turkish flags fluttering from the tops of the masts, with the hills beyond silhouetted against the blue-black sky. Whereas in Bodrum many of the best bars are inside, here they are part of the open-air restaurants, apart from Akvaryum on the corner where you can sit at a genuine bar as well as the outside tables and chairs, or The Daily News behind the Tourist Bureau. Surprisingly, bars are not yet a feature of Marmaris, but that will change - for better or for tourist worse - when the marina is finished in 1988 or 1989. It promises to be the largest in Turkey.

This reflects the remarkable success of Yeşil Marmaris, run by Doğan Tugay and his brother, next to the Kaptan Hotel on the quay which is managed by their courteous, considerate father. Doğan Tugay is the driving force in Marmaris, especially when he joined up with Jim and Jillian Anderson, from Australia and New Zealand, who arrived in Marmaris in 1980 on their yacht *Moana Vahine* which they had sailed across the Indian Ocean and the Red Sea. They moved to Turkey from Greece after a new law forbade foreign yachts from chartering between the islands. Since then their luxurious yacht has been available for charter along the Turkish coast and the three have been instrumental in forming the Aegean and Turkish Coast Yacht Charter Group which negotiates with charter agencies throughout the world, many of whom arrive here for the annual yacht festival in May. Numerous foreign yachts now operate under the group's licence, which has the advantage of guaranteeing safety standards.

Motif and Yeşil Marmaris and the Charter Group operate from:
Marmaris: Barbaros Caddesi 11, tel.: (6121) 2290/91; telex: 52528 GEMA TR; VHF Channel 06, callsign Albatross.
Bodrum: Neyzen Tevfik Caddesi 72, tel.: (6141) 2309; telex 52979 MGTS TR; VHF Channel 06, callsign Albatross.
Istanbul: Yerebatan Caddesi, Salkim Söğüt Sokak 20/6, Cağaloğlu,

tel.: (1) 528.55.10.

The headquarters are in Marmaris and Doğan Tugay knows everything that is going on (he has retreated to an inner office, which recedes further into the rocks, as people clamour for his attention). Jillian Anderson is there as well. Yeşil Marmaris will assist you in providing the type of cruise you want from the wide range of craft at their disposal: bareback, crewed, simple and luxurious. Doğan Tugay also controls the main ferry to Rhodes, though several rival agencies have sprung up recently and are easy to find near the Tourist Bureau and further along the waterfront.

Sailing to Rhodes is an easy trip, little more than a couple of hours on the faster boats, but you are advised to book the day before as your passport may be needed. I can think of nicer Greek islands to go to than Rhodes, but at this point you have to go via Rhodes even if you wish to visit the delightful island of Symi which lies close to the two pincer-like claws of the Datça Peninsula.

If you sail the other way round, be careful not to stay overnight in Marmaris if you are returning home on a charter flight from Rhodes, for the Greeks may make you pay the full scheduled fare as a punishment. The Turks could not care less how long you stay away, but the Greeks are so edgy that a man spreads out a mat soaked in detergent as you alight on Rhodes to prevent you bringing in one speck of Turkish soil. To make this precaution even more preposterous, the Greek gives you a helping hand as you step ashore and a golden, welcoming smile. To go to Rhodes for the day, tour the castle and enjoy a Greek meal, and then return to Marmaris would be enjoyable. Otherwise, try to aim for Cos from Bodrum; Samos from Kuşadası (continue to Pythagorio from the main port); or the ghost island of Castellorizon from Kaş.

As with Bodrum, you are advised to leave the bustle of Marmaris during the day and explore the many places in easy range, preferably by boat (though you can go by car). These are signposted with their destinations along the waterfront: most boats leave at 10 a.m. Places to look for are: Turunc, comparatively quiet with good restaurants; İçmeler Bay, 10 km across with thermal springs; Ceder or Sidere, Cleopatra's Island, reached by taking a bus to the Gulf of Gökova, and then by small boat – about an hour's journey in all.

The Martı Hotel has a private beach and jetty, open to the public if you are using any of their facilities. But seek advice from an agency and, above all, study the maps beside the individual ferries and small fishing boats which show exactly where you will be taken.

Shopping   Marmaris is one of the best centres for shopping, especially for those who come ashore from their yachts, which explains why the prices are not cheap. Leather jackets, silver and black pine honey are recommended. *Kilims* are displayed everywhere, but if you are determined, visit the Halıcı Antique Carpet Gallery, tel.: 1783, off the shopping streets, which is owned by the man who runs the Halıcı, hence the profusion in his hotel.

Where to
stay

Hotel Halıcı, Çam Sokak 1, tel.: 1683; 128 rooms; situated just behind the waterfront near the bus stop. Surrounded by gardens and eucalyptus trees, furnished inside in traditional Turkish style with a profusion of excellent *kilims*, this is one of the airiest and most attractive hotels along the coast. The quiet compensates for the lack of a sea view while the pool is hardly Olympic size but agreeable for a gentle dip and relaxing sunbathe, with waiter service and an American bar nearby. Of course this hotel is used by tourists, but as it is especially popular with Finns the atmosphere is far from formal. In spite of its professionalism and comfort, the Halıcı is reasonably priced from L 12,500 for a single room, and L 18,000 for a double, including breakfast.

Halıcı II is 3 km out of town. A new building with a pool, it is also decorated with *kilims* but does not have as much charm as the original, though it is very pleasant. Prices are from L 24,000.

The Kaptan, on the quayside next to Yeşil Marmaris, is unmistakable. In complete contrast to the Halıcı, this is a simple, no-nonsense hotel with stunning views of the activity on the quayside and the bay beyond from rooms at the front with balconies. Rooms at the back have the advantage of peace and quiet, for the quayside is noisy, especially at a grisly hour around 5 a.m. when the garbage trucks grate, grind, and galumph around interminably. Even so, the Kaptan is inexpensive and there is always plenty to see and do.

Hotel Lidya, Sitler Mahallesi 130, tel.: 2940; 220 rooms. This has all the advantages and disadvantages of a big hotel: a casino with fruit machines; open-air restaurant; good for conferences. You need to assert yourself in such places against world-weary staff, for they are invariably full up.

Hotel 47, Atatürk Caddesi 10, tel.: 1700; fifty-one rooms. A fairly indifferent staff must be persevered with here as well. However, the place itself is new and nicely furnished, the rooms have double beds and some have balconies; there is a restaurant. Prices are from L 30,000 for a double, including breakfast.

You could also try the **Karaca Hotel** in the centre of Marmaris (all rooms with shower); **Atlantik Hotel**, Atatürk Caddesi 11, tel.: 1218; forty-two rooms, on the waterfront; and **Marmaris Hotel**, Atatürk Caddesi 30, tel.: 1308; sixty-three rooms. You will find numerous hotels along the waterfront (more than Bodrum) starting from the Tourist Bureau with Kalyon, only L 7,000 for two, with hot shower, above the restaurant on the next corner: recommended both for the food and accommodation.

Where to
eat

There are numerous restaurants to choose from along the quay, displaying their specialities, so you go where your taste-buds lead you. I have a longstanding favourite – the **Birtat** (half-way along) which I return to for sentiment's sake, but it is expensive. In fact, none of the restaurants is cheap though they may vary slightly in price, and at least the Birtat is reliably excellent, with good *biftek* (steak).

Walking along the waterfront towards the bus-agencies, the **Liman** is a smaller, indoor restaurant, with a no-nonsense atmosphere, and more Turkish. The food is first-rate, though there is less atmosphere.

Best of all if you want genuine atmosphere, and good food at reasonable prices, are the restaurants at the top of the shopping streets which lead from the Tourist Bureau: turn left at the square with the mosque and fountain, and you will see them on either side. Again, as the food is visible, you should trust your own instinct.

A meal in a back-street restaurant like **Hasanın Yeri** can cost as little as L 2,500 per person.

Also recommended are **The Steak House** and **Süleyman's** opposite, in the same location and **The Moustache**, near the Holiday Village, for genuine Turkish food.

Where to stay outside Marmaris

İçmeler: The Martı Tatil Köyü, İçmeler Köyü, tel.: 4910; 280 rooms. This hotel complex with sauna is served by a regular *dolmuş* from Marmaris. Built like a Swiss chalet with a garden running down to a beach and jetty, it is slightly pretentious but good and professional. It is on the expensive side and food is not too brilliant, though it is better at the open snack-bar near the beach. There is water-skiing, windsurfing and sailing.

Efendi Hotel, İçmeler Köyü, tel.: 1057; twenty-six rooms; an attractive new hotel, close to the beach. The front rooms have wooden balconies and it looks good.

Marbas Hotel, İçmeler Köyü, tel.: 2904; seventy rooms; luxurious and recommended.

Turunc: Mavideniz Hotel, Turunc Köyü, tel.: 1421; twenty-four rooms.

İffet Hotel, new, directly on the beach, has twenty-one rooms with private showers and balconies and two restaurants.

Pension Dli Gocek, ten minutes from the beach in farmland, with ten rooms: you breakfast at the nearby Yacht Club.

Villa Gül, family-owned on the beach, with nine rooms, all with balconies, shared toilets and showers. Kitchens are basic and self-catering, but you are close to a market and baker's. It is good for those on a low budget.

Floating Hotel, a modern Japanese monstrosity with 250 rooms anchored at Keci Island. The twenty-minute boat trip to town is free. There are water sports, and the air-conditioned rooms with showers may compensate for the ghastly construction, but I doubt it.

YCA Clubhouse, very attractive low, modern building on the water's edge near Nimada Island.

Turban Holiday Village, Tatil Köyü, tel.: 1843; 246 rooms, mainly in separate chalets. This is one of the best holiday villages in Turkey, in an attractive setting and suitable for families with children who can enjoy the various facilities and water-sports, swimming and sunbathing on a beach backed with pink oleander and pine trees. It is within easy reach of the town, though you may miss the evening promenade which is the jolliest moment of the day along the quayside. Prices vary greatly depending on the season and type of bungalow; they go from L 50,200 for two people.

Remember that as you go inland from the waterfront, the cheaper everything becomes, including the food.

Marmaris to Xanthos

In this part of Turkey you should be advised that buses do not always go directly to your destination, though there are greater opportunities in the peak of the season. There are plans for a big new motorway which will cut through from Marmaris to Ortaca (the main bus depot before Fethiye) but meanwhile the buses from Marmaris go north to Muğla (the civic centre for this area, which should be included in every address, e.g. Datça, Muğla, Turkey). You change buses there and return to the main road from the north to travel south again to Fethiye. Obviously, you want to avoid this detour if possible. If you are on your own, get out at the end of the Eucalyptus Avenue in Marmaris (there's no mistaking that) and hitch a lift, if you are that sort of person. I did so in a small van which carried vegetables and though it bumped along like an ill-tempered tortoise, it made a welcome change. The Özel İdare restaurant near the crossroads has been recommended.

If you are driving independently, the worst of the roads are immediately out of Marmaris where the outskirts are little more than rubble due to some internal mayoral feud which should be corrected at once. Otherwise, the roads are fine.

There's a nice story regarding that magnificent avenue of eucalyptus trees planted nearly a hundred years ago. They have grown so dense that it has become difficult for modern traffic to squeeze past, and the order went out for the trees to be felled. When the young workmen turned up on the appointed day, they downed tools and refused to continue, protesting that their grandfathers and fathers had planted the trees. Surprised by such sentiment, the authorities yielded and on my last visit in 1987 I saw a new detour being constructed to relieve the traffic. The trees remain. Whenever I see that avenue I feel better, for I know of no other tree which conveys the Mediterranean so graciously. And it is typically Turkish that the men should have felt so passionately towards a tree.

Köyceğiz An hour out of Marmaris you turn right to Köyceğiz, a large lake with a small town that share the same name, which has yet to find a personality though it is starting to do so. If you go there, make a point of seeing the white marble lion, its paw resting proudly on a bull's head, which was dredged from the water below Caunus – proof of the wealth that may still be there. This particular lion (they come in many shapes and sizes throughout Turkey) has a marvellous expression of indignant, almost bashful pride.

From here, you continue through farmland and cotton fields to the village of Dalyan.

Dalyan The Dalyan Delta is one of the rarest parts of Turkey, though changing all too rapidly. If there was a moment when I fell in love with Turkey, it was here, so much so that I tried to buy a piece of land on the Dalyan River below the Lycian tombs and nearly succeeded. Since then the area has developed so drastically that I wonder if I should feel for the place in the same way if I lived there today.

Then it was a small riverside village with an excellent restaurant called the **Denizatı**, right on the edge of the water. The Denizatı continues, recently extended, and the friendly former waiter, the beaming İsmet Keser, runs the Piknik bakery under the shadow of a hideous, disproportionate new post office. If you want a fresh Turkish *pide* and a cool refreshing beer from a clean machine, pause at the Piknik.

There are more restaurants now, a new hotel, and the former head of tourism at Muğla, Çemil Zov, has a carpet shop, the Galeri Nakiş, but Dalyan can absorb all this – such expansion is profitable and keeps everyone happy. Also, the simple charm remains: muddy side streets with roses tumbling over walls, fig trees leaning over streams, children hand-in-hand carrying freshly baked loaves, a peasant woman leading a cow, patches of uncultivated land overgrown with weeds and dotted with yellow irises. Happily unplanned and still blissfully ramshackle, there is a satisfying reassurance in strolling through the village of Dalyan.

The danger lies in what is happening further down the delta. To sail the several miles on one of Abidin Kurt's small caiques was a joyful experience, climbing to the ruined city of Caunus on the right, passing through the barriers of the fishery which gives Dalyan its name and controls the grey mullet which features on the Denizatı's menu.

I have travelled through the Danube Delta and caught exciting glimpses of small settlements whenever the tall reeds allowed. In the Dalyan Delta, however, it is possible to absorb the whole invigorating landscape with the cotton fields behind the village and the line of hills in the distance. Travelling at a gentle pace, it is possible to appreciate the wildlife scurrying into the reeds whose roots can be seen below the water, white flashes of ibis, terrapins and an occasional turtle in April when they come upriver. Best of all is the thrill as you approach the sea and see the extraordinary sandbar which stretches for 5 km and is little more than 150 m wide at the northern point where the brackish waters of the delta meet the sea. This narrow entrance is deceptive. With treacherous undercurrents and sinking sands, people have drowned as they swim across to the tempting sandy beach opposite. If you wish to attempt it, wade into the shallow sea and swim from further up. The entrance itself is dangerous, yet so shallow that the YCA flotillas moor at Ekincik where Abidin Kurt collects the passengers in the early morning and transfers them to flat-bottomed caiques, or his big new boat which has been known to stick halfway, adding to the general excitement. Then he ferries them up the delta, stops at Caunus where he or one of his assistants will explain the ruins of the ancient city. Then he continues to Lake Köyceğiz where the yachtsmen dunk themselves in the muggy sulphur water of a covered thermal spring, alleged to cure every illness under the sun including pregnancy, and freshen up with a livelier swim in the freshwater lake afterwards. This is usually followed by a late lunch at the Denizatı and a look at the shops in Dalyan. After this welcome break from their routine at sea, I have seen the mariners snooze happily on their journey back down to the delta, through the channel to their yachts in Ekincik. A number of YCA members who have made this excursion have told me that it was the highlight of their holiday.

For me it is the sandbar which remains unforgettable, due to the strange shanty settlement of wooden huts there which looked as if they were collapsing into the sand, as many were. Unrecognisable, until you were upon them, were two restaurants on stilts. You climbed up some steps to a wooden platform enclosed by a railing and roof but otherwise open to the elements. To eat there at night, while a flickering television set relayed an American gangster series beamed across from Rhodes, was delightfully bizarre.

Abidin Kurt owned a couple of these huts and I stayed there occasionally for we became close friends – partly, I suspect, because he knew that I shared his admiration for this land (his home is at Çandır beyond Caunus) of which he is justly proud. Then the government ordered a clean-up: the huts had to be painted the same colour, a chocolate brown, and smartened up generally, including the outside boxes on the sand which served as lavatories. Perhaps this was a wise move. At least, it led to a third restaurant which opened in the summer, run by restaurateurs from Istanbul, which was slightly more luxurious though it looked much the same apart from the elegant, high-backed chairs. The wind still whistled through. Also, there were several small chalets which actually contained beds and inside lavatories – an incredible luxury compared to the primitive settlement before. I stayed there in 1986, for roughly L 3,000 a night, ate at the restaurants in turn, and thought this was the height of chic. Then it all went wrong.

In 1987, a new decree ordered that every hut should be dismantled, with the owners paying for the cost – the ultimate insult to injury. This means that you cannot sleep there today, nor eat, nor change and wash after swimming. I am hopeful that such advantages will return, yet fear that if they do it will not be on such a simple scale. For all this has been done in the mistaken name of progress, with the tourist development of a big hotel at the southern end of the bar, built with German investment. Presumably, the shanty settlement was not considered smart enough and had to be sacrificed yet, in a paradoxical way, those shanty huts made that sandbar exciting.

Tourists or turtles? None of this might sound important, but it's a drift towards a saturation point when every aspect of delta life will suffer. This is one of the last breeding-grounds in the Mediterranean for the loggerhead turtles, those shy creatures, so clumsy and vulnerable on land when they place themselves at our mercy and find us far from merciful. In the late spring, they emerge from the water and crawl a ponderous few yards across the sand to make a nest, lay their eggs, cover them with their flippers, and then stagger back exhausted to the safety of the sea. Green sea turtles, as well as loggerhead, return to this particular beach, officially known by the name of Iztuzu.

I searched for the turtles one night with a flashlight and was almost relieved not to find one for they hate the intrusion of lights and people and I might have scared them back to the water. But the next morning I could see that the turtles had been there from their tank-like tracks, one of which headed in the wrong direction inland until the dazed animal realised its mistake. A couple of months later, the eggs hatched and Abidin helped to carry the tiny turtles across the blistering sand to the water.

Paradoxically, because these turtles are threatened, they could prove the saving of the sandbar. Turtles are an emotive subject and conservationists throughout Europe, ironically in Germany in particular, have sprung to their defence. It is just possible that there is still time to turn back. A swampy area, about a kilometre square at the southern end, has been drained and concreted over, and the foundations for the hotel laid and building begun. The laying of the foundation stone was attended by a German MP who was criticised by his countrymen for lending such support. There have been disturbing rumours that the contractors deliberately drove their bulldozers over the nesting area in order to keep the turtles away. Noise, lights, people, all the consequences of modern construction would succeed in doing so, and one witness has described the area to me as 'a war zone'. If the turtles stay away there is no problem – for none will remain to be protected. A specious argument with an awful logic.

Tourists or turtles? That is the question. Opinions are divided. The hotel in question, the Kaunos, subsidised by West German finance, envisages 600 beds initially, increasing to 1,800. Then there are

167

further plans for a holiday village, with 1,200 to 4,000 estimated beds, right in the centre of the sandbar. That would be the end for the turtles who would drop their eggs in the sea where they would perish. Altogether, nine hotels are in the planning stage, with the accompaniment of roads, bridges and a possible marina.

The contractors favour tourists, claiming that 1,000 beds mean 'fifteen million dollars in hard cash every year'. The investment is needed, which explains the alleged remark by the Minister for Tourism that such development 'cannot be sacrificed just for a few tortoises', an attitude he may be regretting. The Prime Minister is supposed to have commented privately 'Give me the turtles every time.' Good for him! Needless to add, this is the view of the conservationists and the Friends of Dalyan, led by a remarkable English lady known as Captain June who had her own chalet on the sandbar until it was removed along with the rest. She has risked local unpopularity with her campaign to call an immediate halt to the development, and has secured a vague promise that the Kaunos Hotel might be removed to another position less fatal to the turtles. When I spoke to the Minister for Tourism in 1987, he told me that all development was in abeyance until a survey confirms that it is all right to go ahead. As money talks, and Turkey needs foreign investment, I fear that this will be the verdict and long to see such cynicism belied. As Captain June points out, the money will not go to the local villagers as they expect: holiday makers will pay their Deutschmarks before they leave Germany; the Kaunos Hotel will have its own shop, restaurant, ferry-boat and hovercraft. As at another luxury hotel near Marmaris, the local youths may well be refused admittance. Equally, the prospect of a broad canal cut through the sandbar, to allow the yachts to sail right through to Dalyan, will be a very mixed blessing.

The Dalyan and Ekincik boatmen, and Abidin Kurt who started the ferry transfer with Eric Richardson of the YCA, will suffer accordingly, but so will the local restaurants for the crews will be able to eat on board and, worst of all, they will bring their own pollution with them. As Abidin told me with rare bitterness, 'Such a channel will bring rubbish boats with hippies and cheapies who will leave their shit (literally) and plastic behind them.' It is claimed that yachts are the best form of tourism, leaving only their money behind them, but Abidin is correct in referring to the plastic rubbish which lingers interminably.

On my last visit in 1987, I did not have the heart to go down the delta and find that sandbar threatened with the construction and destruction to come.*

* *Postscript:* Good news. The latest report states that the investment project is being revised so that the turtles will be protected for ever. One can only hope that the speculators allow this wise decision, on the part of the Turkish government, to be fulfilled.

In the long run, tourism will gain if the Dalyan Delta is preserved, and it should be declared a National Park immediately. Meanwhile, its future lies in the balance. Go there for yourself and see if you agree that an area as rare as this must be preserved for future generations.

What to do
The invaluable contact is Abidin Kurt who will arrange for you to be taken on one of his caiques, or the larger ferry-boat, down the delta from Dalyan, or collected from your mooring outside at Ekincik. A day's excursion will include a tour of Caunus, a swim in Lake Köyceğiz, and lunch at the Denizatı – though all are open to arrangement.

If there are several of you to share the expense, you may wish to hire a boat from Dalyan (if that is your starting point), see Caunus and continue past the sandbar to have lunch at Ekincik, now that the restaurants on the bar have been torn down. On the return journey you may wish to continue the short extra stretch, with beautiful woodland on one side, to Lake Köyceğiz for a freshwater or thermal swim.

Write or telephone his office beforehand to make such an arrangement, or telex via Doğan Tugay in Marmaris: 52528 GEMA TR. Starting around 10 a.m., with time for a swim at either end, this would cost you L 50,000 for the day. To my mind, it is well worth it if you are travelling in a party. Abidin Kurt is a marvellous personality and it should be a day to look back on with pleasure if he is able to guide you himself.

Sardes Tourism and Yacht Agency, Belediye Caddesi 13, tel.: (6116) 1050, 1079. This is easy to find in Dalyan, on the left-hand side as you head for the Denizatı on the river or continue out of town. It is represented in Marmaris by Yeşil Travel and in Fethiye by Likya Travel Agency at the Hotel Likya, tel.: (1690) 2233; telex 53018 LIKYA TR. To contact Sardes by radio to book for the river trip, try VHF Channel 6.

Where to stay
Kaunos Hotel and Restaurant, İskele Yanı Dalyan, Köyceğiz, tel.: (6116) 1087. This is a new hotel near the riverside which struck me as wholly agreeable; it is not to be confused with the intended new hotel of the same name at Iztuzu (see p. 167). Someone described it to me as 'noisy', but I doubt if this is justified. You have a choice of double beds or singles, the rooms have baths and showers and are simple, unpretentious and perfectly satisfactory. The exterior is pleasantly laid out with flagstones and a jaunty promenade. Single rooms are from L 7,000; doubles from L 13,000.

Binlik Travel Agency, tel.: (6119) 1001; telex: 53954 ERBU TR; UK address: 182 Lewisham Way, London SE4 1UU, tel.: 01-691 6564. This agency arranges apartments – 'basic, clean and comfortable, but certainly not luxurious' – which you can rent on a weekly or fortnightly basis. Accommodating four to six people with a cleaner, but self-catering, the cost starts from over L 146,500 a week, varying with the time of year, with a discount for early booking. You would be advised to insist on an apartment that is reasonably quiet, and check carefully.

Ali Aktas Pension. On the river, less than 1 km from Dalyan, on the right-hand side, this very simple but very sympathetic pension was where I stayed on my first visit and I have done so ever since. Though basic, with separate showers and lavatories, you have the incomparable reward of eating your breakfast overlooking a small garden of broad beans and vegetables and two lemon trees, with Dalyan River a few feet beyond and the soothing sound of the chugging caiques carrying bales of cotton to be collected at sea. This is a marvellous noise to wake to. On the other side of the river, you have a perfect view of the magnificent Lycian tombs carved in the cliffs by some form of scaffolding in the fourth century BC, one of the most impressive glimpses of ancient civilisation, the yellow-pink sandstone shining in the sunlight.

Adem's Pension (also called Kaunos Pension, *not* to be confused with the Kaunos Hotel), a little further on, is newer and apparently more comfortable. Described to me as 'perfect', it is very pleasant, and right on the water, with a little quay and the same astonishing breakfast view. You may be woken by cockerels or have your lunch interrupted by the excitement of seeing Nureyev step alongside to collect a box of fish. Because of a local decree, it is roughly the same price as every other pension here, including Ali Aktas: L 2,500 for each person, plus L 750 for breakfast, and L 500 for the use of the kitchen. I am told that Adem's should be twice that amount because it is exceptional; the prices may have risen in consequence.

Where to eat
The Kumlubükü Yacht Club, on one of the boat trips from Marmaris, is the type of svelte restaurant one hopes for, run by Ahmet Özkal and a Dutch friend. It is airy and cool with a wooden roof, stone floor, excellent fish salad and barbecued swordfish, and a sleepy dog called Woofy. It opens on 15 April and closes at the end of October.

The Denizatı, tel.: 1021. This is by far the most sympathetic restaurant in Dalyan, due to its superb position on the riverfront, but also to its food and the professionalism of its service. As the grey mullet are caught locally, they are especially recommended, but you can choose yourself from the excellent *mezes* in their glass case, and other fish. A local speciality is the wax-encased sticks of smoked roe of sea bass: an acquired but accumulative taste. Price from L 5,000 per person.

Dalyan Kamping, tel.: 1051. This is further up the river towards the lake, so you have to walk inland a bit and then cut back to the water. Anywhere along the riverfront is attractive, and this makes an agreeable alternative. The price is around L 5,000.

Piknik, near the new post office, is a simple small bakery where you can get excellent fresh *pide* and cool beer, or it's a good place for coffee and biscuits at the tables outside.

The Club House at Ekincik Bay is a fine new restaurant run by

Caunus

Irfan Tezbiner who will welcome you. It is a favourite with the YCA. Though not spectacular, the ruins at Caunus are some of the most interesting along the coast because they are easy to absorb after your brief climb up the hill, beneath the ramparts high above. You can judge the position of Caunus as a port when you look down from the top of the theatre, though the sea has long since receded leaving the delta and marshland below, with a shallow lake where they found the indignant lion which stands in the open air at Köyceğiz today after being submerged for 2,000 years.

Though it is doubtful if Caunus was colonised by the Greeks themselves, it was Hellenised by Mausolus, King of Caria, when the Persians appointed him governor of the province (377–353 BC), though he made his capital at Halicarnassus. Hence the Grecian-style theatre, set into the rock rather than constructed separately in the Roman style, which could have seated 5,000 people (though hardly the 250,000 claimed so chirpily on a British television travel programme). The view from the top is tremendous: towards the sea in one direction, over the cotton fields and the village behind in the other.

Apart from the theatre, there are Roman baths with ancient piping, and the circular foundations of a small temple or pool.

Herodotus believed that the Caunians came from Crete; the writer George Bean that they were indigenous. Whatever is true, they were subjected to the usual sequence of invaders: the Persians in 387 BC who occupied Caunus along with other Lycian ports; Antigonus after the death of Alexander the Great when his generals fought for the succession; and by Rhodes. Then it became virtually a free state under Rome. The mysterious importance of Caunus, which paid higher taxes than Ephesus, must have been due to the profitable sale of salt fish from the hatcheries which existed even then. But the city was doomed by virtue of its position and destroyed by another invader which proved fatal – the mosquitoes from the surrounding marshland, which brought an epidemic of malaria.

A contemporary wit compared the Caunian complexion to that of green leaves, and when the indignant citizens protested he assured them that he had not meant to be insulting – 'How could I call your city unhealthy,' he asked, 'when dead men walk the streets?'

The city was rediscovered as recently as 1842 by a Mr Hoskyn of HMS *Beacon*. In 1946, George Bean found the place still 'singing with mosquitoes'. In 1948 DDT wiped them out, but now they are starting to fly back to join the evening promenade and irritate that perfect moment of the day. They are Dalyan's only blemish, apart from the developers.

Göcek

After you return to the main coastal road, via Ortaca, an hour's drive takes you past Göcek. With astonishing luck, this bay has been bypassed by tourism and remains one of the most unspoilt and blessed areas along the coast.

The village itself is pleasantly simple though it has one good restaurant, several shops and three pensions, but no hotel as yet. When I was there on my first visit in 1987, the modest quayside was being extended and I envisage the time when hotels will start to sprout. I noticed that holes had been laid out in that concrete extension, with saplings already planted though the real construction had hardly started. This foresight is typically Turkish, to plant before you build.

The bay is immense with islands and inlets, and it should be a long time before these are tarnished by the stain of tourism. Even so, the Turkish authorities should seize the rare chance of protecting Göcek from the outset, learning from the mistakes which have been made elsewhere.

Meanwhile, the cheerful sounds of village life welcome you as they must have done for many years: cocks crowing loudly; children chattering merrily as they return from school in their black uniforms and white collars, clutching their books; someone hammering at the back while tailors sit in front of their shops, sewing in the sunlight, watched by their young apprentices. At the entrance to the friendly Aliço Restaurant, a man picks a flower from the cluster of pink roses over the door and continues inside, pressing it to his nose.

To the outsider, Göcek looks devoid of guile.

Where to stay   If you decide to stay here, do not expect comfort. There are only three pensions: the best is supposed to be the one off the market square, recognisable by a sign which promises solar heating. I found it impersonal though clean, and due to bad weather the solar system wasn't working – ironic that solar heating does not provide hot water when you need it most.

From this pension walk down the street (to the right, facing the water), past another pension to the **Özden Pension**, simple but clean, to a room with three beds, overlooking a garden though this is not as cheerful as it sounds for the interior is rather dark. There is a separate Turkish lavatory and wash-basin, even a shower worked by a primitive gas-heater which gives the expectation of hot water rather than the reality, but it meant well. It is very private and quiet and the price is nominal: from L 2,000.

If you do not wish to stay here overnight and want a livelier evening, continue straight to Fethiye, half an hour's drive away.

The offshore islands   **The islands** Just beyond the Aliço Restaurant is the quayside and a jetty and the vast panorama of the bay like an unspoilt Marmaris with shapes looming in the distance which *could* be islands or pine-covered hills and it is hard to tell even when you are near. Deceptively, there are twelve islands altogether. Just as Paradise Island is joined by a causeway to the Marmaris mainland today, there used to be a bridge connecting Devil's Island to Olive Island, where a small plant once manufactured its own oil; now the island is inhabited by black goats.

The water is so pure one feels elated, and either so shallow you can

172

see the bottom or so deep that the clouds are mirrored on the darker surface. The only eyesore is man-made: the mess of floating plastic, the curse of the charter boats.

Tersane Island is the most important, with an Ottoman port noted for its boat building, and is now a popular mooring point for yachts. It has a makeshift restaurant open from mid-May which sports an 'Oriental Corner' for dancing, largely performed by the young manager, Ali.

Cleopatra's Baths The ruins rise out of the water so attractively that it is tempting to believe the legend that Cleopatra did swim here. Plainly that girl was quite a swimmer, dropping her name along the coast as she went. I tried to emulate her, but I am not so nimble and it involves a scramble over rocks on the shore. It is easier to swim more publicly from the jetty, or from the sandy beach on the other side. These ruins are an estimated 2,000 years old and when you study the map and mark a straight line south to the delta of the Nile where Cleopatra was queen in the first century BC, her association with them becomes credible.

The Lycian city An hour's walk inland brings you to the site of this city which goes back 3,000 years with an alleged population of 4,500 people, though little remains today apart from an early domed Byzantine house. The fact that such a city existed reminds one yet again of the busy water thoroughfare in this part of the ancient world.

Where to eat

As far as I remember, the delightful restaurant above the baths is called **Amigo,** laid out on a rough earth terrace below the family home which has a meticulous vegetable garden in front, using every available inch of the small space for garlic, beans, lettuce, potatoes and onions, lined with flowers in whitewashed tins. The combination of flowers and vegetables is typical and so pleasing to the eye that it seems obvious that the two should go together instead of the usual, strict separation.

The settlement is owned by Recep and his nephew, and consists of numerous relatives and children; twenty chickens and fifty goats, kept largely as food for passing boats; and a little white Turkish dog called Bobby, with razor-sharp teeth and a sharp sense of disruption. In the summer, musicians come from Dalaman. It is hardly surprising that everyone seems so happy in such an idyllic setting.

There is a smarter and more expensive restaurant clearly visible a short distance from the Baths, but the **Binlik** restaurant was my next stop, also grander and ostensibly more professional, in another beautiful setting with a small beach. It is run by Salih, a friendly young man, and visited by the *Anatolia* on daily ferry trips from Fethiye at a cost of L 2,500 per person.

It was interesting to see the flat dishes of chicken and fish thrust on poles into the open wood-ovens to cook in the surrounding heat rather than over it, though my suspicion that the chicken was taken out too soon was confirmed when a tourist from Fethiye complained to me. Continuing the mistake, another advanced upon me angrily: 'You are manager?' I spread my arms helplessly, in the way managers tend to do when things go wrong. 'If so?' I asked. 'Do not lie,' she corrected me angrily, 'I can see you must be manager, you sit in the middle of the natives.' *Natives!* I nodded submissively. 'In my opinion,' she continued with a menacing glare, 'in my opinion, the fish is very small portion from the one I point at. Why do you cut the fish?' 'To make it taste better as it cooks in its own juices?' I suggested, maintaining this idiotic pretence. 'The taste has nothing to do with it,' she rebuked me, and strode off.

In fact the old bossy-boots had a point, the chicken *was* underdone and the portion of fish was small. But this was the start of the season and the cook had time to learn. If he has not, make sure that you complain to the real manager, and not some fatuous imposter. Or choose your meat from the charcoal barbecue between the two ovens, which you can judge for yourself.

The journey back across these still, charmed waters was so peaceful, the small Turkish flag fluttering in the slightest breeze, the young bearded boatman smiling at the scene as if it was new to him, that I fell asleep on the *kilim* thrown over the bow, for once perfectly relaxed.

I urge you to spend a day sailing around the islands, either by private arrangement with the boatman which should cost from L 20,000, or on one of the excursions available during the summer. Equally, you can take the ferry-boat from Fethiye, but I doubt if this would have the same exhilaration as your departure from Göcek. Now that Dalyan is threatened, this is the loveliest place along this entire coastline.

Gemile If you are sailing, try to visit this mysterious and little-known island which is due south of Fethiye, around the corner on the way to Ölü Deniz, and still to be excavated by the archaeologists. You stumble on ancient ruins and even paintings if you look below the remnants of a church. There is also the outline of a covered walkway, with arches like an aqueduct, flanked by walls with pieces of mosaic, and pots which are gradually being looted. Pipes suggest an early water supply, or possibly a form of sewage disposal though that strikes me as unlikely.

For the time being, you can enjoy a sense of exploration. 'Scrape away a couple of inches,' someone told me, 'and you'll come across mosaics. Hardly the ruins of Pompeii, but still exciting.' Though I don't wish to be a spoilsport, surely Gemile should be preserved more lovingly?

Fethiye Spacious gardens and waterfront promenades give an air of pleasant relaxation, but the town of Fethiye is new. The old one was largely destroyed in the same earthquake of 1958 which decimated Marmaris, yet Fethiye lacks the sophistication of that resort, and certainly that of

174

bustling Bodrum. The foremost ancient landmarks to survive are the Lycian tombs, such as those of Amyntas, fourth century BC, easily accessible on the outskirts. A very fine example of this graceful form of architecture, with façades like Ionic temples, which can be seen at eye-level, unlike the cliff tombs at Dalyan.

Fethiye, with a population of 22,000 and 140 km from Marmaris, has been described as 'nondescript' and I agreed with this until my last visit when the place began to grow on me. Certainly the English holiday-makers I met there loved the place unreservedly, and though they had not been to Marmaris or Bodrum I suspect they would still have preferred Fethiye which is less brazen.

Near the Rafet 2 restaurant (see following p.) and providing the name of the street – Hamam Sokak – is the Turkish bath. It caters for men and women (strictly separate entrances) and has been recommended as one of the best in Turkey.

Where to stay   **The Likya Hotel**, Karagözler Mahallesi, tel.: 1169; telex 53948. It is wise to book beforehand: there are forty rooms and they are liable to be full in peak season. This is one of the most attractive hotels in Turkey – a pleasant, low-lying building perfectly situated on a point overlooking the bay, just beyond the yacht club. Set in attractive gardens with four gigantic palm trees, its balconies overlook the sea, though you are advised to swim in the pool which is fresher. Prices are reasonable for the comfort offered: from L 25,000 for a double room and breakfast.

Dedeoğlu Hotel, İskele Meydanı, tel.: 4010; thirty-eight rooms. These good, straightforward rooms with showers cost from L 22,000 for a double.

Prenses Hotel, İskele Karşısı, overlooking the sea, tel.: 4479, has similar rooms to Dedeoğlu, with balconies. It is possible to have a room with two beds and another off it with a double, convenient for the whole family. Half-board is compulsory. There is a disco, American bar and a restaurant.

Kordon Hotel, Atatürk Caddesi 8, tel.: 1834. Reasonably priced and recommended by an English couple who stayed there, this is situated in the main street in the centre of town, where it curves to the left. A double room and shower from L 11,000.

Sema Hotel, Çarşı Caddesi, tel.: 1015, just off the main street, near the statue of Atatürk. Ask for a quiet room. Price for a double with shower from L 12,000.

Hotel Kaya, behind the *Oh Yaaa* café near the *dolmuş* stop, is considerably cheaper and good for low budgets: no private bathrooms but only L 3,600.

There are numerous pensions, several behind the Hotel Likya in Karagözler Mahallesi, and the Tourist Bureau (there is one next to the Dedeoğlu Hotel, tel.: 1527) will help you. The Bureau also recommends the **Yat Motel** and **Palmiye**. Obviously, pensions offer excellent value and more local atmosphere at prices from only L 2,700 with shared shower.

The Bureau may urge you to stay at the **Meri Hotel** in Ölü Deniz. Don't.

Where to eat

The wide choice of restaurants is largely divided between those on the waterfront like the **Yat** which is international and used by the flotillas, and those in the centre of town. The Yat is reliable and professional.

Rafet 2, Hamam Sokak 9, tel.: 2676, in a side street off the main road lined with carpet shops. The owner, Mr Yaşar, speaks English. This is an excellent restaurant with a friendly atmosphere, tables and chairs outside. You are made to feel welcome.

Kordon, connected with the hotel (see previous p.), has fresh fish laid out on a circular tray and an excellent reputation.

Sun and **Afrodit** are also recommended; the latter is one street behind Atatürk Caddesi, and is reputed to be good value at a cheap price.

Apparently the restaurant at the Dedeoğlu and the Likya hotels are recommended, though I suspect this is more for Turks dining out than for visitors who look for atmosphere.

Ölü Deniz

Visually this is one of the beauty spots of Turkey, only 15 km from Fethiye and well worth a visit. However, the translation for this idyllic lagoon is the 'Dead Sea', which is disconcertingly accurate, for the water is so placid, with a narrow outlet to the sea, that any pollution lingers and yachts are now discouraged from mooring here. Even so, from a distance it remains a paradise for photographers and travel writers, unless you turn around and face the reverse view of the Meri Hotel which covers the hillside. Then you will find Ölü Deniz unrecognisable if you have known it in simpler days.

Some travel writers recommend swimming from the lagoon at Ölü Deniz, but though it is temptingly shallow for children I cannot recommend it. In glorious contrast, the surf along the beach which stretches across the rest of the bay provides one of the most exhilarating swims along this coast and the water is an astonishing turquoise. This is the bonus after the beauty of the lagoon.

Unless you want to camp (there are several sites at a reasonable cost) I would suggest that you leave Fethiye early in the morning, walk around Ölü Deniz, swim from the glorious beach, have lunch in Fethiye which you have to return to, and continue to Kaş 108 km away, approximately one and a half hour's drive.

Where to stay

Beyond the Meri, you pass the Çavuş, Çetin and Deniz camping sites, and the Belcekız where the bar has classical music. At the Han Camp a meal with wine costs from L 5,000 with music and dancing at night. The Ölü Deniz at the end is reputed to have high standards.

Deniz Camping is run by Anthea Gurkan, a helpful English woman, has fifty-seven beds and is open all the year round. The brochure makes the usual extravagant claim – 'We are at the gates of paradise' – but this is redeemed by the assertion, 'What we cannot offer you: waiters in bow ties; 5-star formality; baked beans on toast and gambling casinos.' She and her husband found the place by accident when there was no road or development and the sand dunes were so high that you could not see the sea beyond. Realising that if they did not move in, someone else would, they did not expect tourism to grow so big so fast. Now the beach is on the verge of becoming one of the most popular resorts in Turkey. Her three sons help in running the site and the atmosphere is informal and friendly.

The Meri, tel.: 1 (local), is popular, especially with coach parties who spend the night and whisk off never to return, but this breeds indifference among the staff. The rooms climb up a steep hill and you could do with an alpenstock or ski-lift if you are at the top, as I was, so I might be prejudiced. There is an attractive-looking open-air restaurant but the food is indifferent and 'international'; judging by the caustic comments in a visitors' book I am not alone in that opinion. Things may have improved, but its great success (it virtually monopolises Ölü Deniz today) does not encourage initiative. Even so, the scenery of the lagoon surrounded by pines is superb. The price for a double room with bath is from L 22,500.

The Çetin Motel has a friendly, young Turkish staff; **Pension Manzara** is new, perched on the hillside with stunning views but is twenty minutes' walk to the sea – take a *dolmuş* going back. **Pension Ünsal**, with eight rooms and three minutes from the beach, is run by a pleasant Turkish family.

Several lesser known beaches can be reached from Ölü Deniz by car: Belcekiz, nearby; Günlük, north of Fethiye; and Katrancı, 17 km. A short distance inland, near the village of Kaya, is the curious ghost city of Karmylassos, once a prosperous Greek community. It was evacuated under the exchange of population decreed by Atatürk in 1923 and an interesting church remains.

Xanthos
History

Once the greatest city of Lycia, Xanthos is 65 km from Fethiye. The men were known for their bravery, though it brought them tragedy rather than victory. Herodotus described their epic battle in 545 BC against the Persians, whose army outnumbered them and forced them to retire inside their walls. Realising that they faced defeat, the men shut their women, children and slaves in the citadel and burnt them to death. Then they sallied out and were slaughtered to the last man. Later, fifty families who were absent at the time started to rebuild the city, fighting to their death when it was besieged by Brutus in 42 BC. Plutarch recorded: 'It was so tragical a sight that Brutus could not bear to see it, but wept at the very mention of the scene . . . Thus the Xanthians, after a long space of years, repeated by their desperate deed the calamity of their forefathers.' Later the city was rebuilt by Mark Antony and the Roman Emperor Vespasian (AD 9–79), who gave the gateway to Xanthos which can be seen today, and also introduced a welcome period of peace and prosperity which lasted until the twelfth century.

What to see   The next invaders were the British, in the form of Sir Charles Fellows who excavated the city in 1838 and carried off the reliefs of the monuments on a frigate which brought them to London. Yet again, a visit to the British Museum (the Lycian Room) is necessary to appreciate these antiquities, and yet again one wonders if such pillage was justified. However, plaster copies of the reliefs can be seen on the Tomb of the Harpies near the great Roman theatre. This shows figures from the underworld, with the faces of women, the bodies of vultures, and the claws of bears. Beside it, also on a monolith, is a fine example of an ancient Lycian sarcophagus or pillar-tomb, from the fourth century BC.

Without their original decorations, the monuments seem incomplete. The theatre is built against the northern face of the acropolis which included a Temple of Artemis, but these Lycian monuments were replaced over the years by the Byzantines. They are worth visiting if you are travelling by car, but if you have had a surfeit of antiquities or it involves a difficult sequence of bus journeys, you could give it a miss without feeling too guilty. The history is more extraordinary than the present reality, though the carved tombs outside the massive walls confirm the Grecian influence around 300 BC, culminating in the classic Temple, with decorations comparable to those of the Elgin Marbles which can be seen in the British Museum in London today.

Patara to Kemer

Patara   The finest beach in Turkey, like a desert by the sea, here there are miles of sand and hardly another person in sight. The only drawback is a windy day when the surf veers wildly in every direction and the sand blows in your face, but this discomfort is in fact a blessing, for it has discouraged construction on such a shifting surface and now Patara as a protected area is saved from development. I should add that windy days are unusual.

There is the bonus too of ruins which are hardly excavated, dating back to the time when Patara was the port for Xanthos and the largest harbour in Lycia, until it was silted up by deposits brought by the Xanthos river. The extent of the ancient city dawns on you gradually as you climb the sand-dunes to the half-buried theatre with an immense well behind it. A magnificent triple-arched gateway greets you as you arrive by road (which is now greatly improved compared to the river-bed effect of a few years ago).

Where to
stay

There is a new hotel, the **Pension Patara II**, about 2 km from the sea, a distance decreed by the Turkish government and a wise one too. There is no sea view, though the hotel staff will drive you there and back, but I imagine this would be a restful place to stay in, if uneventful. Mr Şevki is the owner, as he is of the Patara in Kalkan (see following p.). The price is from L 18,000 for two with breakfast; there is a terrace-bar, balconies, showers and restaurant. As the hotel opened in 1988 it is impossible to report on its success.

Where to
eat

Strictly regulated by the Turkish government, only two restaurants have been allowed, and I prefer the one closest to the sea, also owned by Mr Şevki. Its simple, but imaginative, food includes a Turkish form of ravioli, *manti*.

Kalkan

Partly because it is so small, though expanding rapidly, Kalkan is now a popular resort and many people prefer it to Kaş, twenty-five minutes' drive further south. I find this hard to understand. On the credit side there is a village atmosphere, an echo of the old Greek community which was removed in 1923 leaving the place virtually deserted. Today, glimpses of balconies surrounded by vines and foliage compensate a bit for the electric drills as new buildings fill the empty spaces and crumbling façades. Against that, there is no beach, though you can be ferried to a new terrace on the other side of the bay where you can sunbathe and swim, or take a free boat-trip to the Kalamar Beach Club with swimming in a cove and use of the club facilities, including the bar. What I find unattractive is the harbour, enclosed by an artificial mole of boulders. It lacks the charm of Kaş and suggests a new resort under construction.

Perhaps that was a first impression which has never left me, for I do not entirely understand why I find Kalkan unsympathetic when others like it so much. Plainly this is a matter of personal taste. However, there is one bonus which is undeniable and surprising: a large number of excellent restaurants, eighteen at least, which are better than those in Kaş. So if you do not wish to stay overnight, you can at least go to Kalkan for the sunset view from one of the rooftop bars and enjoy a good meal. Conversely, you may fall in love with the place and wish to stay there.

Where to
stay

The two most popular pensions are:

Pasha's Inn, 10 Sokak No 8 (on the left-hand side at the bottom of the hill), tel.: 77 (local); seven bedrooms which are small but comfortable. The friendly atmosphere is due to the English-speaking owner, Erkut Taçkını, and an excellent rooftop bar where you can also have breakfast. There are Turkish decorations inside. It is slightly on the expensive side compared to Kaş, but this applies throughout Kalkan.

Balıkçı Han, situated around the corner from Pasha's Inn, overlooks the harbour. It is luxuriously decorated in a no-expense-spared style, though the delicate bedroom curtains neither exclude the early light nor encourage privacy. It is very popular, due to the ample and generous personality of Tiraje Evci from Istanbul and her brother Teoman. There is a rooftop terrace for breakfast. Tel.: 75 (local). You could also try:

Kalkan Han, higher on the hill (near the bus depot, overlooking the village), tel.: (3215) 1151. A new hotel converted from a stone building which used to house a bank, this has sixteen rooms, all with showers. Again, the rooftop bar which seems obligatory in Kalkan, possibly due to the night skies which are exceptionally clear – they inspired the claim by Herodotus that this was the place where the moon and the stars are closest to the earth. This is a clean and cool hotel, though it has less atmosphere than the other two. Prices are from L 23,000 for a double room and breakfast, L 18,000 for a single.

Ali Han, simple and comfortable, with ten rooms, is run by a lady who speaks English; good value.

Patara Pension, with eight rooms, overlooks the yacht harbour which welcomes thirty to forty yachts every day. It provides a free ferry service to the Kalamar Beach Club.

Where to eat | Kalkan covers such a small area that there is no difficulty finding the restaurant you are looking for. These are listed in order of recommendation and price.

Korsan is noted for its seafood and lobster; **Beşkapi**; **Balıkçı Han**, on the terrace of the hotel, is reputedly good; **Lipsos**, associated with Pasha's Inn hotel, has an open buffet where you help yourself and is noted for its *mezes*.

Kaş | Known as Antiphellos to the Greeks, and Habesa to the Lycians, this is one of the most delightful places along the coast with a jaunty, jolly personality. Unfortunately, it is changing rapidly and if care is not taken in time it will lose the simplicity which made it so attractive as recently as eight years ago when it had just been reached by road and boasted one hotel, the Ali Baba, which is now one of fifty. In spite of the rapid development, Kaş retains a gentle charm and is never overwhelming; the curved waterfront remains charming even though bulldozers were extending it in 1987.

Big new hotels with up to 200 beds are promised – or threatened – over the next few years, which means that Kaş is changing all the time. Fortunately, most of these will be outside the village, and personally I am glad that the expansion of the harbour is largely for protection from the weather and not for a marina. One addition which I do regret is the blare of bastardised Mediterranean disco music, which can be forgiven when it emanates from a real live disco but is intolerable when it grates deafeningly from a bar next to your restaurant. But one of the late-night bars does play excellent jazz.

Kaş is a good choice of place to stop at, with three exceptional places to visit: Kekova and Castellorizon by boat; and the miles of sand at Patara which compensate for the lack of beaches at Kaş.

The Tourist Office, Cumhuriyet Meydanı 6, tel.: 238, is on the harbour front near the Eriş Restaurant. The director, Namık Aydın, is exceptionally helpful. And there is an up-and-coming travel agency, Turkish Delight, which favours Kaş and British holiday-makers in particular, run by a magnificent Turkish lady, Sezer Duru, who speaks English, and might be able to help you in an emergency. The travel office is at the bottom of Hastane Caddesi as you go into town.

Where to stay If you continue through the town, along the harbour and up a slope with a government building on the right, you come to two pensions and a small hotel which are particularly attractive.

Nur Pension is basic but clean and reasonably priced from L 10,000 for two with shower, and a garden for breakfast outside.

Patara Pension, in the other half of this same building, has charming rooms, with bathroom and erratic plumbing, friendly owners, and a garden full of flowers and kittens. It costs about the same.

Likya Hotel, a few metres beyond, has especially comfortable rooms with large double beds if you ask for them, and hot water from solar heating. A roof garden has a mosaic floor and good furniture. It is slightly more expensive, at L 16,000 a room; one that is extra-special costs L 20,000.

Kaş is liable to be fully booked, and is especially popular with the British, many of whom are booked into the Nur.

Opposite is a cove and a small beach, but beware – it is pebbly! Above is a so-called 'beach club', **Küçük Çakıl**, attractively laid out for sunbathing and soft drinks. A licence, for cool beer at least, is imminent, though this could mar the simplicity.

Mimosa Hotel, Elmalı Caddesi, tel.: 1272, is on the main road coming into town – new, luxurious and allegedly the 'best', with twenty rooms – fourteen with sea views and six of the mountains. Each room has two beds and, surprisingly, 'an extended armchair' which provides a third bed if necessary. There is wall-to-wall carpeting, and a bar and restaurant with charcoal-grilled specialities. The roof restaurant is used for sunbathing by day. A disco and sauna operate in the basement, and a swimming pool at the back is being planned. Prices are from L 17,000 for two people, out of season, rising to L 30,000 in midsummer, including breakfast. L 21,000–36,000 for half-board; no single rooms in high season.

Derya Hotel, Elmalı Caddesi 24, tel.: 1304, is in the centre of town, opposite the Mimosa, and to my mind is preferable largely due to the friendliness of the English-speaking owner who seems anxious to make you welcome. There are nice Turkish decorations with wood and *kilims*, fourteen rooms with balconies, showers and hot water, with the claim that 'everything is prepared by love'. Less pretentious than the Mimosa and cheaper – from L 15,000 for a double room with breakfast.

Ali Baba Motel, Hastane Caddesi, tel.: 1126, is simple but sympathetic, run by Ali Yıldırım. It has a restaurant. Prices from L 10,000

for a double room, slightly less after September. No singles.
Kaş Hotel (near Ali Baba) has the advantage of being right on the sea with a ladder for an early morning dip. L 12,500 for a double room with shower and temperamental w.c.
Hotel Andifli, Hastane Caddesi, tel.: 1042, has communal showers and lavatories. It is simple but also pleasant, costing L 4,000 for one, L 6,000 for two and L 7,000 for three.
Kismet Pension, tel.: 1083, 100 m behind the harbour, is much more basic with shared facilities but reports of it are good. From L 5,000 for one and from L 8,000 for two, depending on the room. It is run by Ali Eris whose son, Yusuf, manages the restaurant with the same name in the harbour.

Where to eat   **The Mercan** is still my favourite at the end of the quayside as you continue out of the village on the way to the Nur and Patara Pensions. It has good seafood and atmosphere. Ducks used to swim past cheerfully and if the development has finished, I hope they do again. Approximate cost for two with wine is L 10,000.

Eriç Restaurant is sympathetic, but you need to order carefully. Though friendly, they can be slightly off-hand. It will cost about L 9,000 for two.

There is an attractive row of restaurants, featuring fish kebabs, off the harbour where you can see the food being prepared so you can easily make your own choice. The Eva Kent, Derya and Resin Eris, at approximately L 8,000 for two, are the most popular. This is referred to locally as The Shady Street, after the trees rather than any nefarious goings-on. It is popular both for lunch and dinner.

If you continue walking for five minutes out of town, there is a track to another cove with a small, simple restaurant set among trees. The water is exceptionally warm, but cool springs a few yards out are wonderfully refreshing.

Unexpectedly, the camp site has the highest reputation of all! It is a ten minute stroll from Hastane Caddesi past the attractive little theatre, which is Kaş's leading monument apart from the Lycian pillar-tomb at the top of a street of shops.

Kekova   Allow a complete day for a boat trip to the waters of Kekova. These are extraordinary: you feel you are sailing back in time, with the ruins of a fortress at the top of the hill above Kale (which means 'castle'), the outline of the ruined city of Aperlae under the water opposite, and Lycian tombs rising out of the sea like prehistoric monsters. Everywhere there are ruins, reminding you of ancient civilisations, such as the Lycian, dating back to the sixth century BC. Until recently, the villages of Üçağız and Kale could only be reached by sea, which adds to the atmosphere, with local children mooring a boat at rapid speed, throwing the anchor overboard to glide towards the quay, jumping ashore with a rope as it touches. There are several restaurants at Üçağız selling fish, or goat if you prefer meat, and the local people seem pleased by any interruption of the day's languorous monotony, dancing to drums and tambourines with spontaneous pleasure. When I first saw Kale there were no restaurants or shops whatsoever; now there are a couple near the jetty which provide a welcome rest after your climb to the castle's crenellated walls. The small amphitheatre has seven rows of seats carved from the rock and the tombs appear to have Greek inscriptions, though these date back to the Lydian language which is still not fully deciphered.

Beyond Kekova Island is Çay Ağzi, meaning 'little river mouth', with a long, white, sandy beach. YCA members often paddle across the river bar by dinghy and take a taxi to the village of Demre nearby. The waters around Kekova Island, which lies parallel to the mainland, are not pretty – they are tremendous. In certain lights the effect is almost sinister, especially if a storm is brewing, when the glowering land suggests that intruders are unwelcome.

Getting there   Today, you can reach Üçağız and Kale by road, 25 km from Kaş, but the proper way to travel is by boat to absorb the enormity of your approach. Either join a boat trip leaving from the harbour, or make your own arrangement to hire a boat for the day if there are several of you to share the expense.

Castellorizon   Another recommended boat-trip is to the island which you can see on the horizon opposite Kaş. Castellorizon (or Kastellorizo) is a geographical curio: a Greek island in Turkish waters so decimated in the twentieth century that the population has to be sustained at a mere 200 or risk a final abandonment. Until recently it was impossible to sail there from Kaş unless you received special permission which was difficult to obtain. Because it is too unimportant for customs and immigration formalities, you cannot stop there overnight – though the island now boasts a hotel, the Megisti. Otherwise, the harbour is a pleasant façade with a few restaurants and shops but little substance behind. Castellorizon has the mysterious appeal today of a ghost island, signifying the sad decline of a port which once contained the fleets which transported timber from Lycia to north Africa.

In such a strategic position, the island was constantly at the mercy of invaders: it was occupied by Rhodes 350–300 BC; by Roman pirates; by Egypt in 1440 and Naples ten years later, then by the Ottomans and Venetians. The Turks became the particular enemy, and after an unsuccessful revolt in 1913, the island was occupied by the French and Italians in the First World War, causing a mass emigration to Australia. The Castellorizon Society there has more members today than the island's entire present population, and many of them return to see the birthplace of their parents.

Yet the island recovered, and a panoramic photograph from the mid-1930s shows a large, bustling port when the population approached 15,000. Disaster returned in the Second World War when the island's position was considered so crucial that the Allies landed and sent the islanders into exile in the Middle East for their own 'safety', forcing them to leave their possessions behind. These were promptly looted and the soldiers set fire to many of the houses to conceal their guilt. Finally, by a cruel stroke of fate, the ship bringing the exiles home sank on the way back – the few survivors returned to find they had lost everything.

'I can never think of Castellorizon,' wrote Dame Freya Stark in her fine book *The Lycian Shore*, 'without a stab as if someone had hit me.'

Now there are signs of a slight recovery and it is fun to visit a typical Greek village with whitewashed houses, blue-framed windows and families of kittens, but as you walk to the impressive church which is out of all proportion today, the grief of this unlucky island is inescapable.

The water is exceptionally clear, but there are no beaches and swimming is best off the rocks at the hamlet of Mandraki beyond the castle headland. If you have time, sail to the Blue Grotto which is supposed to be larger than that in Capri and equal in colour.

A landmark to visit is the reddish Castle of the Knights which gave the island its name. The most easterly island in Greece, it is just 9 sq km.

The Gömbe Mountain Retreat

Today, holiday-makers flock to the sea as if this is the be-all and the end-all, their eyes fixed on the horizon from the start to the finish of their travels. Fortunately, this leaves the interior remarkably intact. Throughout the Mediterranean, there are villages hidden in the hills only a few miles from the water which the sun-worshippers do not bother to visit as they lie on the beach grilling in the sun like sardines.

In the foothills of the snow mountains behind Kaş are a series of extraordinary alpine lakes, with waterfalls cascading down as a backdrop. The surroundings have the bareness of high altitudes, but the lakes are as blue as the translucent waters near Ölü Deniz, which gives a startling effect. Go to the Tourist Office in Kaş for advice on the best way to get there: Mr Aydın personally recommends the Retreat as an interesting change from the inevitable sea.

Demre

Returning to Kaş and driving north-east to Finike, you pass Demre which is worth visiting for the attractive Byzantine Church of St Nicholas, built in the third century but altered over the years and used as a mosque until it was appreciated that this is a truly unique tourist attraction, quite apart from the pleasant building set among orange and lemon trees. St Nicholas, born at Patara further up the coast, was allegedly the original Father Christmas, and his marble tomb rested inside until it was looted by Italian souvenir hunters who took the bones back to Bari in 1087. The top of the tomb had the figure of a child, and the modern bronze statue of Santa near the Church today shows him surrounded by children. St Nicholas was Bishop of Myra nearby, and rumour had it that he gave anonymous gifts to the local children and dropped bags filled with coins as dowries for the poorer village girls who hoped to marry, thus creating the legend of Santa Claus. It is a nice story, and completely harmless if untrue.

At Myra, the former port of Demre, there is a well-preserved Roman temple and a honeycomb of Lycian tombs which are more accessible than those at Dalyan but less mysterious. Avoid the late afternoon when the mosquitoes are out in force, as they usually are when the water has receded. St Paul preached here on his way to Rome but the harbour has silted up since then and the sea is 5 km away, with a good sandy beach.

Finike   Thirty km south of Demre, this could be a convenient stop for lunch at the **Deniz** restaurant around the corner from the **Hotel Sedir**, but unless you coincide with the three-day wrestling contests in the spring – which have a delightful, friendly atmosphere of simple enjoyment – I should advise you to continue onwards.

Olympos   Reached by a terrible, pitted road, the ruins of Olympos are close to the sea. Some people disparage them and admittedly they are overgrown, but the road affords the exciting glimpse of a wall across the stream or a walk along the edge lined with pink oleander where you look down at the tiny frogs to realise that you are standing on the quayside of an ancient city. There is even a temple to Marcus Aurelius concealed in the trees. I find the setting extraordinary, with the constant reminder that this was another of the ancient chain of ports where thousands of people walked and talked along the pavings, with the sea just beyond.

The Chimera   Inland, a steep climb up Mount Phoenix (another name for Mount Olympos), is the hole, only about a metre deep, which produces a flame which never goes out. This is probably some form of gas, but it cannot be extinguished by water and though it is hardly visible by day it can be seen at night by mariners far out at sea, as it was by Captain Beaufort who recorded it in 1811. Dame Freya Stark made the hour's climb by pony in her usual indomitable way, but found the hole small – 'and very sooty, like a hearth. Her fierce days are over.' Hardly romantic, yet since Seneca and Pliny the flame has been associated with the legend of the fire-breathing monster slain by Bellerophon when he rode Pegasus into the sky above. He fixed a lump of lead on his lance which he plunged into the creature's mouth, where it melted from the heat of the Chimera's breath, ran into its stomach and burnt it to death.

The legend is more fun than the reality, unless you wish to search for the half-buried fragments found by Dame Freya including a pedestal inscribed to the Emperor Hadrian by the town council of Olympos, but I fear these will have long since been removed.

Phaselis   Like Olympos, the setting and atmosphere of Phaselis are infinitely rewarding. The ruins are still being excavated and though they are not on the grandest scale, they include an attractive walk through a paved market, theatre, aqueduct and temple. Above all, the three natural

185

harbours shaded by pine-trees made this place attractive to mariners since it was founded by the Dorians from Rhodes in the 7th century BC. In 333 BC Alexander the Great favoured the city so greatly, with its roses in full bloom and its scent of lilies, that he made the port his base for the winter. He was probably persuaded by the citizens of Phaselis to attack the Termessians in the hills above Antalya: they were the hated enemy due to raids in which they looted possessions and carried off the most attractive girls. Phaselis flourished under the Romans who granted its independence, before it became the target for passing pirates and gradually declined.

It is worth the short detour off the main road today (there is a nominal admission fee and a small museum) – it makes a restful pause for a look at what remains, a picnic and a swim.

Kemer   With the best will in the world I cannot recommend Kemer, though it is now one of the most popular centres for holiday villages in Turkey. The Club Méditerranée at Kemer is a model for tactful development with low-lying buildings set among gardens and trees with breathtaking views of the snow-topped Taurus mountains behind and a translucent sea and sandy beach in front. Unfortunately the exemplary French practice has not been followed by the new holiday complexes, largely subsidised by West German finance which could explain the prison camp atmosphere. The Turkish Turban Holiday Villages shine by comparison.

Having dismissed them so brutally, I should in fairness add that I stayed at the Club Robinson in freak but unremittent rain in May, and these are neither the buildings nor the coast to be seen in wet weather! One of the new holiday clubs boasts that it is going to stay open all year round, but this runs the risk of being as forlorn as an English resort in February.

As for the summer months, the clubs are not for me because they are not particularly Turkish, with one striking exception – and that is the enthusiastic young Turkish staff, who go out of their way to make you welcome. That compensates for a lot.

Even the town of Kemer suffers from the concrete-syndrome with its new buildings which are being erected without consideration. In contrast, the new marina which opened in 1986, holding 350 yachts, is well designed and the Olympos Hotel is reported to be the best.

Where to stay   All the following villages, or complexes, can be found in the same area though they are not within easy walking distance of each other. They are all about half an hour's drive from Antalya, a distance of 35 km.

The Club Méditerranée, twin-bedded bungalows with showers and w.c. Noted for windsurfing. The flight from Heathrow to Antalya, and transfer to the Club (about one hour) costs, depending on season, from L 664,000 to 796,500 a week, with a cheap supplementary charge for an additional week. You should check the latest prices with: Club

Méditerranée: 106–108 Brompton Road, London SW3 1JJ, tel.: 01-581 1161.

If you enjoy being organised – games, sports, entertainment – and many people *do* like it, then **Club Robinson** organises superbly. Though one restaurant meal was disappointing, the lunchtime choice was varied, imaginative and excellent. There is swimming in pools and the nearby sea. The chalets stretch interminably down concrete canyons and are poorly designed, yet, given hot weather, a family could enjoy a happy holiday here if they do not mind this impersonality and take excursions to see more of Turkey as it really is.

Milta, a new holiday village, has 402 rooms in a modern complex, decorated in 'rustical' style. The open buffet lunch is excellent; there is a kindergarten, nine tennis courts, and medical assistance is provided if needed. The setting is sensational, with mountains behind and a visual trick which makes the pool look as if it stretches right into the sea.

Alba Club is the only holiday village in the region to open all the year round. With a 900-bed capacity (and a marble Turkish bath), it cost L 7.6 billion. It was opened, along with the Milta, by President Evren on an unforgettable day in May 1987 when there was a cabaret of young Turkish dancers in coloured shirts high-kicking to the tune of 'New York, New York!' and a spectacle in the swimming-pool of divers surfacing and a bearded captain 'in trouble' in a tiny dinghy. It struck me that the President looked decidedly uncomfortable!

The administration is run by an Austrian firm – Alaba Hotels Touristic – and reservations were expected at 78 per cent of capacity with an 'exchange input' of 10 million Deutschmarks. The assurance was given that guests would not be overwhelmingly German, but as no British tour operators were involved at the outset and it is probable that 70 per cent of visitors who come to this coast are German anyway, the promise of mixed nationalities is not wholly convincing. There is considerable emphasis on sport and entertainment, and 500 units with heating for the winter months when there is a 40 per cent reduction.

Palmiye Village is also new, more Turkish-looking and more sympathetic, with good food. Because these holiday villages are new, it is difficult to report on their development and prices. Also, the majority of holiday-makers will be going on agency package tours at considerably lower rates.

Otherwise, the charges are reasonable and could be considered good value in view of all the facilities involved. For a single guest they go from L 51,750 per day, which includes full board.

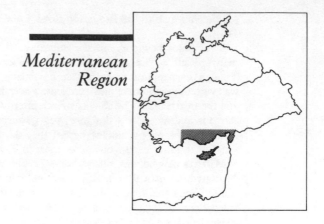

Mediterranean Region

Termessos •   Perge •
        • Aspendos
    Side •
ANTALYA •   • Manavgat

           • Alanya

Tarsus •   • **ADANA**

Uzuncaburç •   **MERSIN** •

Heaven and Hell   • Korykos
(Cennet ve Cehennem) • • Kiz Kalesi
       Taşucu • • Silifke   Iskenderun

      Anamur •

                                              ANTAKYA •

MEDITERRANEAN SEA
(Ak Deniz)   **SYRIA**

             CYPRUS

Mediterranean Region

Introduction

Turkey's Mediterranean coastline does, of course, stretch further west than the starting point of Antalya would suggest, but the region covered in the following section is generally not so highly developed and as a result the towns here have something of a different character to their counterparts on the Turkish Riviera.

There are, of course, beaches and swimming along much of this coastline too, such as the resorts of Side and Alanya, but the places of interest covered in the following section are to be found by turning your back on the sea on occasion. Leaving the resort of Antalya, for example, and heading north-west brings its reward in the ruins of the theatre and necropolis at Termessos high above sea level. On the coastal plains you will find the ruins of the cities of Perge and Aspendos, while past Silifke you can transport yourself to Heaven and Hell (*Cennet ve Cehennem*). Also in this area are the Crusader castles such as Anamur, Korykos and Kız Kalesi which make an exploration of this region particularly memorable.

Though it must be admitted that the romance suggested by the names of some places along the eastern shores of the Turkish Mediterranean region is not always borne out by the reality, the area can still be rewarding in terms of beauty, with the road between Alanya and Silifke hugging the pine-covered mountain slopes which sweep down to the sea.

Antalya to Side

Antalya Antalya is a busy, sophisticated town in its own right with the flavour of the Riviera if not that of an obvious resort. The population is around 200,000. Situated on cliffs with a bay beyond sweeping towards the Taurus mountains, the town has a cheerful atmosphere with wide boulevards lined with date palms and an attractive old harbour which has been restored impeccably with open-air restaurants, terraced bars and promenades. It is an admirable example of modern Turkish architectural style, combining the old with the new.

Founded in the second century BC by Attalus II of Pergamon, it was conquered later by the Romans and Seljuks. There is an excellent museum on the outskirts of the town and you can walk to Hadrian's Gate, which was built in AD 130 to mark his visit. Antalya provides the perfect base for excursions to Aspendos, Perge, Side, and Termessos in particular, and is a good starting point for the independent traveller driving along the Mediterranean coastline, whether west to Bodrum or east towards Antakya.

Where to stay **Talya Hotel**, Fevzi Çakmak Caddesi 30, tel.: 15600; 140 rooms and ten bungalow rooms, with colour television, a mini-bar, direct long distance phone-calls, and air-conditioning; Manager Günaç Gürkaynak. This is unashamedly expensive and luxurious, but the Talya is one of the most sympathetic hotels in Turkey, situated on the cliff-top and well designed. It has an outside dining area like the prow of a ship, marvellous for breakfast with jugs of fresh orange juice and coffee, and a view across the water to the endless, shimmering Taurus mountains as if you are sailing towards them. Candle-lit dinners beside the pool are decidedly glamorous and the food enhances the surroundings. There are four bars, the poolside opens at 10 a.m., and breakfast is served in your room if you prefer, from 7 to 11 a.m.

Usually I resist the luxury-type hotel. With the Talya I yield happily, for though the service is professional the hotel is not impersonal like so many of its kind. Then there is the startling bonus of being able to take a lift from your floor to the swimming-pool, and another from there down the cliff-face, which resembles petrified wood, to the sea and a landing-stage at the bottom. This is luxurious too, with umbrellas and couches for sunbathing, a marble 'health bar' where you can undermine your health with stronger drinks as well, and an exceptional swim in the sea which grows so choppy in the afternoon that the rafts buck like broncos, turning you into a cocktail-shaker if you have drunk too rashly at the bar while providing an exhilarating hangover cure at the same time.

Unless the Talya has suffered from some inexplicable decline, it is worth the considerable expense. The cost plummets in the winter which is still pleasantly warm, encouraging certain tours to offer you a L 6,000 discount every day that it rains for more than four hours between 10 a.m. and 5 p.m. Prices are from L 110,500 for a double room.

Several tours combine the Talya with the Divan in Istanbul for a two-centre holiday, and this must be exceptional value.

Adalya Hotel, Kaleiçi, tel.: 18066. Built in 1869 behind the old harbour, the building was used first as a bank and then as a warehouse. Today this is another triumph of Turkish conversion, preserving the former façade while modernising the interior with air-conditioning for twenty-eight rooms, an American bar and restaurant. It is constructed around a central space with landings on each floor opening on to the bedrooms, rather like a deluxe prison. It is well furnished and highly thought of, yet slightly smug as if the building feels it deserves the many awards it has won. It does, but some people might find the atmosphere a bit stuffy. The bill will be roughly L 55,000 per person – superb value for an exceptional hotel.

Hotel Sera, Lara, tel.: 31170; 150 rooms, with baths, mini-bars and balconies. Turkish Tourism award this hotel five stars (like the Talya) but the modern block is a less attractive building, though it is near the sea at about 11 km from Antalya, a short bus ride. The numerous facilities, pool and tennis court may well be better than their impersonal appearance, which resembles that of a modern airport.

Lara Hotel, Lara Yolu, tel.: 15299; in the same area, with a private beach; sixty rooms. This is smaller, though it is still a large modern block, and seems more sympathetic. The steep steps to a small private beach below is not easy going for children, but Lara Beach is only a few minutes away.

Blue Hotel, on the cliff-top about 3 km from Antalya. This is not even listed in the official tourist guide, yet is particularly attractive, with bungalow rooms off a beautiful garden and a good swimming-pool as well as a man-made area in the sea below. There are the usual facilities, bar and restaurant, and if the Talya is full or too expensive I would try here as an alternative.

Motel Antalya, Lara Yolu 84, tel.: 14609; twelve rooms (probably increasing), all with showers, 5 km on the way to Lara Beach; half-board only. The prices are reasonable, mid-range.

Gala, in the centre of town, is new and small with simple rooms with showers – good value.

Star, Çetinkaya Caddesi, tel.: 11280. Unpretentious, basic, in the centre of town, recommended by Turks. It has large double beds in comfortable rooms. The disco is 'like the ones in Europe'; the cuisine is Turkish and European, with an American bar. A double room costs L 55,000; a single L 42,000.

Where to eat   Take your pick from the restaurants in the old harbour which have the most enjoyable atmosphere.

Kral Sofrası, tel.: 12198, and the **Yat**, tel.: 24855 (smarter and more expensive) charge around L 20,000 for two with wine.

Hisar Tesisi, tel.: 15281, is beside the main street beyond the minaret as you walk down from the top. A converted fortress with cave-like rooms, and an open terrace with views overlooking the harbour, it is popular with the Turks for its good food and atmosphere.

Develiler, Org. Kenan Evren Bulvarı, tel.: 12979. This used to be the best before the competition and may remain so. It is off the main street (which is also referred to as Bahçelievler Konyaaltı), professional, with good food and excellent stroganoff, but the restaurant is indoors. The price is reasonable.

Antalya is behind the mosque off Cumhuriyet Caddesi, and the **Şehir** behind that (through the passage), has the advantage of a rooftop terrace and music at night.

For cheaper restaurants, with a lively atmosphere induced by the number of people eating at open-air tables and chairs, go to the street furthest from the clock tower, Eski Sebzeciler İçi Sokak (meaning 'an old market place'), which is lined with restaurants serving kebabs, such as the **Gaz Entep**.

On the way to the Konya Altı, the ten miles of shingle beach stretching to the Taurus mountains, there are a number of fish restaurants at a reasonable price.

Out of Antalya, on the way to Side and Aspendos, at the village of Belkıs there is the **Belkıs Restaurant**, Büyük Belkıs Köyü–Serik, tel.: 3221.1424. It is pleasant, overlooking the river, with cheerful staff and a range of food, including the traditional stew, *güveç*.

Termessos

It would be a wasted opportunity to leave Antalya without climbing to the mountain city of Termessos to witness some of the most spectacular ruins in Turkey. You drive 34 km on the road to Korkuteli into the mountains, through splendid scenery that becomes increasingly alpine. Then a steep but none too difficult climb on foot until you reach the walls of the ruined city, about 1,500 m above sea level.

The Termessians were tough and needed to be to live in such remoteness. They were feared for their sudden raids on coastal ports like Phaselis (see p. 186), yet they were highly civilised as well, a combination that is increasingly rare in so-called modern 'civilisation'. Massive olive oil containers with linking passages allegedly piped oil all the way to Antalya on the coast; you can see the gymnasium for the athletes, and the small, select odeon for the musicians, once covered with red and black marble. Most breathtaking of all is the theatre, cradled in the mountainside like a gigantic nest with views for miles over the Pamphylian plain. When several thousand citizens watched a performance in such conditions, the stage lit by oil lamps and moonlight, the words of the poorest playwright would have been enhanced. You can also see the arches on the lowest level which released the wild animals.

Yet the most astonishing aspect of Termessos is the tombs. They tumble down the mountainside much as the earthquake left them nearly 2,000 years ago, for Termessos, above all, was a great necropolis – not a city on the hill (acropolis) but a burial ground on the hill, with walkways and gardens where people played music and celebrated the departure of friends and relatives into another world. Many of the tombs are decorated with the shields which symbolised Termessians in battle, others have lions and gryphons or the staring sockets of Medusa heads to scare off grave-robbers, though the tombs are rent so fiercely it looks as if they have been torn apart by wilder elements than man. The necropolis lies on two levels – try to reach the higher which is the most rewarding, but look out for black snakes in the undergrowth.

Termessos was the fortress which Alexander turned away from in disgust after the Termessians released an avalanche of boulders on his men below; he burnt their precious olive groves as he left. When you visit this eyrie you understand why the great Alexander realised he had met his equals. After his death, his general Alcestas sought refuge here but the elders handed him over to his rival Antigonus, who killed him and disfigured his body. Displaying their earlier audacity, the younger Termessians rescued the mutilated corpse and gave it a worthy burial. Today, there is a rock carving of a mounted warrior, supposed to be that of Alcestas in his final battle.

Before long, you may be able to take a cable-car to the top of the Taurus range, ski in the morning and swim in the Mediterranean in the afternoon. Meanwhile, you can go to Termessos in the cooler hours of the morning and return to swim at the Talya or Lara beach.

So far, Termessos is hardly excavated, and it is tempting to hope that it will remain free from mass tourism for a long time to come.

Perge Off the main road, 17 km from Antalya and set inland on a fertile plain, the extensive ruins convey the size of this ancient city when it was colonised by the Greeks after the fall of Troy. Possibly because of the flatness of the Pamphylian plain where the range of Taurus mountains start to veer inland, the ruins do not have the spectacular effect of Termessos but are worth seeing for the theatre and well-preserved stadium, and even more for the main street. There, a channel of water 4 m wide once flowed through the middle, bringing freshness on a summer's day to the people who shopped at the galleries on either side, supported by marble columns to provide shade.

Aspendos This should be seen briefly for its Roman theatre (AD 200), which is the best preserved in the world and is still in use today for the annual Antalya Festival. In the true Roman style, it was built with a wall as backdrop to the stage in front, filled with statuary which has to be imagined today though a reconstructed plan provides assistance. The theatre holds an audience of between 15,000 and 20,000 – an extraordinary figure when you consider it – and the acoustics were and still are remarkable, with the curious visual illusion of a curved dome as you look up at the sky.

The brief detour is enhanced by the sight of a perfect Seljuk bridge over the river where ships once sailed towards Aspendos when it flourished as a river port and Alexander agreed to spare it in return for several thousand horses. It is interesting to note, if one thinks of him simply in dictatorial terms, that Atatürk was so impressed by the theatre when he made a tour of this coastline to encourage Westernisation, that he ordered that it should be restored and used again.

Manavgat   The town of Manavgat is the *dolmuş* exchange stop for Side. Worth a brief detour on a hot day are the waterfalls – pleasing rather than spectacular, with stepping-stones and tributaries abundant with trout, and a terraced café in mid-stream for a cool, relaxing drink.

Side   Side, which means 'pomegranate', has long been popular with Turkish and foreign holiday-makers alike, though its future is threatened by excessive development. The town is a curious amalgam of ancient ruins, some of them tumbled about on the water's edge, and garish souvenir shops selling identical goods. Two large sandy beaches remain the attraction, though one is extremely shallow for swimming, and it comes as no surprise to learn that we have been preceded by Cleopatra and Mark Antony who swam here, too.

Once Side was a modest fishing village with small wooden houses. Today it is swollen by tourism as crowds squeeze their way through the main streets in summer to the blare of disco-pop. This can make it jolly, others may find it bloated. Unfortunately, hotels are growing into vast, ungainly complexes which are coldly impersonal, an attitude reflected by world-weary staff, but a few retain their old character like the Neptune (see facing page).

Those who knew Side in the old days deplore the change and say it is unrecognisable – then they pause, and add that they love it still. Irrevocably spoilt or not, Side sports a boisterous, almost a sexy, charm which Cleopatra herself might have approved of.

Getting there   Side is 75 km from Antalya; by bus you change at Manavgat. But you can go directly to Ankara, Izmir and Istanbul. Cars should be parked in the area near the theatre.

History   In the seventh century BC Side was colonised by the Greeks who came south after the Trojan wars. Then a Pamphylian port of some importance, it had a thriving slave trade around the tenth century AD before it declined. The ruins are largely Roman, with walls and towers so well preserved that they are an essential and startling feature of the town today, one of its advantages. A massive theatre (second century) held an estimated 20,000 people, supposedly the largest in Asia Minor, which indicates Side's size.

What to see   The excellent Museum is both attractive and full of interest, with a fine statue and head of Hermes. A touching, small sarcophagus for a child is decorated with flowers to show that the child is mourned, a swallow to indicate that the family has moved away, a butterfly to suggest reincarnation, and a bobbin of cotton with two notches denoting that the girl was two years old when she died; a mother's bleeding heart lies on the doorway. Another child's tomb has a favourite dog looking wistfully through an open door. Such sarcophagi, and the tear-glasses, echo the celebration of death in Termessos where the

Roman ritual was adopted of weeping into glass containers which were placed beside the corpse so that he could produce them as he stepped into the next world as proof of his popularity. If no one cared enough to cry, professional weepers were employed like the hired 'mutes' in Victorian days who stood, beribboned in black, in grief-stricken attitudes outside the house of the deceased on the day of his funeral.

Where to stay

Local conservationists have fought for the last ten years to save their town from over-development – it is only too apparent that they lost. As it is hard to recommend the biggest and allegedly 'best', I start with one of the few to retain a personality.

The Neptune. It should be stressed that this is not a smart hotel; indeed, it is slightly haphazard, and its brochure does not even list its address or telephone number, but it is very close to the beach in a plot of land which the owner's father, a poor farmer, bought for L 110 fifty years ago. In 1975 the present owner intended to build a private house, but changed his mind when he realised that Side was poised on a tourist boom and built the hotel, step by step, with his ten brothers, planting all the trees and devoting the profits to improving the place generally. The result is happily inappropriate: a large house in the style of a Swiss chalet, with garden houses too, but pleasantly restful with an exceptionally friendly owner and staff. The simple bedrooms have sympathetic decorations; the best overlook the sea, with the promise that 'you will have the nicest experiences in our comfortable rooms – when you get up in the morning, you won't need any music, because the birds will be singing for you.' There are forty rooms, with showers, hot water and balconies, and various bar and restaurant facilities in summer. The price for a double with breakfast is from L 20,000; L 26,000 for half-board.

Cennet Hotel, tel.: 1167. This is a good compromise: not so eccentric as the Neptune, and attractively laid out with 102 rooms on three levels, set in gardens running to the beach with a convenient open-air bar and restaurant. Good for a lunch-time snack of an omelette, slices of döner kebab and salad, coffee and beer for about L 5,000. The gardens are well laid out with tables and chairs in which you can relax after a squeeze through the overcrowded main street filled with tourists and soldiers from a nearby camp who live abroad and have paid for the privilege of a nominal national service of shorter length. It is on the expensive side, at L 65,000 for a double room in summer, but this includes half-board. The beach facilities include wind-surfing and water-skiing.

Defne Hotel, tel.: 1880. One of the immense complexes on the far side of the beach, this has all the facilities. It is similar to the nearby Turtel, but less overwhelming with a mere 110 rooms. Prices from L 37,000 for half-board.

Turtel, Selimiye Köyü, tel.: 2225. This used to be well thought of, but has grown too big. I have nothing against the big hotels in fashionable resorts, with names like The Grand and Angleterre, but these complexes are new and can hardly be called an enhancement, unlike the white wedding-cake affairs you see at Brighton, Cannes or even the Splendid on Princes Islands near Istanbul. The Turtel today has 324 rooms, including 84 suites, two swimming pools (one Olympic size), tennis courts and disco, and boasts that it covers an area of 62,000 sq m. It is a village in itself, with nearly 200 staff, and prides itself on its restaurant. Inevitably the price list is in Deutschmarks. A full-season double room will cost about L 37,500 for half-board.

Hermes Pension is associated with the Hermes boutique in the main square: someone will show you the way. It is run by Mrs Guzel and her family and basic with shared kitchen and washing, but it has a garden and prices are lower accordingly as they are with all such family pensions.

Look out for the sign *Boş oda var* ('Vacancies') for cheap, but not necessarily inferior, lodgings.

Where to eat   **Afrodit**, tel.: 171, at the end of the main street, overlooks the sea. It is popular and busy with a sympathetic atmosphere and owner, Ermin Güneylioğlu.

Numerous other restaurants can be judged on sight as you walk through the town.

Alanya to Antakya

Alanya   With a fortress on top of a high rock protected by crenellated walls, a red tower and a sweep of beach stretching miles to the south, Alanya has been praised as 'the pearl of the Mediterranean', while the rocky peninsula of Kolonoras was known to the Greeks as 'the beautiful mountain'. Some travellers may find such clichés excessive today. Though popular and with plenty of interest, Alanya is not comparable to the resorts further west (Antalya, Kaş, Marmaris and Bodrum) as an ideal base for a holiday.

Due to tourism it has started to become more lively recently, but it is hard to realise that in 1071 this was the leading port for the Seljuks, though they made their capital at Konya. The natural stronghold of the fortress remains much the same, stormed by the Anatolian Sultan Alaeddin Keykubat in 1220 who finally gained admission by one of several legendary methods which include marrying the Governor's daughter, tying lamps to the horns of thousands of mountain goats to suggest an invincible advancing army, or simply doing a deal. On his tour along the coast, Atatürk changed the name of the town from Ala-iyeh to Alanya, called after Alaeddin who built the Red Tower in 1225 to protect the shipyards.

One reason for slight scepticism regarding Alanya is that until recently accommodation has been scarce and often vile, apart from the sprawling **Alantur** 6 km to the south. Fortunately, that position is changing for the better.

Where to stay   **Alantur Hotel**, Çamyolu Köyü, tel.: 1224; a 100-room complex with three swimming pools beside an exceptional beach. Less attractive are the 'pearls' with which you have to pay for your drinks, and the topless Germans who flock here in large numbers.

Alaiye Hotel, Atatürk Caddesi, tel.: 4018; named after the conquering sultan, is a welcome antidote. Small and friendly, it is in the town but only 100 m away from the beach. It has a garden, and all rooms have showers.

Kaptan Hotel, İskele Caddesi 62, tel.: 2000; near the Tourist Office; forty-five rooms, modern and air-conditioned.

Büyük Hotel, Güllerpınar Mahallesi, tel.: 1138; sixty-six rooms with showers, five minutes from the beach; restaurant and bar; half-board only.

Where to eat   Walk along the waterfront and choose the restaurant which most appeals to your eye or pocket.

Towards Antakya   If you are driving south to Silifke, it takes longer than it would appear from the map – over six hours by bus – largely due to the winding roads hugging the mountains which are covered with pines and run steeply to the sea with splendid views. If you are driving independently spare time for leisurely pauses, and avoid travelling at night for it would be a shame to lose such scenery in the darkness.

The Crusader Castles   The most striking feature of the journey south is the castles. **Anamur**, half-way to Silifke is a splendid example, built between two beaches; while **Korykos** beyond Silifke stands beside a beach, eclipsed by the romantic Maiden's Castle (*Kız Kalesi*) which seems to rise out of the sea but was built on a narrow islet 200 m offshore. Once the two castles were joined by a sea wall.

If you wish to make an overnight stop but not in the town of Silifke itself, try the modest but friendly motel at **Bağsak** a few kilometres before Taşucu, which has twenty-two bedrooms, a restaurant and its own bay.

Taşucu   This is a transit point for the ferry to Turkish Cyprus. The tourist bureau, tel.: 234, by the docks will give you advice on current timetables; a hovercraft sails three times a week and the journey takes two hours. The regular boat service is cheaper but longer, going on alternate days, and carries cars as well as passengers. Hotels include the massive new Taştur, tel.: 290, and the Olba Hotel, tel.: 1222, which is smaller and luxurious.

Silifke   A short distance further on is the former Seleucia, founded by Seleucus, one of Alexander's generals who fought for the succession on his death. The acropolis, later a fortress, dominates the hill above the town.

Uzuncaburç

A more rewarding journey is to drive nearly 30 km inland into the hills.

A detour recommended for the beauty of the unexpected ruins which will take you by surprise. Presumably this remote Greek and Roman settlement, known as Diocaesarea during the reign of Emperor Vespasian (AD 9–79) was a military base, yet the ruins suggest the height of civilisation. Probably it was founded originally by Seleucus (around 300 BC) at the same time that he developed Antioch, today's Antakya.

The eastern gateway, leading into the main street, still has five majestic Corinthian columns with the small head of a lion looking down from the elegant frieze above. There is a tower, 22 m high, which was probably defensive and gave its name to the city ('High Tower'), and scattered tombs with the heads of bulls and other finely carved decorations. Most impressive of all is the Temple of Zeus built around 300 BC with thirty headless columns in a design reminiscent of Baalbek in the Lebanon.

As you climb into the hills, you notice two Roman temple–tombs on the left-hand side, which are well worth a closer look for their attractive proportions – two levels supported by four columns, an arch enclosing the sarcophagus, and a perpendicular roof decorated with a frieze. Unfortunately, these have been vandalised over the years.

Dracek

More remarkable and better preserved is the large temple to the Fearless King, reached after a difficult walk down the hill 5 km beyond the village of Dracek further on from Uzuncaburç. Search for a track on the left – though it could be signposted by now – otherwise it is hardly visible. When and if you find the tomb, your effort will be rewarded. This is a handsome building, though set in the wilderness, twice the size of the others. It has the bonus of a handsome phallus carved on the side in honour of Priam (Priape), the God of Fertility, which encouraged prospective brides to come here before their wedding day in the hope of fertility by association – and possibly a curiosity to see the phallus, too. Few visitors come here today, which makes the effort so worth while.

Narlıkuyu

Seven km from Silifke along the coast is this pleasant stop with the mosaic floor of an ancient Roman bath depicting the Three Graces with the encouraging inscription: 'He who drinks from this water will become wise and long-living and, if ugly, fair.' The swimming is good, with a cool, refreshing undercurrent near the surface. There are a couple of good fish restaurants, such as the Ali Baba.

Cennet ve Cehennem

The two chasms of **Heaven and Hell** (*Cennet ve Cehennem*), with curved, slippery sides are to be found 2 km inland. It is not all that easy to descend into Hell, where legend claims that Typhon the Giant was imprisoned. Heaven, slightly nicer, has the ruins of a fifth-century church. It is cool and quiet apart from birdsong, and boys with lamps take you to a dark cave with remarkable stalactites and the sound of an underground river, which may account for the level of cold water at Narlıkuyu.

Mersin One and a half hours' drive from Silifke, Mersin (also known as İçel) is the largest industrial port on the Turkish Mediterranean, with a population of 220,000 and the feeling of prosperity for the fortunate few (Arabs hog the lifts in the best hotels), ritzy poolside restaurants on the beach just out of town with cabaret at night. High apartment blocks as you drive towards such displays of wealth may be a step down but are hardly offensive. The visible blemish in Mersin is the sickly, yellow cloud of gas streaming from a thin factory chimney.

The waterfront has been laid out with gardens and trees, carefully tended by scores of workmen: eventually it will be parkland which will enhance the city further. For more hustle and bustle walk to the older part of town and the square which used to be a covered caravanserai now used for reasonably priced restaurants, though the giant prawns from Iskenderun are not as cheap as you might expect given that it is only down the coast.

Otherwise, little remains to indicate that this was one of the earliest towns in ancient neolithic civilisation, an astounding 6,000 years ago.

Where to stay **Mersin**, Camii Serif Mahallesi; tel.: 12200, has three bars and a roof restaurant – the best in town with panoramic views over the harbour, but expensive and not particularly Turkish.

Toros Hotel, Atatürk Caddesi 33; tel.: 12201; sixty-two rooms. This is half the price of the Mersin but in its modest way is more sympathetic, with Turkish furnishings and a greater Turkish atmosphere.

Where to eat **Babil**, Mezitliköyü; tel.: 75 (local). As so often in Turkey, where the food is on display, you have the chance to walk around the town and settle for the restaurant which pleases or suits your budget best.

Tarsus Today an industrial town, 27 km inland, with a population of 100,000, the name of Tarsus is, I fear, everything. It conveys images of St Paul (whose alleged birthplace is on the outskirts) and Cleopatra preparing for her historic encounter with Mark Antony before they gambolled up the coast. What a meeting that must have been in 41 BC! She sailed up the river in her galley to Tarsus, which was then a port, dressed in the role of Aphrodite, reclining on a couch of gold brocade, and fanned by pretty boys and maidens representing cupids and graces, while thousands waited on shore to greet her arrival. Cleopatra's Gate (also called The Gate of the Bitch) stands in the centre of Tarsus today, though it is doubtful if much of the original is left. The traffic kills the romance and sadly it is not worthy of a detour except for the sake of the history.

Adana Continuing east from Tarsus, you will reach the fourth largest city in Turkey with a population of 1½ million due to recent expansion. It is best to stay overnight if you want to appreciate the atmosphere, which is hardly possible on a hasty visit in the heat of the day. A surprising reservoir, 25 km long, outside the city provides a cooling freshwater swim in the afternoon. Excavations show that Adana dates from the Hittite period but little remains, though the museum contains relics from this and Assyrian times.

Where
to stay

Büyük Sürmeli Hotel, Kuruköprü Özler Caddesi, tel.: 23600, has 170 rooms; big but old-fashioned. **İpek Palas Hotel**, İnönü Caddesi 103, tel.: 18741, is cheaper. For dinner, try the speciality – the hot, spicy Adana kebabı.

Iskenderun

From Adana you cross the plain of Issos where Alexander the Great defeated Darius III of Persia in 333 BC. Alexander founded a city after this great victory, calling it Alexandra ad Issum after himself; this was later shortened to Alexandretta, and then to Iskenderun – İskender means Alexander in Turkish. Once a centre of Christianity, it is now frankly industrial and dull with modern hotels, such as **Hataylı**, Osmangazi Caddesi, tel.: 11551, which has air-conditioned rooms. **Hotel Kamelya**, at Belen on the eastern side of Iskenderun, is noted for nice rooms, excellent food and hospitality.

Thirty km to the south is a fishing village with an attractive sandy beach for swimming, and **Arsuz Turistik**, tel.: 21782 – the best hotel before Syria.

Antakya

The coastline is not as romantic as the names suggest – Iskenderun to Antakya or, better still, Alexandretta to Antioch – for they are belied by the stain of industry rather than tourism. From Iskenderun it is a distance of 60 km to Antakya over the Belen Pass with views over the ancient valley of Orontes.

History

After the death of Alexander the Great in 323 BC, his general Seleucus founded his own capital (in 300 BC) at the mouth of the River Orontes, now the Asi, and named it after his father, Antiochus. (With the unabashed vanity of dictators, he called his province Seleucia after himself.) After the Roman occupation in AD 64, Antioch became the third city, after Rome and Alexandria, of the Empire and the western world, with a population of half a million – astonishing proof of its importance. It grew and prospered with the trade routes to the east, especially as a crucial point on the Great Silk Route for the caravans.

As a centre for the arts, notorious for its self-indulgence, Antioch rivalled Athens. It was also a centre for Christianity, with possibly the first Christian church in the world, 2 km east of the town, where a service is held every 29 June on the feast day of St Peter who preached on this spot and was, by tradition, its first bishop. The city was destroyed in 1268 by the Mamelukes of Egypt, former Arabian slaves, and then started to decline.

What to see

A definite French influence today is due to the occupation by France as part of her mandate over Syria from 1920. Antakya reverted to Turkey just before the Second World War, but retains a boulevardier appearance, with broad avenues lined with palms. Little can be seen of its former glory except, as so often, in the Archaeology Museum which helps to compensate, with the portraiture of the

Roman mosaics taken from Daphne (Harbiye). These are claimed to be the finest examples of their kind, depicting such scenes as Orpheus playing his lyre, surrounded by smiling wild animals who listen entranced. The museum holds many Hittite remains as well.

Where
to stay

Atahan Hotel, Hürriyet Caddesi, tel.: 11036; twenty-eight rooms; L 8,500 for a double. Apparently people can look into bedrooms from the rooftop restaurant opposite (!) but the hotel's own restaurant is recommended. Try also the **Divan Hotel**, İstiklal Caddesi 62, tel.: 11518; with twenty-three rooms.

Where
to eat

Zümrüt, in the same street as the Atahan Hotel, has an outdoor terrace. There are also a number of cheaper kebab houses in the same central street.

Harbiye (formerly Daphne) with woods and waterfalls provides a cooler and pleasanter setting for an evening meal. The **Deliban Hotel** (tel.: 5455) is luxurious yet reasonable.

By now you have reached the Syrian border. If you wish to continue to Aleppo, it is vital to have obtained a visa, and nowadays this is not too easy.

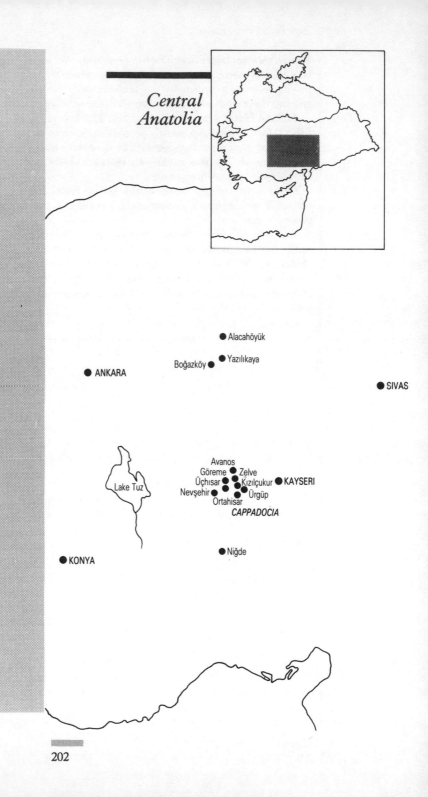

Central
Anatolia

● Alacahöyük

Boğazköy ● ● Yazılıkaya

● ANKARA

● SIVAS

Avanos
Göreme ● Zelve
Üçhısar ● ● Kızılçukur ● KAYSERI
Lake Tuz   Nevşehir ● ● Ürgüp
Ortahisar
CAPPADOCIA

● Niğde

● KONYA

Central Anatolia

Introduction

In Central Anatolia you are in the heartland of the country, both geographically and politically, since the Turkish capital of Ankara, the seat of government and administration, falls within this region.

In addition, Konya is the centre for the sect known as the Whirling Dervishes: a sect which, although officially discouraged today, holds a ceremony in the town each December to commemorate the death of their founder Mevlana, Celaleddin Rumi, who lies buried here.

There is evidence in this region of the various influences at work throughout the country's long history. Christian frescoes can be seen in the churches at Göreme, Seljuk style in the buildings in Sivas and Konya, and Ankara's Museum of Anatolian Civilisations bursts with treasures from, among others, the Hattian, Hittite and Phrygian periods of the region's history.

The Hittite sites around Boğazköy are certainly memorable, but the highlight of any visit to Central Anatolia is undoubtedly the Cappadocia region between Nevşehir, Kayseri and Niğde. The surrealistic terrain around Göreme, although seemingly other-worldly, is the result of natural and human factors at work on the landscape. The rock churches of Güllüdere and Kızılçukur, and the underground cities of Kaymaklı and Derinkuyu, together with the strange ravines, rock cones and the weird shapes which the Turks call 'fairy chimneys' are unforgettable and provide a fitting climax to a visit to this region.

Ankara

Ankara's location at the heart of Anatolia makes it one of the most convenient centres in Turkey, easy to travel east, west, north and south. Atatürk's decision to make this his capital in 1923 was a shrewd one, for this is a truly Turkish town even though the previous layers of civilisation – Greek and Roman – are visible. The first impression may be that of a modern city, but the roots stretch back to paleolithic

Main areas

and neolithic ages, with excavations revealing remains from the Hattis succeeded by the Hittites.

Today the modern city is dominated by the Mausoleum of Atatürk, while the ancient Citadel houses a twelfth-century mosque. The layout of the city makes it easy to explore, with the main road or boulevard - inevitably named Atatürk Bulvarı - continuing to Ulus Meydanı ('the square of the nation') as the main focal point, with the citadel on the hill above where the back streets boast a more colourful atmosphere; the first Parliament building; and the Çankırı Caddesi, the continuation of the boulevard, leading to the Roman ruins and ancient baths on the way to the airport.

The embassies and richer residences are situated on the hill of Çankaya in striking contrast to the *gecekondu*, the rough dwellings erected overnight on the outskirts by incoming families in search of work.

A curiously underrated city, Ankara has a busy, friendly atmosphere enhanced by parks and artificial lakes where people go boating, and the Atatürk Forest Farm with picnic sites and a replica of the house in Salonika where Turkey's national hero was born. In hot weather, if the din of the city becomes overwhelming, you can drive to recreational areas outside, especially Gölbaşi Lake with fish restaurants along the shore. There is no denying that Ankara is a governmental town but it can be enjoyable too.

Getting there

As the capital of Turkey, Ankara is the centre for a network of communication: there is an excellent bus service to and from the entire country and planes from Istanbul. Numerous trains either stop en route to Van or Erzurum, or go direct, like the special deluxe Blue Train from Istanbul which takes seven and a half hours, and the Anatolia Express, which goes at night with a sleeping car. Though trains are inexpensive, it is advisable to make sure of a booking. One word of warning: do not take any train that is not marked as an *ekspres*, or it could be days before you arrive.

What to see
Atatürk's Mausoleum

A neoclassical temple which took nine years to build on top of a hill called Reşat Tepe, the mausoleum (*Anıt Kabir*) is reached through a broad avenue flanked by statues of lions, set in an impressive ceremonial square surrounded by columns with the words emblazoned above the entrance: BEYOND ALL DOUBT, GOVERNMENT BELONGS TO THE PEOPLE. With soldiers and sailors on guard, the mausoleum has the awe-inspiring solemnity of a shrine, visited by Turks with open reverence, yet some of the modest touches are the most interesting to the foreign visitor. These include Atatürk's personal possessions and the splendid vintage limousines in which he toured the new republic.

Hittite Museum

Also known as the Museum of Anatolian Civilisations, on the slope of the Citadel, this could hardly be a greater contrast to the Mausoleum with the foremost collection of Hittite treasures which go back several thousand years. It is one of the finest museums of antiquities in the world, and alone justifies a visit to Ankara. The exhibits start with the Palaeolithic period before 7000 BC; the Neolithic period 7000–5500 BC with a reconstructed house from the recently discovered town of Çatal Höyük, and a fresco of kissing leopards; then the Chalcolithic period with its painted pottery. The Bronze Age, 3000–2000 BC, is splendid with golden artefacts, the bronze statuette of a bull (2400 BC), the innovation of a horse's bit, along with the famous latticed sun discs with the figures of stags. This is a useful way of assessing the various stages of Turkish civilisation as you move forward in time to the Assyrian period, 1950–1750 BC, and then to the hall which deals with the Hittites, 1700–1450 BC, which has the special appeal of being recently discovered. The Inandik Vase showing a wedding procession, and a surprising act of sodomy, painted in relief, were found by the director of the museum in 1967.

Friezes have been taken from the archaeological site of Boğazköy representing the divine bulls who pulled a celestial chariot. The central hall is devoted to Hittite sculpture, including the famous lions and sphinxes which guarded the city gates. Yet again, it is the detail which lingers in the memory, such as the vessel shaped as a two-headed duck, 1600–1500 BC, a work of sheer perfection. From the later period, the statue of a guardian lion from Malatya is memorable, too.

There is much to see and a knowledgeable Turkish friend would be a help. Of interest to those going to Lake Van are the Urartian objects, the bronze cauldron with bulls' heads, based on a tripod with cloven feet, resembling a Phrygian cauldron also in the museum, indicating a consistency in Anatolian design. Cauldrons were a crucial part of daily life, and there is another from Gordion (100 km from Ankara and once an important town on the route to the West) dating back to the Bronze Age. Gordion was occupied by a series of invaders, so that eighteen levels of civilisation have been excavated, like the layers of a *mille-feuille*. The name came from Gordios, King of the Phrygians, and it was here that Alexander the Great cut the Gordion Knot, known to sailors today as a Turk's Head, fulfilling the legend that the man who untied this rope would conquer all of Asia. Sad to say, Alexander cheated. Unable to loosen it with his fingers, he did so with his sword, proclaiming, 'I've done it!', and the propitious thunder and lightning convinced everyone that he had.

The final exhibitions concern the Greek and Roman times, with the exception of a life-size figure of the Phrygian Goddess of Animals, smiling as she holds a bird in her hand.

When Dan Leno, the music hall comedian, showed his visitors around the Tower of London, he always steered them determinedly towards the refreshment rooms: those in the Ankara Museum provide a welcome climax at the end of the east hall, where you can enjoy a drink, listen to birdsong, and try to untangle the numerous civilisations you have crossed, like a traveller in time.

Where to stay

In view of Ankara's importance as the seat of government, there are numerous modern hotels to accommodate visiting foreigners and conferences. Inevitably, these suffer from impersonality – like the Büyük – and tend to overwhelm. The Ankara Hilton is joining them in 1988. Consequently, several of the biggest hotels are omitted here, such as the Büyük, Dedeman and Stad. Several other large hotels have more atmosphere and personality.

To start with, one which is modest yet highly recommended in the middle-price range is **Bulvar Palas Hotel**, Atatürk Bulvarı 141, tel.: 134.21.80–88; 177 rooms. This has the immediate advantage of being on one of the main boulevards, with a small terrace in front where you can have a drink and watch the passing parade. Also it is more old-fashioned, with a genuinely Turkish atmosphere and friendly staff who make time to see that you are enjoying your visit. There is a choice of rooms which they are happy to show you: some with only a wash-basin, some singles on the street which are noisier, others behind or on a corner with the luxury of two windows. Avoid the restaurant in the basement, which has no atmosphere, but the facilities on the ground floor are sympathetic with good Turkish food. Prices range from L 27,000 for the cheapest single to L 38,000 for a double with shower, or L 50,000 for a more luxurious corner room.

Top range

Top-range hotels include:

Etap Altınel Hotel, Gazi Mustafa Kemal Bulvarı 151, tel.: 230.32.35. Prices from L 98,250 for a double room with shower. (The Etaps are usually reliable.)

Best Hotel, Atatürk Bulvarı 195, tel.: 167.08.80; prices from L 71,500.

Büyük Sürmeli Hotel (*not* the super-luxury Büyük Ankara), Cihan Sokak 6, tel.: 230.52.40; prices from L 76,000.

Kent Hotel, Mithatpaşa Caddesi 4, tel.: 131.21.11; prices from L 62,500.

Etap Mola Hotel, Atatürk Bulvarı 80, tel.: 133.90.65; prices from L 53,500.

Mid-range

Erşan Hotel, Meşrutiyet Caddesi 13, tel.: 118.98.75; prices from L 26,800; conveniently situated in the centre and largely used by businessmen – bland but comfortable.

Anıt, Gazi Mustafa Kemal Bulvarı 111, tel.: 229.23.85; prices from L 17,850.

Gülpalas Hotel, Bayındir Sokak 15, tel.: 133.31.20; price for a double room with bath from L 22,500; quiet, with only forty-one rooms, some without baths.

Taç Hotel, Çankırı Caddesi 35, Ulus, tel.: 324.30.95; prices from L 13,500 without bath and from L 17,850 with.

Lower range

Ulus is a good area for small quiet hotels in the back streets, like the Taç (above). Other names to look out for are:

Devran, tel.: 240320 near Gazi Lisesi high school on Sanayi Caddesi;

Bulduk Hotel, Sanayi Caddesi 26, tel.: 310.49.15; and **Akman Hotel**, Tavus Sokak 6 (near Devran), tel.: 2441; modern with a bar and parking space. These have the advantage of being close together if one of them is full; all cost around L 13,500 for a double room, possibly slightly more with a bathroom.

Where to eat

Liman, İzmir Caddesi 11, Kızılay, tel.: 230.27.05, is good value for its fresh fish, with a friendly atmosphere. It costs around L 14,650 a head with wine.

Yakamoz Diplomat, Köröğlu Sokak, Gaziosmanpaşa, tel.: 139.48.68, is also good for fish at about L 17,600.

Uludağ Lokantası, Denizciler Caddesi 51, Ulus, tel.: 312.45.65, is the place for kebabs at about L 7,300 a head.

R.V., Tahran Caddesi 12, Kavaklıdere, tel.: 127.43.44, in the Embassy quarter, is noted for the excellent choice of European and Turkish dishes, and its general elegance. It is expensive, from L 17,850 with wine.

Also in the area of Kavaklıdere are **Pera Restoran**, **Villa a la Turka** (slightly less expensive at Ulus), **Yeni Karpiç**, **Yıldız**, **Divan**, **Havuzlu**. These are all Turkish, with reasonable prices.

Hotel receptionists may try to induce you towards **China Town**. This does have excellent food, but it is pretentious, catering for tourists and foreign personnel stationed in Ankara, and accordingly it is very expensive.

Excursions from Ankara

The Hittite sites
Getting there

Day trips from Ankara to the Hittite sites are possible: it is easiest to go on a bus tour organised by a travel agency in Ankara. If you are driving independently, they are on the route to Samsun on the Black Sea. You turn off at Sungurlu, 175 km east of Ankara; if you have travelled independently by bus, take a *dolmuş* or taxi from there. The ruins are so extensive that a taxi with a guide makes sense.

Boğazköy

Also called Boğazkale, this is a modern village 210 km east of Ankara and only 3 km from the ancient capital of **Hattusa**, dating from 1600 BC, which expanded to Ankara, Kayseri, Tarsus, Mersin and part of Lebanon 300 years later.

The Hittites settled here due to the position, which was easy to defend, building a fortress on the hill – **Büyükkale** ('citadel') – of stone slabs which fitted on top of each other without the need of mortar. Thousands of clay tablets were found here signifying a library, and this was probably the site for governmental buildings and the royal residence too, the largest of all the Hittite buildings, 160 m long by 135 m. There is so much to absorb that you would be wise to be selective. The grand archway of the famous Lion Gate has gone, but

Alacahöyük

the entrance to Boğazköy is still guarded by two stone lions outside, intended to frighten away intruders.

Though the sphinxes from the Sphinx Gate at Boğazköy are now in museums, the originals at the other Hittite site of Alacahöyük 36 km away remain, with a relief at the base of a double-headed eagle, a brace of hares in its talons. Excavations have revealed fifteen layers of civilisation starting with the burial chambers where the Hittite kings were placed, surrounded by golden jewellery – these are now in Ankara. A visit first to the Hittite Museum in the capital helps to put these sites in perspective.

Yazılıkaya

Within easy reach of Boğazköy, this has a chamber carved out of the rock with friezes of processions. For once, these are best seen at noon, so try to time your visit accordingly.

It has to be admitted that, due to the age of the remains, the figures such as the sphinxes have been worn by time and you need to travel with your own enthusiasm. If you do, you should be rewarded, but the reconstruction is in the mind's eye.

Where to stay

Staying overnight at Boğazköy could be interesting, if primitive. The **Aşıkoğlu** is both a restaurant and a hotel with eight simple rooms. **The Turist** is equally simple, but both are clean.

At **Sungurlu**, 19 km away on the main road to Samsun, there is a convenient and attractive hotel, **The Hitit**, tel.: 424.09, simple but recommended, with a good restaurant and comfortable rooms. Prices are from L 4,000 for a double room and it is wise to book. **Hattuşaş** is a bit grander, with thirty rooms, twelve with shower.

Konya to Sivas

Konya

Formerly known as Iconium, Konya is 260 km south of Ankara. It is an interesting stop if you are continuing south to Silifke or Antalya. The Seljuk capital from the eleventh to the thirteenth centuries, it offers several things to see, mainly connected with the spiritual leader Celaleddin Rumi, known as Mevlana ('Our Master'), who founded the Mevlevi Dervishes, better known to us as the Whirling Dervishes.

Mevlana Mausoleum

His tomb, with the beautifully tiled conical dome of the old monastery, now a museum, is one of the most perfect in Turkey, with a band of Arabic inscriptions wrapped around the incomparable turquoise Iznik tiles. This was where the religious order of the Mevlevi Dervishes was founded, leading to a cult that developed controversial political undertones though Mevlana's original beliefs sound exemplary. He was married to one woman, which was unusual, believed in the equality of women, and preached that all men are free. Yet it is easy to understand why the Dervishes are an anachronism today, with their costumes representing death (the conical hat a tomb and the swirling skirt a shroud), and their whirling movement emulating that of the heavenly bodies. Combined with the chanting, the movement sent the dancers into a state of trance. Finally, the order was banned by Atatürk and is discouraged today as a suspect secret society. It persists, however, and is celebrated with ceremonies in December which commemorate the death of Mevlana on 17 December 1273.

Theological School   The other place of special interest is the carved entrance to the İnce Minareli Medrese ('Slender Minaret'), only the base of which remains after it was struck by lightning. The gigantic doorway opposite, however, is one of the best preserved and most sensational examples of Seljuk baroque art, dating from 1258, with some of the best stone and wood decorations in Turkey and a particularly fine swirl above the arched entrance.

Much belongs to legend regarding this ancient city on the Anatolian plateau. It is claimed that it was the first town to emerge from the Flood, which would take some proving or disproving, and that when Perseus produced the Medusa's head from his bag, he did so here, nailing it to a pillar like an icon – hence Iconium. Early Hittite remains *have* been found and the Alaeddin Mosque can be seen on the ancient citadel, built in 1220.

Where to stay   **Başak Palas Hotel**, Hükümet Meydanı 3, tel.: 113.38; forty rooms, is pleasantly old-fashioned and rather like a rabbit warren, but central and inexpensive. It is recommended by those who stay here.

Özkaymak Park Hotel, Otogar Karşısı, tel.: 337.70; prices from L 22,350 for a double room with bath.

Yeni Sema Hotel, Yeni Meram Yolu, tel.: 132.79; is situated just outside the town, and is liked by those driving independently. There is a first-rate restaurant in a garden, but coach-parties like it too.

Where to eat   Try the local specialities when you can find them on the menu, such as *fırın kebap*, oven-roasted mutton; *etli pide*, pitta bread with meat, and *peynirli pide*, pitta with cheese.

Köşem, Alaettin Bulvarı 26 (not far from Başak Hotel), is a favourite with Turkish businessmen – it has three rooms and an open-air terrace at the back and is inexpensive.

Derya Kebap, in the same area, is very popular with Turks, cheap and merrily crowded.

Fuar is for eating out of doors in Luna Park.

Kayseri   Formerly the Roman Caesarea, 326 km south-east of Ankara, this is the capital of Cappadocia. Its archaeological museum is of great interest, and the Köşk theological school is a Mongol building of classical simplicity. The Great Mosque of Ulu Cami has been restored since it was built in the twelfth century.

The citadel (*hisar*), which dominates the old town, is made of forbidding black volcanic stone and was built in the thirteenth century and greatly repaired by Sultan Mehmet II in the late fourteenth.

Kayseri has a long history largely because of its position at the crossroads of the main trade routes in Anatolia, with roads leading east from the Aegean coast that intersect with roads going north and south between the Black Sea and Mediterranean. All major roads still converge on Kayseri. The first Hittite capital, Kanesh, was situated at Kültepe, north-east of Kayseri. Although there were early settlements at Kayseri, the first certain history occurred when the last King of Cappadocia changed the city's name to Caesarea, in honour of his ruler, Caesar Augustus, in the first century AD. In Byzantine times, Kayseri became important as the birthplace of the great St Basil. The city was sacked by the Arabs several times in the seventh to tenth centuries and was then taken over in turn by the Seljuks, Mongols, Crusaders, Egyptian Mamelukes until its final conquest by the Ottomans, under Selim I, in 1515.

Today, little remains of the old town and Kayseri largely comprises drab modern buildings and avenues that have sprung up in recent years.

There is a fine example of Seljuk caravanserai north-east of the city. The **Sultan Han**, 46 km on the road to Sivas, is well worth stopping for, built by the Sultan Alaeddin Keykubat in the thirteenth century and one of the finest examples of Seljuk architecture, with its intricately carved archways and immense walls.

Situated on the main caravan route, it served to provide good accommodation for travellers, merchants and their animals. The caravanserai was a self-sufficient fortified town, inhabited by cooks, doctors and all the workers needed to service the caravans. In return for paying a tax to the Seljuk sultan, the merchants were allowed to use the caravanserais free of charge.

If you are not driving independently, you could take a taxi from Kayseri, but you should agree a price with your driver first.

Shopping   Above all, Kayseri is a busy trading city with some of the best markets in Turkey, culminating in a central open square in the covered bazaar with bales of recently dyed wool and a fine selection of carpets. If you see something you like, buy it here, for it is unlikely to be cheaper anywhere else, especially the attractive black-and-white tablecloths with patterns stamped by wooden blocks.

Bargain as you shop, for this is a feature of Kayseri. Hard bargaining is so traditional here that if your companion is beating down a craftsman to the point of embarrassment in another part of Turkey, all you have to do is shake your head humorously and say that he or she comes from Kayseri and he will get the point immediately and burst into laughter, entering into the spirit of the game. Be warned, however, that you are very likely to be pursued by carpet sellers throughout your stay in Kayseri.

Where   **Turan Hotel**, Turan Caddesi 8, tel.: 119.68, is old-fashioned (an
to stay   advantage) with a roof terrace and a Turkish bath; prices are from L 22,500.

Where to eat

Hattat Hotel, Istanbul Caddesi 1, tel.: 193.31, is more modern and slightly more expensive, but popular with passing travellers. Try the speciality, *sucuk*, a spiced sausage, or *pastırma*, dried beef with garlic and very pungent spices. The hotels have the best restaurants. **Cumhuriyet,** 27 Mayis Caddesi, and **Kardeşler Lokantası** in the same street, also have good reputations.

Sivas

This no-nonsense town is full of life. It is not the place to which tourists would go deliberately, but is all the more rewarding for that, truer to Turkey than any coastal resort.

The places to look for are the entrances to two theological schools: the **Çifte Minare Medrese** (1271) is no more than a façade, but what a façade! It represents the best of Seljuk design with a beautifully carved entrance and two tall minarets above. The **Gök Medrese** (Gök means 'sky'), also built in 1271, also has a superbly carved doorway whose intricacy never overwhelms, with the windows and walls built in traditional Seljuk style as well.

Where to stay

Köşk Hotel, Atatürk Caddesi 11, tel.: 111.50, is modern, comfortable and reasonably priced. It has forty-four rooms with baths, and is the best in town.

Sultan Hotel, Belediye Sokak 18, tel.: 129.86, is less expensive.

Cappadocia

Cappadocia is situated in Central Anatolia between Nevşehir (274 km south-east of Ankara, and the largest town), Kayseri and Niğde. Göreme is the centre for the churches and the museum, and Ürgüp is probably the best place to stay. Avanos is famous for its pottery and onyx from a nearby factory.

To rush through Cappadocia by bus, allowing brief stops for passengers to descend and photograph this weird landscape, would be as heretical as dashing through the National Gallery in London on roller-skates. The strange conical shapes may look similar, but they vary over a large region and time is needed to absorb them, especially in the changing light, for they can look dusty on a dull day, yet radiant when the sun is shining. An overnight stay is recommended, for the towns of Cappadocia are full of character.

The landscape has been described as lunar – I am guilty of this myself – but that is too easy, even though there are few earthly places like it. It is a land in upheaval as if the ground was shaken apart, burst upwards, started to melt, then froze – and this is roughly what *did* happen thousands of years ago when the mountain of Erciyes erupted and covered the land below with lava. Since then, the tormented shapes of pumice have been sculpted by the erosion of the weather, creating the famous towers with a protective layer of harder tufa on top, referred to euphemistically as 'fairy chimneys', though they look decidedly phallic.

It takes the eye some time to recognise the human factor, with the gradual realisation that these shapes were houses, and the open holes were doors and windows. People have lived in these homes since 3000 BC and the man-made caves are still used as coolers for local lemons and apricots, which can be stored for months. These odd dwellings were a natural refuge in an area where wood is scarce and pumice easy to mould before it is exposed to the air when it hardens.

The Hittites were among the first to settle in Cappadocia but, above all, this was an early centre for Christendom. Christians settled here in tens of thousands to escape persecution from the Arabs further east. This is what makes Cappadocia so remarkable today, with its churches richly decorated with frescoes of such familiar scenes as the Last Supper. These are some of the most extraordinary frescoes in the world.

Getting around Moving from place to place in the Cappadocia region can seem something of a problem: the places of interest are quite far apart and, if you're travelling independently and relying on public transport, it can seem at times as if you're spending most of your time searching or waiting for a means to take you where you want to go. There are several daily buses from Ankara to Kayseri and Nevşehir, but Kayseri is a distance of some 70 km from Cappadocia and separated from it by hills. There are *dolmuş* services from Nevşehir which go close to Göreme (a fifteen-minute walk is about the closest you'll get), but by far the best idea is to base yourself in a town such as Ürgüp and organise a taxi to take you to the areas you want to see.

Zelve The valley of Zelve is particularly beautiful with the ruins of a Byzantine church as well as a Muslim mosque at the entrance to an enchanted chasm with the cliffs honeycombed with caves. It comes as a shock to learn that people lived here as recently as 1950, when they were evacuated because it became unsafe.

As you travel through Turkey your admiration grows for the people who settled in such places as Termessos and Sümela; the Christians were foremost in their exploitation of the natural upheaval, turning it to their advantage as they carved whole communities out of the rock. This is what happened on the surface.

Underground cities The strange troglodyte civilisation above was equalled by the subterranean cities *below*, where the Christians descended when the hordes poured in from the East around the seventh century. When you consider that the Christian population was around 30,000, the scale of these cities becomes more comprehensible – they had churches, ventilator shafts, water tanks and passages which stretched for several kilometres, such as the ones from Kaymaklı to Derinkuyu, which lived up to its name of 'deep well' with seven storeys reaching a depth of 85 m. Yet these were temporary homes to last only until the hordes departed. They were sealed by rolling gigantic millstones across the openings and no smoke was allowed to escape for fear of discovery, denying the inhabitants even the comfort of a fire in winter. If evidence of Christian faith is needed, you will find it here. Personally as I crawled to a lower layer, I found the narrow tunnels so claustrophobic that if I had been a Christian I should have preferred the risk of pillage, carnage and rape in the open air.

Finally the Eastern invaders were driven off by the Byzantines. When the Seljuks followed in the eleventh century they allowed the Christian communities to live in peace.

Inevitably, Cappadocia is popular with tourists so yet again you are advised to go there out of season if possible.

Göreme

The valley of Göreme was disfigured recently by a modern structure of glass and tubing to symbolise the conical shapes of Cappadocia. To everyone's relief and amusement it collapsed in a storm.

The frescoes

Göreme, untarnished, offers some of the most interesting frescoes. The small Elmalı Church (the Church of the Apple) has various scenes from the life of Christ including the crucifixion, though many of these are crumbling from age. The Church of St Barbara opposite has attractive designs in red. Yılanlı Church is in bad repair, but the vaulted ceiling has a delightful fresco of St George complacently lancing a green dragon; and the Tokalı Church near the museum is an impressive structure, the largest in Cappadocia, with five vaults and a series of frescoes which have been restored.

Karanlık Kilise

The most impressive is Karanlik ('Dark') Church, where the frescoes are well preserved owing to the absence of light, apart from that filtering through a small window. They are dominated by the face of Christ surrounded by angels in the hollowed-out central dome, though the most entertaining is the Last Supper, with a huge fish resting on a dish surrounded by Christ and the Apostles. Its beautiful simplicity is shared in the scene of Christ's birth, with the cattle peering over the crib. This church, above all, should not be missed.

Other villages

Should you have time, other astonishing places to visit are **Güllüdere** and **Kızılçukur**, where twelve churches have been carved from the lava rock which sprout up like clusters of conical fungi out of the earth. Even if you only drive through them, the villages of **Ortahisar** and **Üçhisar** are astounding. **Acıksaray** en route to **Nevşehir**, has the façade of the monastery carved into the rocks like a miniature Petra.

Where to stay

Overnight stops could be made at **Avanos** or Nevşehir. The **Hotel Venessa**, Orta Mahallesi Avanos, tel.: 1201, is at the bridge over the River Kızılırmak. This is for tourists, a lively, busy, sympathetic hotel with seventy-three rooms with showers and spectacular views. The **Evim**, tel.: 92, is next to the bridge as well, on the opposite side.

At Nevşehir you can try the **Orsan Kapadokya Hotel**, Kayseri

213

Ürgüp

Caddesi, tel.: 1035, on the road to Ürgüp. It has eighty rooms and a pool; a double room costs from L 22,500.

Providing an excellent base, Ürgüp cannot be called an *attractive* town – the surroundings are too overwhelming – but you feel you are in the heart of somewhere unique, as indeed you are. In spite of the souvenir shops, it remains surprisingly unspoilt, though more and more places are now adapting to tourists.

On the road to Yeşilhisar there are more cave churches to be seen in the towns of Mustafapaşa, Camil and Soğanli. The latter features a church which is unusual even by the standards of this extraordinary region for, unlike other churches in the area which are cut into the rocks, this one, known locally as the Church with the Beret, is a crag which has been sculpted and shaped into a building, that even boasts a cylindrical dome as part of its structure.

Where to stay

The **Turban Holiday Village**, tel.: 1490, costs from L 10,000 for a double room. On the hill, a few minutes' walk out of town, it is a modern complex with well-designed buildings which look suitably futuristic in such a surreal setting. It has the advantage of a swimming pool. But it is undeniably big, and very much on the coach-tour circuit with foreign tourists who descend like locusts.

Büyük Hotel, Kayseri Caddesi, tel.: 1060, has forty-nine rooms. Old and reliable, it has comfortable, large rooms. The food is international and the décor Tyrolean. It is popular with groups as are most of the big hotels, so it is often full.

Tepe Hotel, Teslimiye Tepesi, tel.: 1154, is on the outskirts, with double rooms from L 8,000. It has a swimming pool against that extraordinary background.

The new **Boytaş**, en route to Nevşehir (Karayazı Köyü, tel.: 1259), has been described as 'possibly the ugliest building in Turkey'.

The above are the big hotels in Ürgüp, but the smaller pensions in town have far more character with a real chance of absorbing the Turkish atmosphere rather than the tourist jostle. As you walk down the hill from the Turban Holiday Village (which is a pleasant thing to do anyway), you will come across an old Ottoman house slightly inset on the corner. This is known as **Born Hotel** or **Pasha's Palace**, 100 years old and looking it, with a pleasantly crazy informality. Prices are from L 3,000.

Hotel Park, Avanos Caddesi 20, tel.: 1883, is really a glorified pension. It is run by Mehmet Arık, and all rooms have a lavatory and a shower. Prices are from L 8,000 for a double room.

Where to eat

Look for the busiest restaurant and wait if you have to. Apart from a few places which cater specifically for tourist groups, like the **Kaya** restaurant – an underground series of caves which holds 300 and could be boisterous fun – there are no particular restaurants to recommend. But there are plenty to choose from in the centre of Ürgüp, serving good, basic Turkish food and a lethal local wine which will leave you in a state of daze. Try the local speciality of *güveç*, small pieces of lamb with tomato, pepper and aubergine, baked in one of the round earthenware pots which they specialise in at Avanos, and which perform miracles in the course of the cooking.

A favourite Turkish dance hall in Ürgüp seems to have vanished and the replacements are intended more for tourists. Even so, on a good night you could have a marvellous time, another reason for staying inside the town rather than out of it. Altogether, Cappadocia is a rare experience.

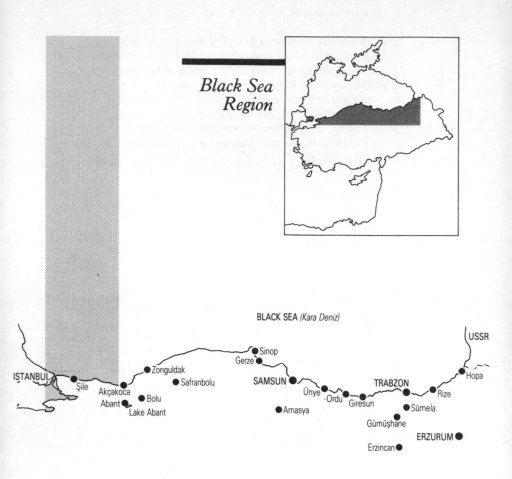

Black Sea
Region

BLACK SEA *(Kara Deniz)*

USSR

ISTANBUL
Şile
Akçakoca
Abant
Lake Abant
Bolu
Zonguldak
Safranbolu
Gerze
Sinop
SAMSUN
Ünye
Amasya
Ordu
Giresun
TRABZON
Sümela
Rize
Hopa
Gümüşhane
ERZURUM
Erzincan

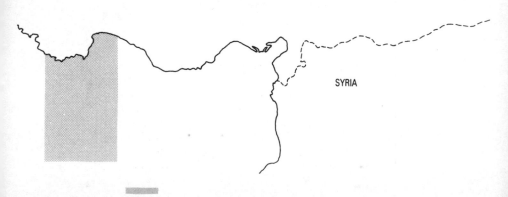

SYRIA

Black Sea Region

Introduction

The Black Sea coast is like another country. Largely spared the corruption of tourism, the towns and villages have a timeless quality which makes them most sympathetic.

The lush greenery of the region once again highlights another aspect of the diverse Turkish terrain. The Black Sea area might be termed the garden of the country, producing as it does an abundance of hazel nuts, maize, tobacco, cherries, tea and wild rhododendrons along a coastline laden with vegetation. Admittedly, the produce of the area is not all so attractive: the regions around Ereğli and Zonguldak are the country's major coal and steel centres and, for this reason, the following section does not suggest road routes between Safranbolu and Sinop.

It must also be said that the lushness of the green coastline is the result of the rainfall in the area. There is heavy snow in winter and the summers are mild. In recompense, it is the rain which scares away those tourists who only wish to fry, and the local people are so anxious to have their share of the fruitful tourist cake that they make you doubly welcome.

It's an area you can usefully view from both sea and land. Take the passenger ferry from Istanbul to Trabzon, from which you can appreciate the cliffs and mountains sloping down to the coast, or drive along the road which is, for the most part, good and head inland to explore towns such as Bolu, Safranbolu and the charm of Amasya.

Along the coast

History In the wars of succession which followed the death of Alexander the Great in 323 BC, an adventurer called Mithridates fled to the Pontic mountains to escape the fate of his uncle, who was executed by the Macedonian general Antigonus in 302 BC. Mithridates remained there and eventually declared himself King of Pontus, ruling from the fortress of Amaseia (today's Amasya). The dynasty thus established continued to thrive for more than two hundred years until the death of Mithridates VI Eupator, during which time the Pontic kingdom gradually occupied the coastline, made Sinop its capital in 183 BC, occupied Cappadocia and penetrated as far inland as Iznik, and steadfastly refused to succumb to Roman rule. In 70 BC, during the last of three Mithridatic Wars, Sinop and Amaseia were finally forced by an army led by Lucullus to surrender to Roman domination, and within a year all the Pontic kingdom had been absorbed into the Roman Empire.

A later dynasty was created by Alexius Komnenus and his descendants, who ruled from Trabzon until it was occupied by Mehmet II in 1461.

Travelling along the coast
By boat

To take a passenger boat like the *Izmir* from Istanbul is one of the most enjoyable experiences in a lifetime of travel. You leave at 5.30 p.m., slip from the Golden Horn into the Bosphorus, cross under the great bridge to Asia with the Dolmabahçe Palace on the side, go past Tarabya, with fleets of small fishing boats and old wooden houses on the water's edge, and finally enter the Black Sea (*Kara Deniz*) which really *is* black and can be surprisingly rough. Then down to dinner, to savour the first of many excellent meals with the satisfaction of knowing that you are heading for a different coastline. Seldom is travel so carefree, for this is a working passenger boat used by Turks with an air of easy informality, and a friendly captain who welcomes your visit to the bridge: something that would be discouraged on the tourist cruise ships of the Mediterranean with their regimental bonhomie. There is the chance to make Turkish friends and enough time to absorb the various ports of call – Sinop, Samsun, Giresun and Trabzon – without a sense of being rushed.

This boat journey may not be luxurious, and the cabins are basic, but the cost is extraordinarily good value at about L 31,500 single fare for a two-berth luxury cabin. The boat leaves Istanbul at 5.30 p.m. on Monday evening and arrives at Trabzon at 8 a.m. on Wednesday. For further details, contact Turkish Maritime Lines in Istanbul (144.02.07 or 145.53.66), or one of their local branches before you leave home. There is also a car ferry line which runs from mid-May to mid-September, leaving Istanbul at 7 p.m. on Thursday and arriving at Giresun at 12 noon on Saturday.

By car

The advantage of travelling along the coast by road, on the other hand, is the opportunity for a closer look at the magnificent alpine scenery, much of which remains wild. The chain of Pontic Mountains that runs parallel to the coast accounts for the heavy rainfall.

By bus

There is a good regular bus service from Istanbul along the coast, which is fast and inexpensive; also from Ankara to Samsun, a distance of 420 km.

By air

If you want to fly, twice weekly flights go from Istanbul to Samsun, and a daily one to Trabzon. There are also flights to and from Ankara.

Şile to Safranbolu

Şile　Şile, 70 km from Istanbul, is a popular beach resort, with nightclubs and entertainment, for those escaping the confines of the city. The beach at Şile is typical of those which line the coast of the Black Sea; near to the shore, at least, the water is closer to a Mediterranean blue.

Where to stay　You could consider the **Değirmen Hotel**, Plaj Yolu 24, tel.: 148, which has seventy-three rooms and charges L 8,500 for a double room, or stay at the **Ömerler Köyü**, tel.: 2528.

Where to eat　The Black Sea is rich in varieties of fish. Anywhere along the coastline, look for restaurants offering the opportunity to try *palamut* which is particularly good, with firm flesh – something between tuna and mackerel. *Hamsi* are the smaller anchovies, very plentiful in season which is when they should be eaten, as fresh as possible – they are disastrously tough if they have been frozen.

Akçakoca　Another popular beach resort, this time 240 km from Istanbul. Part of this coastal road could still be under construction. An inland route over mountain passes allows you to avoid the industrial, coal-mining centre of Zonguldak and could provide greater interest.

Abant　Turn inland from the coast and head south towards this lakeside mountain resort at an altitude of 1,500 m for a change from beaches and sea views. The **Yedigöller National Park** offers spectacular scenery of a different variety, with rushing rivers, seven lakes (*yedi göller*), and forests of oak and birch as well as pine.

In this park you may find a rare tulip growing in the wild; tulips (from the Turkish word *tülbend*, or turban, which the flower resembles) were to be found in Turkey long before the Dutch adopted them.

Where to stay　The **Turban Abant Hotel**, tel.: 5573, would make a good place to stay, with its sauna and pool. On the shores of the lake, surrounded by pine forests, it is relaxing and good value at L 9,000 per person.

Bolu　Heading north-east from Lake Abant brings you to Bolu, originally the capital of Bithynia, and known in Roman times as Claudiopolis. Not a great deal of the city's historical past remains to be seen, but you could always take a look at the Ulu Paşa mosque in the market place which was built for the Ottoman sultan Yıldırım Beyazıt at the end of the fourteenth century.

Where to stay　The **Koru Hotel** (part of the exemplary Turkish Automobile Club), Ömerler Köyü, tel.: 2528, charges L 11,500 for a double room. There are several smaller hotels, such as the **Yurdaer Hotel**, tel.: 2903, and **Menekşe Hotel**, tel.: 1522, both on Hürriyet Caddesi.

Where to eat　There are a number of restaurants to choose from, but two recommended by the Tourist Board include: **Filiz**, E:5 Karayolu Boludağı, tel.: 1026, and **Idris**, Belediye Meydani, tel.: 1202.

Safranbolu　Presumably the first part of the place name derives from the saffron for which this town is famous; the -*bolu* part is the Turkish corruption of -*polis* ('city'). Below the modern town is a village famous in Turkey for its old whitewashed houses, caravanserai and evocation of the past. The site has recently become a protected area.

Sinop to Ünye

Sinop The fine natural harbour at Sinop did not prevent the destruction of the Turkish fleet in 1853, when the Russians sank every ship but one and killed 3,000 sailors, an act of aggression which led indirectly to the Crimean War a few months later. Today the port has a jaunty atmosphere and it is pleasant to linger, with beaches below the forests and good restaurants. Sinop is totally unpretentious. Take a walk from the jetty into town, past rows of cobblers and barbers, and you come out the other side of the peninsula, a site overlooking a bay which, elsewhere, would be treasured for tourism but when I visited was occupied by a rubbish dump. There is a pleasant tea-garden, an archaeological museum which houses some beautiful gold icons, an atmosphere of leisure, and a Byzantine fortress which dominates the town where prisoners were chained in water up to their necks ('This is very discouraging things for the prisoners to escape,' says the brochure, a claim one would not dispute).

Sinop was also the birthplace of the third century BC Cynic philosopher Diogenes who, it is claimed, carried a lantern through the streets of his adopted home of Athens in broad daylight in an attempt to find an honest man – a cynical gesture indeed. Diogenes also had something of a cheeky line in repartee, judging from legend. When asked by Alexander the Great if there was anything he could do for him, Diogenes is said to have requested the great man to get out of his light. Not altogether as eccentric as such tales as his living in a barrel would suggest, Diogenes developed his philosophy that man should live according to the simplest and easiest practical means at the expense of convention: a tenet modified and incorporated in later Stoic philosophy.

Where to One recommended hotel is the **Melia Kasım Hotel**, Gazi Caddesi *stay* 41, tel.: 1625, with fifty-seven rooms.

Gerze A forty-minute drive from Sinop is Gerze, a fishing village with good swimming from attractive beaches, but the reason for stopping here (there is a simple but adequate hotel) is to explore the surrounding countryside which is beautifully alpine with farms, woods, hills and mountains.

Samsun The coastal road along the shore from Sinop to Gerze takes almost two hours to drive. The biggest port along the Turkish Black Sea and 150 km from Sinop, Samsun is frankly an industrial city with dirty docks and stinking water and a population around 200,000. It was burnt to the ground by the Genoese in the fifteenth century, so little remains of interest, though it was here that Atatürk landed to organise the War of Independence on 19 May 1919. The date is commemorated as a national holiday which gives Samsun a certain *cachet*, though there is little to show for it apart from a fine statue of Atatürk on horseback sculpted by the Austrian, Krippel. There is a large area set aside for the annual fair in July on the waterfront, but at other times it is bleak.

Unless you have business in Samsun you are advised to stay elsewhere, possibly driving inland to Amasya.

Where to stay

If you do decide to pause in Samsun, the **Büyük** ('Turban') **Samsun Hotel**, Sahil Caddesi, tel.: 107.50, is new, sanitised and posh, with air-conditioning and a pool. Prices are from L 22,350 for a double room. The **Burç Hotel**, Kazımpaşa Caddesi 36, tel.: 154.80, is slightly cheaper.

Amasya

Turning inland from Samsun and driving a distance of some 150 km, you will be rewarded by your arrival in Amasya. Cobbled streets and overhanging vines make this one of the most scenic towns in Turkey, set in a gorge dominated by the cliffs carved with rock tombs and with wooden houses overhanging the River Yeşilırmak. Once a Hittite town, it is thought to have been founded by the Amazons and became capital of Pontus.

What to see

The fortress, on an outcrop of rock overlooking the River Yeşilırmak dates from Roman times, and the site reveals a well, cistern, dungeon, subterranean tunnel, the remains of a mosque and, perhaps most noteworthy, the rock tombs in the southern and eastern walls of the fortress which are illuminated at night. These date from the third century BC and were the burial places of the kings of Pontus. Above the tombs is the citadel and the summit, from which the views of the surrounding countryside are spectacular, can be reached by car.

Historical monuments in the town include the fifteenth-century theological school with fine reliefs, and a number of mosques, perhaps the best of which are the Fethiye mosque, a former Byzantine church converted into a mosque in 1116 which is to be found in the street of the same name, and the Sultan Beyazıt mosque set in a pretty garden close to the river. Opposite the Beyazıt mosque is the Gök Medrese, now a museum, which, among other relics, includes in its collection six mummified figures of Mongol rulers of Amasya which are to be found in the adjacent Türbe of Sultan Mesut.

Perhaps the most attractive feature of Amasya, apart from its charming wooden houses clustered along the riverbanks, is the fact that it is some way off the beaten track and, consequently, relatively unspoilt by the tourist hordes.

Where to stay

The **Turban Amasya Hotel**, Emniyet Caddesi, tel.: 4054, has thirty-six rooms, many of which have balconies overlooking the river.

Ünye

While not one of the newer Turban hotels, it is well run and moderately priced. The restaurant, which also has a dining terrace, is good and the service excellent.

Turning back once again towards the coast, Ünye is set in an attractive bay with hints of a coming resort, such as restaurants and camping sites near the beach. Surprisingly, the caves nearby accommodate seals. The road afterwards twists around the peninsula with peaceful fishing villages and unspoilt beaches below.

Where to
stay

The **Belediye Çamlık Motel**, attractively situated near the shore, has a good and inexpensive restaurant, and rooms with baths overlooking the sea. Prices are from L 9,000.

Giresun to Hopa

Giresun

Some 52 km east of Ordu lies this quiet Turkish town set on a small peninsula and overlooked by its Byzantine castle. The fortress is worth a visit, if only for the panoramic view it affords of the surrounding areas. It is from here that the Roman general Lucullus is thought to have taken the first cherry trees to Europe; the coastline is also famous for the green hazel nut plantations.

Where to
stay

The **Giresun Hotel**, Atatürk Bulvarı 7, tel.: 3017, charges from L 13,500 for a double room.

Trabzon

On a fine, calm day, the shoreline en route to Trabzon resembles that of an Italian lake, where the forests run close to the water's edge. The first impression of the town can be disappointing if you expect the enchanted scene described by Rose Macaulay in her classic travel book *The Towers of Trebizond*: 'Still the towers of Trebizond, the fabled city, shimmer on a far horizon . . .' Today those towers belong to a flour mill and industrial chimneys – so much for romance. Yet Trabzon is most appealing once you are there. It is hard to pinpoint exactly why, except that it is cheerful.

History

The history of Trabzon (also Trebizond and Trapezus) has been chequered; always a significant port, once on the caravan trade route to the East, it is now a transit point for goods bound for Iran. At one point the town became the capital of Pontica under Emperor Hadrian and, after the fall of Constantinople to the Crusaders, the Emperor Alexius Komnenus moved here to form a separate state which lasted until the surrender to Mehmet the Conqueror in 1461. It had lingered for eight years as the last Christian outpost in Asia, following Mehmet's capture of Constantinople. In 1917 it was occupied by the Russians before the revolution put an end to ideas of further expansion into north-east Turkey. In spite of all these occupations, the people of Trabzon appear to have walked a skilful tightrope of independence. This is reflected in the city's early name of Trapezus, which may have given us the word 'trapeze' due to the narrow promontory in the town which divides two ravines.

What to see
The main square is typical, with tea gardens where families pass the time, protected by the shade of luxuriant trees which range from palms to pine, with a splendid statue of Kemal Atatürk in the centre.

The church of Ayasofia Above the town, 3 km from the centre and overlooking the sea, the church is surrounded by a pleasantly informal garden. Built in 1250, it has beautiful proportions, became a mosque after the fall of the Komnenus Empire in 1461, and serves as a museum today. The superb Byzantine frescoes were restored in 1957. The sculpted frieze at the south porch portrays the story of Genesis with an eagle perched above as the symbol of the Komnenus power.

Atatürk's Summer House Also on the outskirts is another museum, a white building with the hint of an Italian lakeside villa, surrounded by rose gardens and pines which have grown so tall that they partly obscure the view over the Black Sea below. The rooms of Atatürk's summer house are kept immaculate, full of interesting photographs and souvenirs, but it is the obvious pride and pleasure of the visiting Turks, young soldiers and old peasant ladies in head-scarves, which make this house a pilgrimage, even though he only stayed here twice. British visitors will be interested in the photograph of Atatürk with King Edward VIII, when he was Prince of Wales, on his visit to Turkey. The house was presented to the Turkish leader by the grateful people of Trabzon.

Where to stay
Özgür Hotel, Kıbrıs Şehitleri Caddesi 29, tel.: 113.19, is situated off the main square. A few visitors have disparaged it as 'old-fashioned', others (including myself) think it exceptionally sympathetic with comfortable rooms and a rooftop restaurant overlooking the park. Prices are from L 19,750.

Usta Hotel, İskele Caddesi, Telgrafhane Sokak 3, tel.: 121.95, is allegedly the best in town with a good, lively, rooftop restaurant. Prices are from L 17,850.

The monastery of Sümela
While you are in Trabzon, make time to drive south, inland, over the Zigana Pass (every bit as romantic as it sounds), en route to Gümüşhane, Erzincan to the west and Erzurum to the east. Before the dusty Anatolian plains with nomadic flocks of sheep, you will cross an exhilarating landscape which could be a wilder version of Bavaria or the Swiss Alps.

The climb is tremendous. It is what the 10,000 soldiers of Xenophon saw when they looked down from on high during their exhausting trek back to Thrace in 401 BC. Crying *'Thalassa!* [The sea, the sea!]', they wept and hugged each other with relief.

The foliage here is known for twenty-six shades of green, and this is easy to believe, but it is the man-made touch of the astonishing monasteries which makes it unforgettable. Turn off the main road to the village of **Maçka**, named after the heavy stick which the inhabit-

223

ants used to defend themselves. This is an attractive village with a fast-flowing river under ancient arched bridges. Continuing along the narrow valley brings you to the ruined monasteries of **Vazelon** (16 km) and **Kuştul** (21 km to the east), but **Sümela**, 20 km further on, is the most remarkable.

From below, Sümela is little more than a smudge, apparently a painted façade on the cliff-face scarcely visible between the trees. Once you have climbed to the ruins, 1,220 m high – a steep walk which takes half an hour – the extent of the monastery is more evident, though at first there is a feeling of disappointment that the buildings are in such disrepair and the frescoes so faded, crumbling and completely covered in graffiti. But gradually this is replaced by a growing admiration for the monks who chose such remoteness, and led such a rarefied existence. Legend has it that in the fourth century AD the site of Sümela was suggested to a Greek monk, Barnabus, in a vision in which the Virgin Mary asked him to find a sanctuary for her sacred icon, painted by St Luke, in the Pontic mountains. Barnabus and his nephew Sophronius sailed to Trebizond with the icon and went to look for the place in the mountains that Barnabus had seen in his vision. They found it here in a large natural cave and built the sanctuary. The monastery was then supposedly founded under Justinian in the fifth century, though no evidence remains of it.

If you are not driving, you may have to take a taxi to Sümela from Trabzon as there are not many *dolmuşes*; but don't miss seeing it, for it is one of the most spectacular sights in Turkey.

As you look down on the valley from one of the empty arches, the reason for living here can be appreciated: the isolation from the outside world; the ease of defence; the solace of the thousands of books in the famous fifteenth-century library. Then, the dormitories and courtyards would have been thronged with people; the monastery, second only to Mount Athos, was chosen by Alexius Komnenus II for his coronation. The Greeks were extradited from here in 1923 (under the exchange agreement) and the wooden roof of the abandoned monastery was burnt seven years later. But enough remains for your imagination to work on, and the climb whets the appetite for a picnic beside the river below at tables and chairs laid out with typical consideration. There, Turkish families barbecue their meat or trout from the fish farm nearby.

At the top of the Zigana Pass, where the air is keen and the meadows covered with pink and white wild flowers, there are open air barbecues famous for freshly slaughtered mutton. This is fine if you like your meat as tough as leather – but at such a summit the toughness hardly matters!

Rize　　An hour's drive east of Trabzon, Rize gives you the chance for a swim in the clear water at **Araklı** and lunch in the open-air **Plaj Restaurant** beside the beach, popular with Turkish families. Rize is a

224

total surprise: far from a 'picturesque' fishing village which an old guide might lead you to expect, it is a tough, active city with a busy market, a vast square teeming with people, and two statues of Atatürk. Most astonishing of all is the Botanical Garden at the top where you can enjoy afternoon tea surrounded by palm trees with a panoramic view over the coast. The garden is exotic enough, but turn around and you might be in Sri Lanka or China with hills covered with terraces which provide the bulk of Turkey's tea.

Hopa   The last port before the Soviet border, Hopa is 89 km to the east. Here watchtowers can be seen, signalling that this is very much the end of your Black Sea journey. There are two small pensions at **Kemalpaşa**, just beyond.

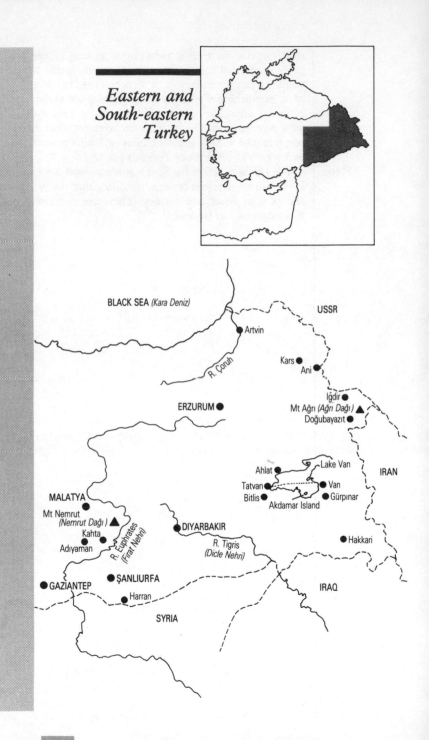

Eastern and South-eastern Turkey

BLACK SEA *(Kara Deniz)*

USSR

Artvin

Kars

Ani

R. Çoruh

Iğdir

ERZURUM

Mt Ağrı *(Ağrı Dağı)* ▲

Doğubayazıt

Ahlat

Lake Van

IRAN

Tatvan

Van

Bitlis

Gürpınar

MALATYA

Akdamar Island

Mt Nemrut
(Nemrut Dağı) ▲

Kahta

DIYARBAKIR

Adıyaman

R. Euphrates
(Fırat Nehri)

R. Tigris
(Dicle Nehri)

Hakkari

GAZIANTEP

ŞANLIURFA

Harran

IRAQ

SYRIA

Eastern and South-eastern Turkey

Introduction

When you travel east, you realise that Turkey is more a continent than a country. The landscape is more immense: vast open plains with nomadic flocks of sheep, towns enclosed by massive basalt walls, and Mount Ağrı, supposedly the Biblical Ararat on which Noah's Ark came to rest, looming above Doğubayazıt.

In fact, everything in this landscape seems to be on an immense scale. Superlatives abound in connection with places of interest: Lake Van, the largest lake in Turkey which can take up to six hours to cross by ferry boat, Diyarbakır, allegedly the hottest place in Turkey in the summer, and Mount Ağrı, at over 5,000 m the highest mountain in the country. Perhaps it was this larger than life quality about the region that persuaded Antiochus I of Commagene to erect the colossal statues at the summit of Mount Nemrut or, more likely, his larger than life ego. Whichever it was, the toppled heads now litter the ground, taller than the visitors who make the trip up the mountain to see them.

This immensity of scale in the region is also reflected in the distances you will have to cover between major cities and areas of interest. A journey that may not look far on the map may take you almost a day to cover because the distance involved is so vast and because the roads in the region are less good than in the more developed areas.

This is generally true of all facilities in the region. Since it is not one of the most highly developed in terms of catering to the tourist industry – although this is rapidly changing as more and more visitors travel further eastwards to explore the less accessible regions of the country – you should expect facilities to be more primitive and hotels scarcer. You should not expect to live in the lap of luxury in Eastern and South-eastern Turkey, but any absence in terms of comfort is more than compensated by the exhilaration of a visit to this area.

Though harsher, Eastern and South-eastern Turkey is invigorating, and the countryside surrounding Lake Van is idyllic. Unstained by tourism, this is an area to be visited by the discerning traveller who relishes adventure and is prepared to explore local villages on foot. A more serious problem is caused by the conflicts on the borders of neighbours such as Iraq and Iran, which make it unwise to venture into areas where safety cannot be guaranteed.

Around Erzurum

Erzurum

This harsh city, set in a reddish plateau and surrounded by dark hills, makes the traveller realise that he has arrived in a very different part of Turkey. The looks of the people and their taboos, such as alcohol, are alien to the West – or, rather, Western permissiveness is alien to them, especially during Ramazan.

Erzurum is the largest city in the east, with a population of around 200,000. It is now, and always has been, on the route to Asia and a crucial military headquarters, though there is an important university too. Outwardly, the city would not seem to encourage tourism, yet once you know it and the people who live here you are made welcome though their toughness is undeniable. They have, after all, had to adapt to a cruel climate of freezing winters and fiercely hot summers, earthquakes, and a series of invaders, including the Russians who have occupied Erzurum on two occasions, the last as recently as 1916.

What to see

There are numerous places to visit, particularly the **Çifte Minareli Medrese** with a superbly tiled and patterned entrance, one of the most decorative in Turkey, with two minarets. The minaret of the **Yakutiye Medrese** also has a patterned portico and minaret, another fine example of a classic Seljuk doorway.

For winter sports, there is a new centre 6 km away at **Palandöken** in the snow-covered hills.

Where to stay

Hotel Oral, Terminal Caddesi 3, tel.: 197.40, charges L 17,850 for a double room.

Büyük Erzurum Hotel, Alirevai Caddesi 5, tel.: 165.28 and **Efes Hotel**, Tahtacılar Caddesi 30, tel.: 170.81 are also reliable.

The **Tufan** restaurant is recommended.

Kars

It is 211 km to Kars from Erzurum via Horasan, though some would favour the much longer route (480 km) via Artvin to the north, which you can take if you have ample time to spare (see facing p.).

Close to the Russian border, Kars has served as a battlefield for numerous invaders: Seljuks, Mongols and Tamerlane. Above all, the twelfth-century fortress has been fought for by the Russians, and was defended during the Crimean War in 1855 by a British force led by General Wilson who became a national hero in England as the newspapers reported his bravery; his Turkish allies were less impressed.

In 1877 the Russians occupied the city, but Kars benefited from the Russian Revolution because Lenin and Trotsky returned the province in 1921. Due to Atatürk's diplomacy with his fellow 'revolutionaries' it stayed in Turkish hands. Kars today has the dubious reputation of having two of the worst hotels in the world, and recent reports do not indicate any improvement.

At night it is supposed to be dangerous to walk in the streets, though other visitors will tell you differently. The castle built by Sultan Murat III still dominates the city and you can walk around it but, because it is in use by the Turkish Army, you are not allowed to enter the garrison.

Where to stay No hotels can be recommended. To say the **Yılmaz** is the best suggests a glimmer of virtue; possibly it is the least awful: Küçükkazımbey Caddesi 114, tel.: 1074/2387. At least it serves alcohol which is a necessity in Kars.

The **Kemal Palas** is the poor alternative.

Ani The main reason for going to Kars is to visit the ghost city of Ani. Ignore reports that it is difficult to get permission; you only have to ask at the tourist bureau (they will understand when you specify Ani), at Faikbey Caddesi, İnönü Karakolu Karsısı, tel.: 2724. They will give you a form which you must take with your passport to a security office 50 m away on the opposite side of the road. They will also arrange *dolmuş* transport if you need it.

Ani was on the ancient silk route to the East and its walls still enclose the remains of numerous churches and mosques where the population was an estimated 100,000. This figure is hard to credit today as you look at the abandoned ghost town, destroyed by Ghengis Khan in the fourteenth century when its people fled, never to return again. Shepherds are the main sign of life in this Armenian city today apart from the visitors, awestruck by the desolation.

Artvin Driving north-west to Artvin from Kars takes five hours on empty roads through beautiful countryside (about L 73,750 return by taxi), or you can go directly by bus from Erzurum. It is a fascinating town on top of a hill which overlooks the River Çoruh as it flows towards Russia, with revelatory views of the surrounding country. In season you can fish for trout on unspoilt stretches of water, hunt wild boar, or pick some of the 1,800 varieties of wild flowers. Try the local sweet made from mulberries called *pestil*. On the last Sunday in June, a unique contest occurs in the mountains when bulls fight each other supposedly to the death – it sounds gory but, apparently, the bulls are sensible enough to turn tail and flee if they feel they're getting the worst of it.

Equally, you can avoid Erzurum altogether by flying straight to Trabzon and driving to Artvin via Hopa, along the coast. Should you wish to continue to Erzurum, you can drive directly through the

Doğubayazıt

Tortum and Çoruh valleys, an exhilarating journey made accessible only recently, and stop at one of the simple hotels in Tortum.

From Kars, continue back towards Erzurum until you reach the turning to the south for Iğdır (at Karakurt or Ladikars). To get to Doğubayazıt you should allow at least eight hours' driving. You can stay at a good hotel near Iğdır, but the reason for coming here is the **İshak Paşa Palace and Mosque**, the most romantic in Turkey, which looks at times as if it is floating in the mist above the plateau with Mount Ağrı (Ararat) beyond, its summit in perpetual snow. See it at dawn if you can and walk towards it for an hour and a half before the visitors descend by *dolmuş* later in the day. It opens at 8 a.m.

The building, started by his father, was completed by İshak Paşa in 1784, a rich and powerful landowner, on the silk route to Persia and virtually his own master. This Arabian Nights palace, therefore, is late Ottoman and not as timeless as its magical exterior suggests. Constructed directly in the natural rock and perfectly self-contained with defence walls 12–15 m high, its proportions are dramatic. But despite its defences, the Russians removed the great steel and gold-plated door in 1917 and took it to Moscow where it can be seen in the museum today.

The palace, in the Seljuk style, is so magnificent that an Iranian ambassador who stayed there was tactless enough to report to Selim II on his arrival in Istanbul that İshak Paşa's palace put all the rest to shame. Not surprisingly, İshak Paşa promptly fell from favour, in spite of his explanation that such grandeur was necessary for the Sultan's representative in the east.

Where to stay

Surprisingly, Doğubayazıt, a town of 10,000 people, has a good choice of hotels, due to truck drivers en route for Iran and to Eastern Anatolian Tours.

Ararat Hotel, Emniyet Caddesi 48, tel.: 1139, has the advantage of a Turkish bath and restaurant; prices from L 6,000 for a double room.

Where to eat

The Istanbul Lokanta in the main street is a good place to eat.

Mount Ağrı

The mountain – the use of its old name, Ararat, is sometimes resented – looms temptingly beyond and the town of Doğubayazıt is the base for those in search of Noah's Ark. Apparently there *is* a strange formation high up on the mountain which does resemble a fossilised vessel, but when you appreciate that the mountain covers over 1,550 square km, embracing a smaller one beside it, the problems of finding it are understood more clearly – they have defied scores of adventurers, including a former astronaut. Apart from the danger of crazed Iranian brigands and wild dogs which are equally fierce and just as hard to reason with, you will require permission to climb, which is frequently refused. If you are determined, there are agencies which organise climbing parties: Trek Travel, Taksim Meydanı, Istanbul, or Ahmet Ağa in Doğubayazıt itself, whose guides take you up the southern slope with two camps, before attempting the summit which requires proper climbing equipment. If you are serious about this, you will have made your own preparations; if the idea suddenly seems irresistible, make them on the spot.

Lake Van and environs

There is an elation about the province of Van which makes you feel that you are close to the Biblical creation of the world. This is not mere fantasy. Once this region was the centre of the Urartian civilisation, and the word Urartu was derived from Ararat. Climbing that mountain in September 1876, a British explorer, James Bryce, had a similar sensation as he looked down at 'the whole cradle of the human race, from Mesopotamia in the south to the great wall of the Caucasus' to the north: 'If it was indeed here that man first set foot on the unpeopled earth, one could imagine how the great dispersal went as the races spread themselves . . . No more imposing centre of the world could be imagined.' One knows exactly what he felt, with constant confirmation as you drive around Lake Van, known as 'the upper sea' to the Assyrians. On Akdamar Island on the outside of the church, carved friezes record scenes such as Jonah and the whale; St George and the dragon; Adam and Eve (slightly vandalised) and other figures from the Old Testament – these alone make a visit to Van worth while.

There is even more than that – a sense of limitless space dependent on the seasons and acceptance of natural disasters such as earthquakes. Yet far from being desolate, the space is reassuring, as soothing and as pastoral a scene as you could hope for.

Van The town of Van is down-to-earth rather than near to water; the lake is 5 km away so there are none of the jolly quayside bars and restaurants you might expect. There will be one day, and all too soon, for the surrounding area is bound to become popular although it is blessedly remote now and frequently cut off altogether in the winter snow. It is a busy, no-nonsense town centred on two main streets with some very good shops, especially for eastern *kilims*, but they are expensive and you need to bargain with skilful persuasion for the owners know that such goods are in growing demand.

What to see On the outskirts, 3 km west, you will be overwhelmed by the vast rock fortress with the castle of Tushpa. This was the capital of Urartu in the ninth century BC, later occupied by a series of conquerors: the Medes and then the Persians. In the tenth century AD it became the capital of Armenia before it was seized by the Mongols and destroyed by Tamerlane. Gamely, it continued to survive until the fortress became a battlefield between the Russians and the Turks in the First World War and lost the will to resist any further.

Little remains apart from the impressive foundations of huge slabs laid on top of each other, but it is worth the climb – especially at sunset – to look down from the ramparts at the plains and detect the outline of an ancient harbour when the water reached below.

The excellent museum at Van offers proof of the artistry of the Urartians as well as their power, when they ruled an empire stretching north to the Black Sea and the Caspian. The Urartian designs are very fine.

Where to stay   **Hotel Akdamar**, Kazım Karabekir Caddesi 56, tel.: 181.00, is a lively unpretentious hotel with a good bar and restaurant including a roof terrace. It is not luxurious, but has a sympathetic atmosphere. The price for a double room is L 17,850.

Büyük Urartu Hotel, Hastane Sokak 60, tel.: 206.60, is cheaper at L 14,500.

There are several cheaper hotels. The **Tekin Hotel**, Küçükcami Civarı, tel.: 130.10, has the advantage of being quiet; a double room with a shower costs L 11,500. Also, **Beşkardeş Hotel**, Cumhuriyet Caddesi 54, tel.: 111.16, and **Çaldıran Hotel**, Sıhke Caddesi, tel.: 127.18, are both around L 8,900 for doubles with shower.

Where to eat   **Kösk**, with an outside garden for hot weather, is recommended though slightly expensive.

Şafak, Maras Caddesi, near the tourist office, specialises in Turkish dishes.

Lake Van   The road around the lake is excellent with no tourist eyesores (so far). The lake is huge – the largest in Turkey – and takes four to six hours to cross by ferry boat from Tatvan, with the train continuing to Iran on its arrival. Take your own food if you wish to eat, for the restaurant and bar facilities are poor. The lake is known for its buoyancy due to the high degree of sodium carbonate, which makes it good for washing in but vile to drink. You can see clusters of women washing their clothes on the shore and fishermen are known to trawl the larger items behind their boats. Certainly you emerge from a swim feeling cleaner and softer. The water is so peculiar that few, if any, fish can live in it; yet the notorious Van cats – which have one blue eye and one yellow – are alleged to swim in the shallows, though the local people are perplexed by the idea.

Akdamar Island   The island should not be missed. It is easy to reach in summer by the motorboat ferry from **Gevaş** (a twenty-minute journey) or by one of the smaller fishing boats from the nearer jetty on the mainland opposite. There is a pleasant, inexpensive *lokanta* where you can wait until others arrive to share the cost.

Far from being barren, as some travel brochures indicate, the island is delightful – a mass of wild flowers in the spring, with groves of olive and pine trees where Turkish families arrange their picnics, and a few helmeted soldiers with guns posing smilingly for photographs. The sensational image of the church with the water and the range of snow capped mountains beyond is one of the most satisfying combinations of land, water and man-made monument in Eastern Turkey.

The tenth-century church of the **Holy Cross** with the carved reliefs outside echoes the Armenian style of Ani, though the decorations inside have been worn away by the years. Otherwise the carvings are well preserved, and fascinating in their detailed portrayal of the Old Testament: two lions lick Daniel's feet, David is dwarfed by Goliath, and a frieze of animals is entwined with vines and bunches of grapes. It is a joyful celebration of life itself.

Excursions from Van

If you are driving independently, there are several points to see. An exemplary Seljuk tomb with a rounded base and a conical top may be seen from the main road 44 km from Van as you approach Akdamar Island, and is worth stopping for. Built in 1358 for a princess, it is exceptionally well preserved. At **Ahlat**, on the other side of the lake en route to Tatvan, there is a vast graveyard of such tombs and a sea of tombstones, fascinating for those with an interest in this architectural style but not worth a special detour otherwise.

Semiramis Canal Driving from Van to **Mejingir** and **Gürpınar**, you reach the Semiran Suyu – the Waters of Seramis. This is the source of the Semiramis Canal, constructed by King Menua as early as 800 BC, when Urartu was 'the most powerful state in western Asia'. Stretching to Van 55 km away, it irrigates the surrounding region – further proof of Urartian skill. With the Seramis waters pouring *out* of the earth, like a waterfall in reverse, it is tempting to splash in them, and they prove surprisingly warm even in early spring.

Hoşap Continue driving towards the border and you come to the splendid picture-book castle of Hoşap on the other side of the river near the village of **Güzelsu**, spanned by a double-arched bridge of black and white stone which dates back to 1500.

The castle is well worth the climb, built on Urartian foundations by the Mahmoudis in 1643, and has an impressive entrance with a stupendous carved stone doorway. The view from the top reveals the crenellated walls which protected the community of 8,000 people who remained up to the First World War. The busy courtyards directly below convey the type of enclosed existence which flourished here so recently.

Başkale Başkale, 50 km further on, claims to be the highest town in Turkey, at 2,500 m, and now has two basic inns which are convenient if you need to rest.

Hakkari If you are able to, and this may be difficult in view of the current political situation, continue to Hakkari, 45 km south-east of Van, near the Iranian border and set in an invigorating region of lakes, mountains and wild rivers. The road is good, except when covered in ice, snow or a fall of rock, and beautifully empty apart from the odd group of children who sell a root resembling asparagus. The battlements of an early Urartian fortress at **Çavustepe** are visible on the hills above and are now being excavated.

Bitlis to Şanlıurfa

Bitlis This final route covers a great sweep of south-eastern Turkey, which will constantly surprise you. Leaving Lake Van behind, drive out through Tatvan. You climb through wild countryside, once densely forested, to the cheerful town of **Bitlis**, 1,545 m high with a population of 28,000 people. It is dominated by the castle on the hill. The **Turist Hotel** in the centre is simple but clean, with eighteen rooms, and could provide an interesting stay if you have the time.

Diyarbakır A huge romantic city of half a million people, Diyarbakır's lasting impression is of strength. It is enclosed by tall, black basalt walls which give it a medieval appearance and stretch for 6 km; they are best seen from a horse-drawn phaeton. With seventy-two towers but only five gates into the city, it is a rare example of early military defence, dating from AD 349. Such defence was necessary, for Diyarbakır has been fought over by successive states like dogs with a bone: the Hurrians around 1500 BC, then the Urartians, Assyrians, Persians, Alexander, and his generals after his death. The Arabic tribe of Bakr seized it from the Romans, and gave the city its present name.

Getting there There are daily flights from Ankara and a weekly one from Van; if you travel by bus you leave Van around noon, stop at Bitlis 165 km further on, with another half-hour stop later, and reach Diyarbakır at the splendid hour of dusk.

What to see Today the large market is one of the most active in Turkey, patronised by Turks rather than tourists, with streets devoted to single crafts, practised in front of your eyes. Though this is unmistakably the East – peasants in baggy trousers and groups of veiled women dressed entirely in black advance towards you – there is considerable sophistication too, with students eager to talk in a small tea garden off the main street, a courtyard almost opposite which sells exceptional *kilims*, restaurants and numerous hotels. Everyone is helpful.

The landmarks include the elegant exterior to the **Ulu Mosque** with rows of decorated arches and columns, which was built in 1091 but is more graceful than most great mosques in the Seljuk style.

A word of warning: in the height of summer, Diyarbakır has the reputation of being the hottest place in Turkey. This is wholly believable as you continue south from the bus depot on the edge of town and start across the dusty plain to Şanlıurfa, embraced by the Tigris and Euphrates. This is the ancient Mesopotamia, soon to be revived again with one of the most important irrigation projects the world has ever seen.

Where to stay   **Demir Hotel**, İzzetpaşa Caddesi 8, tel.: 123.15, has a friendly manager, a garage, a bar, a roof restaurant for local dishes and a terrace for music and dancing. It is not luxurious but comfortable: insist on changing rooms if you are not satisfied. Prices are from L 26,800 for a double room.

Aslan Hotel and adjacent **Aslan Palace**, Kıbrıs Caddesi 23, tel.: 139.71 are excellent value, costing from L 5,000 for a double room. **Saraç Hotel**, tel.: 123.65, next to the Demir, is half the price and **Hotel Ertem**, tel.: 129.72, opposite the Saraç, is cheaper still.

Where to eat   A wide selection of kebab houses is easy to judge. Recommended ones include **Hacı Baba** and **Babaman**.

Şanlıurfa
(also known as Urfa)   A splendidly robust city with Biblical and archaeological interest, Şanlıurfa's name possibly goes back to the Hurri dynasty which was replaced by the Hittites around 1400 BC and renamed Edessa by Alexander's successors. As a Christian and scholastic centre, Edessa was attacked by Arabs from the East in the seventh century and then recaptured by the Byzantines. Surprisingly, Edessa became a Crusader state in the eleventh century under Baldwin of Flanders. He was routed in his turn by a Seljuk governor who founded the Zengid dynasty, whose son decimated the Christian population. This led to the promise of a Second Crusade though it failed to arrive, and the city remained under Muslim rule.

Today there is a powerful undercurrent of activity, but the impression at dusk is one of relief after the heat of the day, and peacefulness with the stone turning to the colour of faded yellow roses. It is especially peaceful around the famous **Pool of Abraham**, filled with sacred carp which jostle for the type of chick-pea sold by small boys or the caretaker. The pool is 200 m long, supplied by water from a sacred spring: no one is allowed to catch the bloated fish. Rumour has it that a drunken soldier tried once and ended up in prison; another version says that he died.

The **Halil Rahman Mosque** enhances the setting, with a seventeenth-century theological school whose series of graceful archways is reflected in the water. There is a good, interesting atmosphere to absorb at night, with food that owes much to Arabia. The museum has the usual, attractive sculpture garden.

Where to stay   **Turban Urfa Hotel**, Köprübaşi Caddesi 74, tel.: 3520, has fifty-five clean and comfortable rooms with showers, some with air-conditioning. The restaurant and terrace bar have good views. Prices are from L 6,000.

Guven, nearby, is cheaper, with prices from L 4,000.

Harran   Harran, 45 km to the south, on the way to Akçakale on the Syrian

235

border, is noted for its curious beehive-shaped, domed dwellings and its Biblical connections. Just as Abraham is supposed to have been born at Şanlıurfa, this is believed to be his resting place and that of his family, based on the claim in Genesis: 'and they came unto Harran and dwelt there.'

Gaziantep   Should you continue via Gaziantep, a prosperous town of Hittite origin and the centre of the pistachio nut industry, be sure to visit the Archaeological Museum on the edge of the town donated by Hasan Süzer of the Pera Palas in Istanbul. It contains a fine collection of Hittite reliefs; another of Antiochus, always hobnobbing with the gods, shaking hands with Apollo; and even the bones of a mastodon to shock you with the realisation that such mammals roamed the pine forests which existed here in the Ice Age.

Where to   **Hotel Kaleli**, Hürriyet Caddesi, tel.: 134.17, is probably the best.
stay   **Murat Hotel**, İnönü Caddesi 39, tel.: 152.76, is also recommended.

The **Keyvanbey** restaurant, Hürriyet Caddesi, tel.: 126.51, has an attractive upstairs terrace.

Adıyaman to   This region goes back to the beginning of time as we know it: the
Malatya   paleolithic and neolithic ages, 8,000 years before the birth of Christ. Numerous landmarks remind one of more recent times. The perfect Roman bridge at **Cendre** (or Cendere), so simply yet strongly designed, is a single arch of ninety-two stones weighing over 10,000 kg (10 tons) each – a pleasure to look at for minutes on end. It is still in use today, with the River Kahta swirling underneath. It was built as a tribute to the Roman Emperor Septimus Severus by the people of Commagene with pairs of columns at each end to commemorate his wife and sons. When one son killed his brother on becoming emperor in his turn, the twin column beside his own was destroyed.

Eski Kale   The fortress for Arsameia, the capital of the Commagene kingdom, may still be seen on the clifftop. A hundred metres away is a stunning relief of Mithridates shaking hands with a smaller Hercules – it is so well preserved that it is hard to credit that it dates from 50 BC, especially as it stands impressively in the open air rather than in a cloistered museum. Nearby is a rock inscription recording that Mithridates, the father of Antiochus I, was buried here. The memorial to Antiochus himself crowns the summit of Mount Nemrut which can be reached from Adıyaman or from Malatya to the north, a large modern city of 150,000 served by an airport.

Where   Mount Nemrut is the reason for coming here and this is the final
to stay   and worthy destination. You can stay easily at either of the main towns, but Adıyaman is the best point from which to set off for Nemrut.

Arsemia Motel, Nemrut Yolu Üzeri, tel.: 2112, charges from L 6,000 and has a pool.

Nemrut Tur-Tes. Motel, Adıyaman Khata Yolu, tel.: 863, and the **Antiochus Motel**, tel.: 1240 (west of town and basic), are both recommended.

In Malatya, try the **Kent Hotel**, Atatürk Caddesi 151, tel.: 121.75, an extremely friendly hotel with a lobby covered with exceptional *kilims* which are for sale and hard to resist. Rooms are from L 5,000.

Sinan Hotel, Atatürk Caddesi 14, tel.: 129.07, is about the same price.

Mount Nemrut

Getting there

A road is being constructed to take you directly to Mount Nemrut from Malatya, making it too easy! Doubtless this will be followed by a cable-car to make it easier still. Meanwhile, you can take a bus to Kahta and stay there overnight (try the Merhaba or Kommagene pensions, both around L 3,000), or change there for a *dolmuş* to the mountain, but the best route is from Adıyaman in a *dolmuş* costing L 25,000 for the return trip, with time to visit the other places mentioned. This becomes reasonable when shared with others and at least, if you are driving independently, it saves your own car from some shattering roads. Until recently, visitors made their way by mule and even now the new road is covered by snow for most of the year, so you are advised to go there in July or August, though it is passable in late May and September when there are fewer people. The *dolmuş* can be arranged at the tourist bureau in Adıyaman at Hükümet Konağı, tel.: 1008. Take a flashlight and warm clothes – Nemrut should be seen at dawn.

From the pleasant Antiochus Motel on the main road, where they serve a furious little wine called *Lav* after the lava erupting from a volcano on the label, you set out at 1 a.m. in the shared *dolmuş* in the darkness. Roughly, and that is the operative word, roughly 40 km later, you bump into the village of Kahta where it is possible to stay overnight. This is the half-way stop, and from here you can walk for the next six hours if you have a guide, but this is not recommended unless there is a full moon and you are incurably romantic, and energetic too.

Otherwise, you leave the main road for a boneshaking track with glimpses of rabbits and deer-like growling dogs in the headlights, and turn left at Gerger, continuing past the army post at Narince.

At the summit

When you reach the summit of Mount Nemrut, having travelled for several hours, it is not the cold which hits you, but the wind. And though the final climb on foot is only a few hundred yards, it is steep and slippery and there is no track visible, so you are grateful for the beam of light from someone ahead to guide you forward. And when you reach the top, it comes as a surprise to find that this is not the top

237

at all, for a tumulus rises like a pyramid 50 m higher, a sepulchral mound which might contain the tomb of Antiochus himself though every attempt to excavate it has been thwarted by the trembling shale which threatens to cause a landslide. Obviously a way will be found in the future, and that could be a revelation.

As you wait, cringing in the wind, shielded by one of the stone statues, the craziness of the scene begins to dawn on you, even though the dawn itself seems to have been delayed. This was an act of personal megalomania worthy of the pharaohs and their pyramids, erected by Antiochus I of Commagene shortly before the birth of Christ. Plainly he envisaged it as the divine right of kings, for he was descended from Alexander the Great on his mother's side, and from Darius I of Persia on his father's who was Mithridates I and founded the kingdom of Commagene, ruling the land between the River Euphrates (now the less evocative Fırat) and the range of Taurus Mountains.

At the top of the highest peak, at 2,500 m, Antiochus built his statues of the Greek and Persian gods – or, rather, those he considered worthy to be his ancestors, Hercules, son of Zeus, and Zeus himself – and between them he erected his own statue, proclaiming 'I, Antiochus, caused this monument to be erected in commemoration of my own glory and that of the gods.'

With blocks of marble brought from Gerger below, eight for each god, and black marble for the reliefs at the base of the tumulus carried from an eastern quarry tens of kilometres away, an army of slaves must have crawled like ants up the mountain face to fulfil his vanity. Today, the row of statues sits headless, defeated by the erosion, storms and earthquakes over the last 2,000 years which have taken their revenge against such mortal insolence. The last to fall was that of the Goddess of Fortune which tumbled down during a thunderstorm in 1962 and lies there on the ground today. The rest of the heads – there are five altogether – have been placed upright and are no less impressive in their state of upheaval for they seem to have stood there since the start of time. The original figures were ten metres high but the scale of the heads must surely have been disproportionate for they are tremendous. That of the bearded Zeus is supposed to be the largest in the world, taller than a man, only comparable to those on Easter Island. If this is vanity, it is magnificent.

The figures sat on a terrace with the sacrificial altar below, and the ground is scattered with the statues of formidable eagles and lions – one majestic open-mouthed beast apparently howling his defiance in the wilderness, another covered with astronomical symbols. The head of the goddess sprawls on the ground garlanded with flowers and there are strange conical shapes beyond her.

You wait and wait. Gradually, a thin line appears on the barren plain of Mesopotamia: the River Euphrates. There is dawn at last, yet no sunrise. Suddenly it explodes, neither black as someone had warned me, nor green as another had insisted, but the molten glow of a raw red force thrust from the earth as if its core had been shattered. Then you know why Antiochus placed his gods to face such power, like the opening of a furnace door, for if a man had never seen such a sunrise before he would fall on his knees in awe.

Hail to Antiochus who proclaimed that 'no living human being shall be able to build anything higher than this shrine,' for though the heads have fallen, his own among them, and though man has created higher memorials since, he gave us a glorious affirmation of the inevitability of life and death – 'What I have done is proof of my belief in the presence of the gods.'

It is all over in a matter of seconds as that throbbing sun – you can almost *hear* it – is torn away from the earth and rises palely into the sky. You are left for a few moments more, shaking from the experience, regardless of the wind which seems to have abated.

Yet again, Turkey has astounded you.

Useful Reading

For pleasure, even if not strictly relevant

Eric Ambler, *The Mask of Demetrios*
John Buchan, *Greenmantle* (interesting if you are going east)
Agatha Christie, *Murder on the Orient Express* (though only a few scenes are set in Turkey, it whets the appetite and you can see the room where it was written in the Pera Palas Hotel, Istanbul)
Graham Greene, *Stamboul Train*
Francis Yeats-Brown, *The Golden Horn*

Modern classics

Lesley Blanch, *The Wilder Shores of Love*
Christina Dodwell, *A Traveller on Horseback in Eastern Turkey and Iran*
John Freely, *Strolling in Istanbul* and *Stamboul Sketches*
Philip Glazebrook, *Journey to Kars*
Rose Macaulay, *The Towers of Trebizond*
Alan Moorhead, *Gallipoli*
Tim Severin, *The Jason Voyage*
Freya Stark, *The Lycian Shore*
Richard Stoneman, *Across the Hellespont*

Architecture

Ekrem Akurgal, *Ancient Civilizations and Ruins of Turkey*
George Bean, various books
Godfrey Goodwin, *A History of Ottoman Architecture*
Richard Krautheimer, *Early Christian and Byzantine Architecture*
Michael Levey, *The World of Ottoman Art*
Steven Runciman, *Byzantine Style and Civilization*

History

Noel Barber, *The Lords of the Golden Horn*
O. R. Gurney, *The Hittites*
Halil Inalcık, *The Ottoman Empire: The Classical Age, 1300–1600*
Lord Kinross, *Atatürk: The Rebirth of a Nation* (the definitive biography of Kemal Atatürk)
Stuart Legg, *The Heartland* (hard reading, but revealing about the hordes from the East)
Michael Psellus, *Fourteen Byzantine Rulers*

Steven Runciman, *A History of the Crusades* (three volumes) and *The Fall of Constantinople*
Michael Wood, *In Search of The Trojan War*

Turkish

Yashar Kemal, *Mehmed my Hawk* and *The Sea-Crossed Fisherman*
Aziz Nesim, *Istanbul Boy*

Turkish Rulers

Byzantine Emperors

324–37	Constantine the Great	780–97	Constantine VI
337–61	Constantius	797–802	Eirene
361–3	Julian the Apostate	802–11	Nicephorus I
363–4	Jovian	811	Stauracius
364–78	Valens	811–13	Michael I
379–95	Theodosius the Great	813–20	Leo V
395–408	Arcadius	820–9	Michael II
408–50	Theodosius II	829–42	Theophilus
450–7	Marcian	842–67	Michael III
457–74	Leo I	867–86	Basil I
474	Leo II	886–912	Leo VI
474–91	Zeno	912–13	Alexander
491–518	Anastasius	913–59	Constantine VII
518–27	Justin I	919–44	Romanus I
527–65	Justinian the Great		(co-emperor)
565–78	Justin II	959–63	Romanus II
578–82	Tiberius II	963–9	Nicephorus II Phocas
582–602	Maurice	969–76	John I Tzimisces
602–10	Phocas	976–1025	Basil II
610–41	Heraclius	1025–8	Constantine VIII
641	Constantine II	1028–34	Romanus III Argyrus
641	Heracleonas	1034–41	Michael IV
641–68	Constantine III	1041–2	Michael V
668–85	Constantine IV	1042	Theodora and Zoe
685–95	Justinian II	1042–55	Constantine IX
695–8	Leontius	1055–6	Theodora (second
698–705	Tiberius III		reign)
705–11	Justinian II (second	1056–7	Michael VI
	reign)	1057–9	Isaac Comnenus
711–13	Philippicus Bardanes	1059–67	Constantine X Ducas
713–15	Anastasius II	1067–71	Romanus IV Diogenes
715–17	Theodosius III	1071–8	Michael VII Ducas
717–41	Leo III	1078–81	Nicephorus III
741–75	Constantine V	1081–1118	Alexius I Comnenus
775–80	Leo IV	1118–43	John II Comnenus

243

1143-80 Manuel I Comnenus
1180-3 Alexius II Comnenus
1183-5 Andronicus I Comnenus
1185-95 Isaac II Angelus
1195-1203 Alexius III Angelus
1203-4 Isaac Angelus (second
reign)
1203-4 Alexius IV Angelus
(co-emperor)
1204 Alexius V Ducas
1204-22 Theodore I Lascaris
1222-54 John III
1254-8 Theodore II Lascaris
1258-61 John IV
1261-82 Michael VIII
Palaeologus
1282-1328 Andronicus II
Palaeologus
1328-41 Andronicus III
Palaeologus
1341-91 John V Palaeologus ⎫
1341-54 John VI Cantacuzenus ⎬ co-
1376-9 Andronicus (IV) ⎪ emperors
1390 John (VII) ⎭
1391-1425 Manuel II Palaeologus
1425-48 John VIII Palaeologus
1449-53 Constantine XI
Dragases

Ottoman Sultans

1324–59	Orhan Gazi
1359–89	Murat I
1389–1403	Beyazit I
1403–13	*Interregnum*
1413–21	Mehmet I
1421–51	Murat II
1451–81	Mehmet II The Conqueror
1481–1512	Beyazit II
1512–20	Selim I The Grim
1520–66	Süleyman I The Magnificent
1566–74	Selim II
1574–95	Murat III
1595–1603	Mehmet III
1603–17	Ahmet I
1617–18	Mustafa I
1618–22	Osman II
1622–3	Mustafa I (second reign)
1623–40	Murat IV
1640–8	Ibrahim
1648–87	Mehmet IV
1687–91	Süleyman II
1691–5	Ahmet II
1695–1703	Mustafa II
1703–30	Ahmet III
1730–54	Mahmut I
1754–7	Osman III
1757–74	Mustafa III
1774–89	Abdül Hamit I
1789–1807	Selim III
1807–8	Mustafa IV
1808–39	Mahmut II
1839–61	Abdül Mecit I
1861–76	Abdül Aziz
1876	Murat V
1876–1909	Abdül Hamit II
1909–18	Mehmet V
1918–22	Mehmet VI
1922–4	Abdül Mecit II (*Caliph only*)

Classical Place Names

Classical name	Modern Turkish equivalent
Adramyttium	Edremit
Adrianople/Hadrianopolis	Edirne
Alexandretta	Iskenderun
Amaseia	Amasya
Antioch	Antakya
Antiphellos/Habesa	Kaş
Ararat	Mount Nemrut
Assos	Behramkale
Caesarea	Kayseri
Claudiopolis	Bolu
Constantinople	Istanbul
Daphne	Harbiye
Diocaesarea	Uzuncaburç
Edessa	Şanlıurfa
Ephesus	Efes
Euphrates River	Firat Nehri
Gallipoli	Gelibolu
Halicarnassus	Bodrum
Hellespont	Dardanelles
Iconium	Konya
Magnesia ad Sipylus	Manisa
Myra	Demre
Nicaea	Iznik
Pergamon	Bergama
Phocaea	Foça
Physkus	Marmaris
Seleucia ad Calycadnum	Silifke
Smyrna	Izmir
Tigris River	Dicle Nehri
Trebizond	Trabzon
Troy	Truva

Index